To Rod
It's a great life!
Liza Copeland

Cruising
for Cowards

CRUISING FOR COWARDS

An A - Z of OFFSHORE STRATEGIES, BOATS AND EQUIPMENT PREFERRED BY EXPERIENCED CRUISERS

by
Liza & Andy Copeland

Illustrations by Harold Allanson

1997
Romany Publishing

Canadian Cataloguing in Publication Data

Copeland, Liza
Cruising for Cowards - An A-Z of Offshore Strategies, Boats and Equipment Preferred by Experienced Cruisers

ISBN 0-9697690-3-2

1. Sailing. 2. Sailboats 3. Boats and boating - Equipment and supplies. I. Copeland, Andy, 1934 -. II. Title.

GV811.4.C66 1996   797.1'24   C96-910601-7

Illustrations by Harold Allanson

Also by Liza Copeland
Just Cruising, Still Cruising, Comfortable Cruising & a video Just Cruising

Romany Publishing   Tel: (604) 228-8712
3943 W. Broadway   Fax: (604) 228-8779
Vancouver, B.C.   Website: www.aboutcruising.com
Canada V6R 2C2

Book and cover design by Sport BC Graphics, Vancouver, B.C.
Printed in Canada by Hignell Printing Ltd., Winnipeg, Manitoba

For Duncan, Colin and Jamie,
who have made our cruises such a success,
and Alison who kept everything running on
the home front during our six-year circumnavigation.

Acknowledgements

Many people have helped with this book, spending long hours discussing all aspects of cruising and working on the manuscript; it's hard to thank them enough. It was wonderful having Andy join me in the writing; his technical knowledge knows no bounds and adds huge scope to the content covered. Harold Allanson has been a delight to meet. Seeing some of his work I phoned him out of the blue with "Would you like to illustrate my new book?" "Sure," he replied. Neither he nor I envisioned the extent of the illustrations. Not only did his cockroaches flourish in personality I met someone as dedicated as myself to perfection. Many thanks also go to Marion Munro, at Sport BC Graphics, and the staff at Hignell Printing whose artistic skills and hard work have contributed hugely to the quality of the final result. I would also like to thank Doris Colgate, Steve Callahan, Tom Linskey and Anne Hammick for their kind words of approval.

I have had many dedicated editors and proofreaders. Kim Davies has been pillar of support spending hours not only on the text, but also confirming the smallest detail. Peter and Glenora Doherty, offshore sailors and long-term members of Bluewater Cruising Association, took endless trouble with suggestions and keeping me in line with consistency. Mike and Doreen Ferguson, liveaboards for fourteen years, offshore sailors for five, Dave Seller, a Pacific veteran, and many other offshore cruisers had several suggestions.

Dave Miller of North Sails, Dave Bonner, sailmaker whilst cruising, and Carol Hasse of Hasse and Company Sailmakers were most informative regarding current trends. Barbara Storch generously shared ideas from her course on Sailing for Wimps.

Again Brenda de Roos, Diana Gatrill and Trevor Jenkins spent many hours proofreading while June Mauthe contributed her time on the computer. Caroline Baker and Jean Lee have been trojans in scrutinising the final copy. Nancy Garrett, my next door neighbour, was not only full of her usual enthusiasm but also provided frequent dinners to help us through, and spent half the final night checking and rechecking the manuscript.

CONTENTS

Note: All prices are quoted in U.S. dollars

Preamble

Of course you're not a coward, you are planning to go cruising! However, there must be some reason why you haven't left the dock. Maybe you have information overload on boats and equipment, or are overwhelmed by the decisions of leaving the real world. Perhaps you are worried about whether you will actually enjoy life afloat. If you have any of these concerns and more *Cruising for Cowards* is for you.

Rather than overwhelming with technicalities the Copelands have focussed on the strategies, boats and equipment that are preferred by those who are experienced cruisers. Written to meet the needs of both coastal sailors and circumnavigators, they answer common questions such as: What kind of boat to buy and how to find it? What equipment is necessary? How much cruising costs, how funds are managed and work along the way. How cruisers provision, maintain their boats, plan routes to avoid storms, communicate with home, cope with the constant requirements of travel and live together on a small boat 24 hours a day.

Liza, an educational psychologist and boating seminar speaker, and Andy, formerly a fighter pilot in the Royal Navy and currently a yacht broker, are both life-long cruisers and racers and have sailed over 80,000 nautical miles together. Their six-year circumnavigation with their three children is recounted in the best selling books *Just Cruising* and *Still Cruising* and in *Just Cruising*, the video.

Since returning they have been deluged with questions on how to cruise successfully; hence the writing of *Cruising for Cowards*. The topics covered reflect the areas of greatest concern. They are listed in alphabetical order and the Table of Contents gives a detailed account of all subheadings.

With its entertaining personal anecdotes that illustrate both technical and practical issues, together with Harold's hilarious cartoons, you will find this book not only gives a wealth of realistic cruising information, it also marvellously entertains.

AGE AND STAGE IN LIFE
Who is out there?

*We are frequently asked, "What kind of person do you find cruis-
ing and what is the most common age?" The answer is that
you meet all sorts, of every age and background. There are young
couples, those taking time out in mid-career, families with children of all ages and retirees.*

The youngest we came across doing a long passage was a two-month
old on the Atlantic Rally for Cruisers. There seems to be no upper age
limit. Our friend Dusty Trembly is almost 83 and singlehands a 44 footer.
Recently he decided that instead of completing a second circumnavigation he would come to Vancouver to cruise in the Pacific Northwest.
He is a little worried it will be too tame. I assured him that Hecate Strait
could be guaranteed to give him some excitement! During his circumnavigation he regularly returned home to Denver to do ski patrol
just to make sure he stayed fit.

1

Those over 45 years of age appear to be the biggest group cruising; most either have investment or rental income, or are on a pension. Retirement is a tidy package with a career finished, no deadlines and an income secured, but at this stage some may find starting the lifestyle very demanding. Health considerations can also become a concern with advancing age. When people mention that they will wait until retirement to cruise, we urge them at least to buy their boat beforehand and to make any modifications required; also that they work at physical fitness.

What is the best age for children to cruise? If the opportunity to go cruising presents itself we urge you to take advantage of it whatever the ages of children. It is too wonderful a family experience to be missed. However, if you have flexibility, it seems generally agreed amongst cruisers that the optimum ages are six to twelve. Although it works well to have children under six on board, with certain safety considerations, they tend not to remember very much and can limit travel opportunities. By age six children are far more independent and aware, both of boat routines and of different cultures and cuisines. They delight in the adventure of the lifestyle and love sharing it with their parents. For the older child those hormones start working at the onset of puberty, even in the middle of the ocean, and the rather daunting teenage years begin - daunting for their parents anyway, particularly in a confined space! In addition, a high school curriculum is often much more demanding than an elementary, with specific facilities required. Many teenagers miss team sports and peers are scarce just at a time they are becoming important.

Not only do cruisers come in all ages, they come from the whole spectrum of jobs, backgrounds and cultures. Whether you are a prince, pauper, wheelbarrow manufacturer, plumber or doctor, the sea is an excellent equalizer. Cruising guarantees a variety of characters among fellow cruisers and wonderful camaraderie. Not only will you share the good times and many memorable experiences together but you will also have support through the difficult periods. By necessity, cruisers have to be handy and with such a diversity of skills among them there is always someone who can help fix a problem. It is the same with the children. Although age, gender and grade are social dividers in regular life, cruising kids of all ages and nationalities become friends naturally and spontaneously despite any language barriers and get together for school and chores, as well as general entertainment.

A typical crew consists of a couple. Although the male generally calls himself skipper, both male and female work companionably as a team. Both share the chores and maintenance but usually have their own areas of expertise; both take watches and are equally capable of navigating and handling the boat. They enjoy the lifestyle - living on a boat, sailing the oceans and visiting ashore, and making mutual decisions about when and where to go. In the minority are families, same sex crews and singlehanders. Cruisers are 'out' from months to forever. The average time for a circumnavigation is four to six years but many take longer depending on career plans or schooling for children.

The number of cruisers sailing the oceans is increasing dramatically every year. Certain areas have become particularly popular, such as the Mexican coast and extended Caribbean cruising that includes the South American and Central American coasts. Last year over 500 boats reputedly crossed the Pacific and with such races as the Darwin/Ambon having opened up Indonesian cruising, more yachts are heading across the Indian Ocean. The Atlantic Rally for Cruisers has encouraged Atlantic crossings and the increase in round the world rallies, such as the Europa, has not only swelled the cruising population, it has also publicized the feasibility of extended world sailing. Sailing magazines and active cruising clubs, particularly those with publications such as by the US Seven Seas Cruising Association, the UK Ocean Cruising Club and Canadian Bluewater Cruising Association, encourage others by printing a variety of articles by those offshore. In short, cruising is becoming quite commonplace!

Now you know you will happily fit into the cruising community. Of course, making the decision to actually join it is another issue!

(See Anxieties about the Lifestyle, Decisions about Leaving and Boating Experience.)

ANCHORS (GROUND TACKLE), ANCHOR WINDLASSES, RODES AND ANCHORING

A good anchor and rode, and anchoring practice is part of your insurance for a safe boat and a calm life. A night's worry over the set of the anchor is guaranteed to spoil the next day's cruising or sightseeing.

ANCHORS

Types

Most cruisers carry at least three anchors - their **main**, everyday anchor, a **storm** anchor and a **kedge.**

There are dozens of different patented anchors available and many have their merits. Virtually all cruisers, however, stick to proven anchors which have stood the tests of time. The **Bruce** or **CQR** are overwhelmingly the most popular main anchors used by offshore cruisers. They are both plow anchors which achieve their holding power by penetrating broad flukes. The **Delta** is also gaining popularity.

The British **Bruce** is known for setting quickly and remaining buried when the boat turns with the current or wind. It also holds well if a short scope is necessary. It was ranked the strongest out of 14 anchors studied by Boat US and is used to anchor oil rigs in the North Sea. An occasional problem can occur if a rock or other object gets caught in its 'scoop', preventing penetration.

Bruce

The genuine **CQR** also performs well in many bottom types, digs deeper the harder the pull and stays holding if the boat turns, but one should avoid buying one

CQR

of the many cheap imitations. It is at its least effective in soft, buttery mud.

The **Danforth** style and aluminum anchors are comparatively light and hold well in a soft bottom with a straight pull but may fail to rebury if the boat turns, or reset if the anchor has dragged. They are good in all types of mud (the weakest point of both the Bruce and CQR) which is why they are so popular in North America, but are not good in rock, coral or sea grass. They are particularly prone to damage if force is required to dislodge them from the bottom and

Danforth   can even be distorted by a change in direction in pull.

Because they are relatively light and therefore easy to throw out of a dinghy they are popular and effective as kedges (manoeuvring anchors).

Many use a **Fisherman** as a storm anchor. Although these old fashioned anchors are awkward to stow, carry and use, and rely on weight (twice that needed compared with the Bruce and CQR), once set they hold like a rock. They work well in a variety of bottoms and unlike many other anchors they will cut through heavy weed and catch where there is only a shallow layer of mud or sand over rock. The patented fisherman which comes apart in three pieces so it can be stowed in the bilge, is recommended.

Fisherman

Bow Rollers

Cruisers commonly have two bow rollers and ideally have a self-stowing system for the rode and an anchor locker or chain pipe which can be sealed when underway. Both the **Bruce** and the **CQR** anchors stow well on bow rollers but must always be lashed or pinned securely on passages. Many also have a system for a stern anchor, particularly useful in the Mediterranean as it allows one to Med Moor bow-in.

Seasoned sailors always err on a larger size of anchor, including shackles, swivels and chain, than is recommended for the size of the boat, particularly if the boat has high windage.

5

Strategies

Anchors are sometimes used in combination from the bow, or bow and stern, to hold the boat in a certain direction because of current, an uncomfortable swell or for security in strong winds. For example, we used an 18-lb Danforth kedge in series with the Bruce at times, shackled to the crown with 20' of chain. This combination gives tremendous holding power yet it was easier to recover than two anchors streamed separately from the bow and avoids the problem of the rodes twisting together as the boat swings with the tide. In some areas, particularly in the Mediterranean (hence the term Med Moor), or in small windless anchorages such we have in abundance in British Columbia, anchoring from the bow (or stern) with lines ashore is common (see **Docking**). Many boats can anchor safely in this way in small but deep anchorages.

If more than one anchor is set it is important to consider the other boats in the vicinity carefully. Many a time we've seen havoc created in a crowded anchorage when the tide or wind changes and all the boats swing but one! A similar result can occur with different rode lengths.

At Sea

For use in storms while at sea a **drogue** deployed from the stern to slow the boat down or a **sea anchor** used from the bow to hold the boat into wind is often carried *(see Safety - at Sea)*. Aboard *Bagheera* our Danforth kedge and chain are stowed aft. When shackled to our long warps this not only acts as an effective drogue but also ensures that the warp does not skip out of the water.

Dinghy

You also need a small anchor for the dinghy. Folding grapnel types and small Bruce or Fisherman anchors are commonly used.

ANCHOR WINDLASSES

Pulling up the anchor by hand in the heat of the tropics can be gruelling; in colder climes the driving rain is even less pleasant.

Either manual or electric windlasses are almost essential in many areas where anchoring depths can exceed 30 metres. The manual models are powerful but very slow and increasingly electric windlasses are appearing on cruising boats. We came to this decision aboard *Bagheera* when we changed to an all chain rode to cruise the Pacific. We were fortunate that on arrival in Fiji in 1987 just after the second political coup we met a chandler who was happy to sell all his stock at a bargain price. We thus became the proud owners of a Nillsen Maxwell electric windlass although had to wait until Australia to find chain to suit!

The correct combination of anchor, chain and windlass is important. Again most err on the heavy side; marine stores and manufacturers have reference tables to help you. Remember a windlass is designed to pull up an anchor, not move a boat or break an anchor out. It is important not to over-stress an electric anchor windlass. We seldom anchored in more than 20 metres. An exception was in the Maldives where it was a minimum of 30 metres at the drop-off of the reef. The snorkelling was superb but our anchor windlass had started to complain by the end of the week. The small town of Male was not a place with spare parts around the corner and Andy had to be very resourceful to repair it.

When buying an electric windlass consider the advantages of the vertical varieties over the horizontal. Although the horizontal ones are easy to install the vertical designs are more efficient as more of the chain is in contact with the gypsy. They can also take leads from different angles and have the motor below deck where it is protected from the elements so is less likely to corrode.

Our electric windlass is useful in many ways. It not only saves our backs in deep anchorages, it also takes Andy aloft in the bosun's chair to complete regular rig inspections - like most men he is no lightweight to pull up the mast! - and it is also used to hoist the inflatable dinghy on deck either for security at night or for stowing before long passages. Best of all, it became no chore to shift anchorages at a whim, whereas with the manual windlass the work involved made us hesitate to move except when absolutely necessary.

ANCHOR RODES

These can be all chain, or a combination of rope and chain. The ideal safe scope used for rope and chain is generally considered to be 7:1, slightly less can be used with all chain in shallow water, no less than 4:1 for all chain in depths over 10 metres. On our Bruce we had 100 metres of 5/16" high test chain, with 40 metres of 3/8" BBB chain and 70 metres of octoplait rope for a storm anchor. Again, always consider the size of the anchorage, vicinity of other boats and weather conditions.

An all chain rode is considered a 'must' in the Pacific and Indian Oceans to avoid chafe from the coral and coral fissures and is increasingly being used in the Caribbean. If weight forward is a concern one can go down a size by using high test chain with increased strength and much reduced weight. For a storm anchor heavy chain combined with good quality nylon rode eases the shock loads but one has to keep the rope clear of coral and guard against chafe at the bow fairlead. After a few years chain will need to be re-galvanized to protect it from corrosion. On a long trip this is a job to plan in advance, as good galvanising facilities can only be found in major first world cities.

Chain should be marked with colour coded paint or Dacron thread to gauge the scope let out.

When anchors are set, a **nylon strop** clipped onto the chain about two metres down from the bow roller and fastened to a bow cleat is commonly used to take the load, reduce jerking of the chain and minimize noise.

A **rubber snubber** may also be used on this strop to increase its elasticity. On a foul bottom, such as the many in the Mediterranean we found littered with ancient chains and old wrecks, it is prudent to put out an **anchor buoy**. A plastic bleach bottle works well.

ANCHORING

Anchoring is one of the trickiest manoeuvres on board. It is something to practise and perfect in a deserted anchorage as the unexpected is always lurking close-by in a crowded one! Nothing is more embarrassing or demoralising than the verbal exchange that can ensue between the person on the bow and the person at the helm when attempting to anchor, with the volume of course at an ever escalating pitch. Developing a set of hand signals that are distinctive can work wonders, eradicating the need for any verbal exchange - well, most of the time! Also significant is a mutual understanding that the perspectives from the bow and stern can be very different! A good way to overcome this is to change places regularly.

Study the chart, assess the anchorage and find a desirable spot for the boat to lie. In the tropics look for white sand and avoid anchoring in the coral. The common anchoring practice is to motor upwind, checking the depth to estimate the scope required. The anchor is dropped just as you begin to back down. Go back slowly keeping enough tension on the rode to dig the anchor in with the chain lying straight but not so much that the anchor drags because it has been jerked out before properly buried.

When using the engine to back down, the 'paddle wheel' effect of the propeller will initially make the stern swing one way or the other. Our stern kicks to port so we always turn the bow to port (i.e. the stern turns to starboard) to compensate at the last moment before the anchor goes down. You can also straighten up with a quick burst on the throttle. Tension on the rode will naturally align the boat.

When the desired scope has been let out depending on the depth, the size of the anchorage, the weather, available room and state of the tide, the anchor needs to be dug in by using increased revs on the engine. If the rode becomes really taut without movement then the anchor is set. Take a transit with the shore and if practical dive to see how the anchor is lying. Then relax - enjoy a snorkel in the brilliant turquoise water or a wander ashore on the white sands under the swaying palms....

Two anchors can be used for increased security in bad weather, to hold the boat into a swell, to prevent rolling all night or in anchorages where there is a strong reversing tidal current.

You will be anchoring far more than you may think; how much will depend on your cruising grounds and budget. We anchored approximately 80% of the time during our six year circumnavigation and we are typical cruisers. Some of the time there were marinas but because they were expensive we generally only went in once a week to do laundry, shower and allow the boys a free rein from the boat. Some of the time we were stern-to a wharf with no other facilities. Most of the time anchoring was the only option.

Despite all the practice and precautions everyone has their anchoring stories and I'm sure you won't be an exception! Ours happened at random around the world - in Portugal, Madeira and Kenya.

Our first disaster was in Cascais on the Portuguese Atlantic coast. Formerly a fishing village close to where Andy grew up, it is now a chic tourist area. All was peaceful when we retired, a light wind blowing *Bagheera* gently offshore. During the night the wind changed, not only in strength but also in direction. When we awoke we were on a lee shore with short steep waves that were building. It was time to get the anchor up and leave but it was not so easy. Andy pulled and pulled

but the anchor would not come free. We circled around this way and that trying to break it out. The water was murky, we couldn't see a thing. Suddenly a huge breaking wave thrust *Bagheera's* bow high in the air. Simultaneously the manual windlass was ripped from the deck. In extremely rough conditions Andy had to dive to the bottom. He found that we had snagged on a huge old ship's anchor chain which probably had lain untouched for more than a century!

The Madeiran affair was a nightmare. The anchor had been bedded in for a week outside the harbour. While we were touring the island (utterly beautiful, one of our favourites) a cruiser dropped his anchor over ours, changed his mind, and lifted ours with his. When a squall came through *Bagheera* dragged, pounding on the rocks behind and a third of the rudder was smashed. There were no haul-out facilities available so we took the boat into the harbour and removed the rudder in the water. Andy was terrified it would sink to the bottom and we had a mass of lines rigged only to find it floated! It took ten days of rebuilding, fibreglassing and sanding but the yachting community as always were a wonderful support and someone even came along with two-part foam which was unavailable locally. The only problem was it made the rudder even more buoyant and it was extremely difficult to reinstall in the water!

In comparison the Kenyan episode was a peaceful event.

We had a date one evening with the Women's Group in Kilifi, north of Mombasa, but the boys had been out to a safari park and we were running late. As soon as they were on board we powered at full speed over to the other side of the inlet where Tony and Daphne, wonderful friends to visiting cruisers, were hosting the evening in their home. We had been to the anchorage several times and knew there was a long drop off. At dusk, close to a couple of other boats, Andy dropped the anchor and quantities of chain rattled over the windlass. We leapt into the dinghy and rushed ashore. It was a wonderful evening with exotic food and a BBC film. As we returned to the beach down the numerous steps Jamie ran ahead. Suddenly he called out, "There's a boat on its side." It took only two seconds to deduce which one!

Always one for action, Andy had everyone unload extra weight, the jerry cans of water and fuel and other portable gear. We knew we were on falling tides and as we had obviously dragged we were concerned that there wouldn't be enough water for *Bagheera's* 7' draft. At that extreme angle it was an extraordinarily uncomfortable night. I finally managed to sleep in Colin's cabin, as the boys had been invited to stay ashore, but the fishing reels that are normally well above the berth kept prodding me in the back. Also the floor was a gooey mess. The galley lockers had been open, the ones with all the sauces, herbs, tea and coffee...

All was quiet at 5:00 am, as it had been all evening. By 6:00 the mast was beginning to lift and by 10:00 we had happily returned to our upright state and loaded everything back on board. As our friends had coffee in the cockpit they analyzed the event and soon came to the same conclusion we had arrived at several hours earlier, but had been too embarrassed to admit. We hadn't dragged at all, there had just been too much chain out! Incidentally the film we had watched was Jeffrey Archer's *Not a Penny More, not a Penny Less*. I had always admired Jeffrey Archer for the unexpected twist at the end of his stories - but now I'm not so sure!

ANXIETIES ABOUT THE LIFESTYLE

For cruising to be successful it is critical to analyze the motivation and expectations of all concerned.

Setting the date to leave the dock is probably the single most difficult aspect of cruising. (Although Andy now says the traumas of returning are equally as bad!) A date not only imposes a time frame to get everything completed but it also confirms the intention to go. Irrevocable decisions regarding jobs, finances and your home have to be made, and the boat organised.

Up to this point, one, or even both of the parties may not really have thought the decision through. Andy and I were lucky. Not only did we both want to go cruising in foreign lands but we had done so before, so we had both realistic and similar expectations. I have learnt that this mutual understanding and agreement is unusual. Heading off on the oceans is often only one person's dream while the other party goes along with the idea but doesn't really expect or want it to happen.

The anxieties that arise from setting a departure date can be traumatic and in fact have put many off cruising altogether. Particularly difficult are the different focuses. Those that are convinced about the lifestyle generally concentrate on concrete issues. Is the boat ready? Is more equipment needed? Are there sufficient tools, spares and charts for the route? Copious lists are made, and added to, but as items get crossed off the top at least an equal number appear at the bottom which can cause intense anxiety. Urged on by the dream of shedding a lifetime of responsibilities ashore, these people are so consumed by a passion for chasing the sunset and exotic sights in far distant lands they can't wait to head out, at the risk of being unprepared.

In contrast, many partners may have emotional anxieties that are hard to define, and rationalize, even to themselves. Although they recognize the lure of the 'footloose and fancy free' lifestyle they are quite content with their current life and find it difficult to be enthusiastic about casting off the lines. They like their home and the comfort it provides, enjoy their job and are secure with the familiar, predictable local community, family and friends. They have agreed to go cruising in theory, and can see the positive sides, but they did not really seek change in their lives and the reality of cruising is more than daunting.

As the date approaches the risks seem greater to the less committed partner. How will they cope with the anticipated feelings of inadequacy on board, boredom, loneliness, hard work, discomfort and panic about being out of the sight of land, to say nothing of having to live with their partner 24 hours a day - which they've never had to do before!

Rushing around the chandlers and supermarkets with endless lists they wonder how they will possibly cope without a car, let alone a dishwasher, washing machine, dryer and familiar kitchen appliances. In addition they don't want to sell their home and lose the memories associated with it.

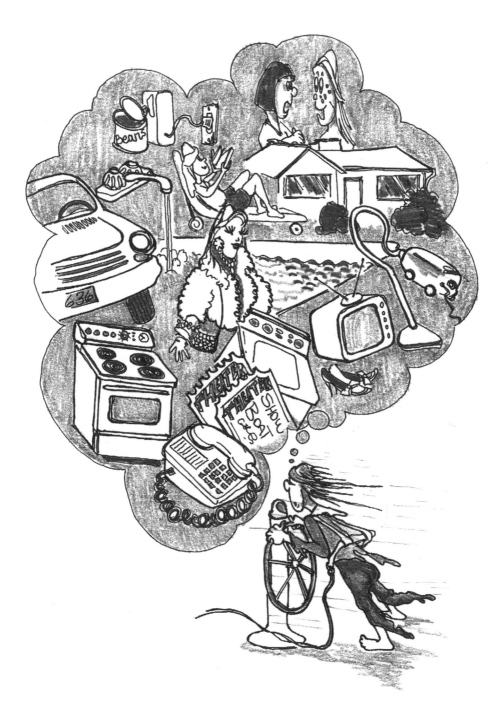

As well as coping with their own anxieties they also have to contend with everyone else's reactions. These can be hugely varied, from the "Wow!" of speechless wonder to exclamations of horror. Many people are quite mystified about why one should want to do it at all and find it hard to be sympathetic to your self-imposed stress. When children are involved there is frequently extra 'advice' that implies total irresponsibility, particularly if the children are being taken out of school or are very young. Some cruisers even find they are subject to hostility. In Andy's case, for example, several men said, "Of course I would be going off too but I have my own business." Andy soon learnt it was not diplomatic to say, "But I just sold mine!" In my case many women made it quite clear that I had let their side down by actually agreeing to go, completely ignoring the fact that I had spent a good deal of my life on boats both cruising and racing, that I obviously enjoyed being on the water and that the decision was mutual!

Life is tense for almost everyone before leaving. We've all panicked about whether we are doing the right thing, whether the lifestyle is really for us. It takes us all some time to adjust to life on board. Extreme reactions, however, are generally minimized with time, discussion and planning well before the departure date. Acknowledging, understanding and accepting different aspirations is important and the major decisions must be made with mutual understanding. Gaining boating experience and technical knowledge so that one is comfortable and competent on the water does wonders for building confidence *(see The Decisions about Leaving)*.

When the lines are finally cast off it is as though the burden has been left on the dock. So many of the concerns that were major issues are no longer important; those that are outstanding can generally be attended to by phone. If one is easing into the lifestyle gradually, as recommended in ***Route Planning***, forgotten equipment and supplies can be bought along the way. Shopping becomes enjoyable, part of the adventure of exploring ashore. When a big grocery shopping trip is needed, a taxi fare costs nothing compared to running a car. You will soon realize that the chores are not as formidable as anticipated. A boat is considerably smaller than a home, and once you have learnt to remember to secure the ketchup, coffee and soya sauce before heading out (shock-cord or fiddles across the inside of the lockers works wonders) the time spent on housekeeping is not such a burden. Even laundry takes on a different light when completed in the cockpit and hung out in the sun to dry, with the wind being a natural iron. (Maybe it's a good idea not having a full length mirror around initially!)

As you are in the cockpit or ashore a good deal of the time, any concerns about being claustrophobic will prove to be unfounded. Although passages can be uncomfortable on occasion they are generally soon over and forgotten. The more you are involved with watches and navigation the quicker time will pass; being able to cope with sea-sickness and having the correct clothing will make you considerably more comfortable.

Far from being lonely, most cruisers quickly make friends along the way and within no time develop some very special relationships with others, a camaraderie which often lasts a lifetime. At the same time whether by phone, radio or visits, you will have no problem keeping in touch with friends and relatives back home. In fact, those relationships become closer because there is so much to share. As you plan your own day, whether it is to be busy or relaxing, you will wonder how you coped with the routine pressures of society and why you were ever reticent about leaving!

Soon you will be enjoying the adventure of cruising and seeking out new cultures and products. You will also be realising there is no time to be bored. Organising this lifestyle, like any other, requires work to be done in order to have the fun.

BILGES, BILGE PUMPS AND THROUGH-HULLS

BILGES

Bilges need to be kept clean and dry. In hot climes water soon fouls from the action of bacteria on any dust, fuel or other contaminants which find their way under the floor boards. Any unpleasant odour will considerably increase one's tendency to seasickness, so must be treated immediately with bleach (an item that should be permanently on your provisioning list).

Adequate limber holes are necessary for water to drain quickly to the lowest part of the bilge. It is a good idea to have effective strum boxes or filters at all pump intakes, so that debris, such as labels from cans and bottles stowed in the bilges, cannot disable your pumps.

PUMPS

Big is best where pumps are concerned; a powerful bilge pumping system, both manual and electric, is usual. A high-quality manual diaphragm pump which can remove at least 25 gallons a minute when combined with a dose of adrenaline will move enormous quantities of water. This pump should be mounted in the cockpit near the helm so that, if necessary, one person can cope, and must be positioned high enough so that it is comfortable to operate for long periods of time. Frequently these are placed so one has to be a contortionist. On larger boats, a second manual pump may be fitted at the forward end of the cockpit.

Know how to use the engine's raw water pump to move bilge water in an emergency. In addition, powerful pumps can be fitted which drive directly off the engine through an electromagnetic clutch. These may be valved to act as fire pumps using sea water or as emergency bilge pumps drawing from the bilge. Remember to place outlets for bilge pumps as high as possible so that when heeled they are not immersed. This ensures that seawater cannot syphon into the boat.

Cautious sailors who have the room will carry a portable gasoline fire/salvage pump. Buy one that is self-priming and run it regularly to make sure it will start in an emergency. A dripless stern gland is also recommended for any boat going offshore (*also see Engines and Propellers*).

As modern yachts leak very little, it is easy to underestimate the huge volume of water which may have to be removed after a knockdown or a damaging collision with a solid floating object. Remember electric and engine-driven pumps may not work if the batteries have been immersed (gel batteries are better in this situation) or if the engine cannot be run. At this point you may have to resort to manual pumps and buckets, or the gasoline fire/salvage pump.

THROUGH-HULLS

Below water through-hulls and sea-cocks are potential weaknesses and should be kept to a minimum. In fibreglass and wood hulls they should always be bronze, not plastic. On every haul-out the through-hulls should be inspected for security and corrosion, and the sea-cocks checked for smooth operation.

Sea-cocks should have hoses double-clamped (in stainless steel) and be protected from damage, for example, from being stepped on or from heavy objects falling on them. A soft tapered wood plug secured close to the inside of each through-hull will make available a temporary means to stem the flow in the event of a sea-cock failure.

Everyone on board should know the location of the sea-cocks so that in the event of an unexplained flooding they can be closed immediately, with the exception of the engine intake which will be needed to run mechanical and electric pumps.

In the event of catastrophic damage to a through-hull or in case of a larger breach in the hull, a plan of action should be prepared (*see Safety-collision mats*). Note that if the hull has not been damaged other sources of a leak could be the rudder post, the shaft log, the keel bolts and the transducers for the sounder and log. Leaking cockpit lockers and the hull-to-deck joint are also possibilities.

THE BOAT

Put ten experienced sailors around a table, ask them for their definition of the ideal cruising yacht and you are likely to get ten different answers. The old salt who maintains that heavy displacement and full keel are essential for ocean cruising is nowadays as far out on a limb as the modernist who insists on an ultra light, water ballasted rocket ship.

In fact, there can be no such thing as the perfect vessel for all conditions. At any popular cruising destination there will be all kinds of yachts which have safely made an ocean passage and it is hard to argue that only one type is suitable. In the end, the only requirement on which all agree is the need for quality construction and reliable equipment.

Those who have been offshore in a variety of types are tending more and more to demand modern designs with good performance.

When deciding what boat to cruise in, behaviour at sea is not the only quality which must be considered. Days on passages are greatly outnumbered by those spent at anchor or day-sailing. The boat is your home, so comforts and living space are important.

Hull materials, displacement, keel shapes, beam, rig, rudder types, interior layouts and freeboard all affect the behaviour and comfort of your cruising home in both positive and negative ways. In the end, most people will buy a yacht which to them looks good, feels good, is affordable and has a reasonable combination of the particular characteristics which they consider important for their planned type of cruising.

The search for the ideal yacht is difficult for the less experienced. They will be beset by conflicting advice from all sides and by pressure from brokers determined to make a sale. By all means get as much advice as possible, but always find out the source of that advice and the true knowledge of the advisor. Too many armchair sailors are experts without the backup experience; they have read extensively but have limited sea time. Others may have had a successful voyage in only one type of vessel and cannot see the virtues of other designs.

Seek out cruisers with several years experience who are currently cruising; if possible visit some of the destinations such as the Caribbean or Mediterranean and look at what they are sailing. Read cruising magazines such as *Yachting World, Yachting Monthly* and *Practical Boat Owner* from the UK and *Cruising World, Ocean Navigator, Sail, Blue Water Sailing, Lattitudes & Attitudes* magazines from the USA. Gain experience by crewing aboard others' boats and go on a bare boat charter in one of the remoter destinations.

CONSTRUCTION AND DESIGNS

Most yachts doing long passages today are moderate displacement monohulls between 35 and 45 feet. Most are made of fibreglass, have a fin keel and separate rudder, usually spade or hung on a semi-skeg. The majority are production or semi-production boats. Sloop rig with headsail furling gear and a removable or permanent inner forestay, for hanked on sails, has largely replaced the old twin headstay concept. More than one spar is uncommon.

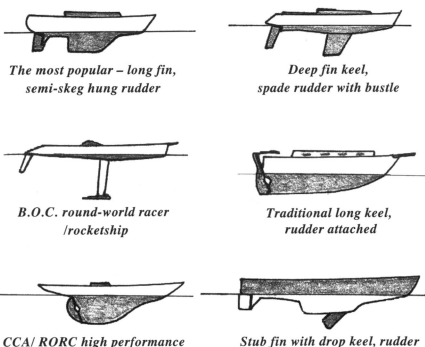

The most popular – long fin,
semi-skeg hung rudder

Deep fin keel,
spade rudder with bustle

B.O.C. round-world racer
/rocketship

Traditional long keel,
rudder attached

CCA/ RORC high performance
full keel, rudder attached

Stub fin with drop keel, rudder
on full skeg

The last fifty years has seen huge advances in designs and in construction methods. New materials have enabled boats to be stronger and lighter, research has refined hull, keel and rudder shapes and mass production has made it possible for almost anyone to get out on the water, rather than the privileged few.

All yachts are compromises and with almost every design feature there are benefits and drawbacks. Considering the fact that few naval architects have extensive offshore cruising experience it is surprising that so many modern designs are good passage making vessels, although it is probably because they have evolved from ocean racing types. Traditional heavy displacement, long keel boats are getting far less popular except amongst newcomers to ocean sailing.

Having sailed almost all variations of monohull and several multis, built of a variety of materials, our choice for a world cruise with three young children was based on quality of construction, sailing efficiency and our limited budget. We decided upon a new 40' Beneteau

First 38s sloop, built of fiberglass in France in 1985. She weighs 17,900 lbs, has a keel stepped masthead rig, fairly deep fin keel of 7', spade rudder and a beam of 12'9'.

On quality of construction, Beneteau equates, we feel, with the Toyota of the car world, both being affordable but built to hold together for a long time. Beneteau have cornered most of the quality charter market world-wide simply because of their boats' reliability and ability to take punishment; though for offshore passage making only some of their models are suitable. We have been very happy and impressed; after more than 75,000 nautical miles and fourteen years of use *Bagheera* has had no structural problems and looks better than many untraveled boats half her age. Her sailing efficiency is assured from the design features, particularly the moderate displacement and freeboard, the keel shape and rig. We knew she would be fast, upwind and down, and would sail us out of trouble if necessary.

Our budget could cope with this new boat. Beneteau is one of the largest sailboat builders in the world and has pioneered efficient quantity production of fiberglass vessels. There are several other manufacturers, particularly in Europe, who build affordable yachts which also make satisfactory ocean passage makers.

What should be looked for in a fibreglass boat?

1) A very rigid structure. Fibreglass is a flexible material and any movement will lead to leaks and structural deterioration. Early glass boats had very thick hulls with ribs and stringers built up to try to stiffen them; later, 'sandwich' cored hulls were developed which are effective if built well. The most satisfactory way is the modern grid system where a massive 'backbone' structure is bonded to the inside of the hull, although this is expensive in tooling for the builder.

2) The integrity of the hull-to-deck joint is critical. The strongest but also the most expensive to build is an inside shelf moulded around the perimeter of the hulk when it is laid up. To this the deck is chemically bonded either by glassing or, even stronger, by using one of the recently developed adhesive agents, after which the toe-rail is bolted at close intervals. This means the builder has to take the hull mould apart and hand finish the mould joint area instead of simply lifting the completed hull out of a one piece mould.

Cheaper to build but not as robust are the hulls with an outside shelf or lip, to which the deck is attached. In this type of construction

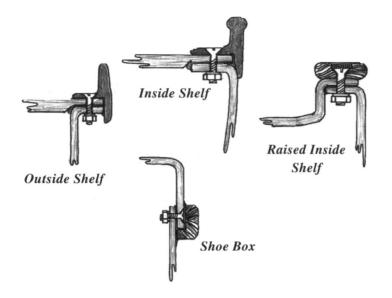

Inside Shelf

Raised Inside Shelf

Outside Shelf

Shoe Box

the rail protrudes beyond the hull so it is very vulnerable to damage and adds little to the strength of the join.

The 'shoe-box' hull-to-deck join is also cheaper for the builder. In this case the deck has a vertical flange which fits over the hull sides like a box lid. Unless this join is massively glassed over or bonded it will quickly weaken in any movement of the hull.

3) Bulkheads should be bonded not only to the hull but all the way around their perimeter, thus tying the hull and deck together.

4) Rig loads must be transferred to the hull with no load taken by the deck.

5) The deck coring should be balsa or one of the high density marine closed-cell foams, although any areas where fittings are secured should be solid glass. Plywood, found in many vessels because it is cheap and easily worked, gives little insulation and no resistance to rot, so is not satisfactory as a coring material. This is tough to investigate as dealers may not know or want to admit to the presence of plywood, so it might require a call to the manufacturer.

6) Hatches and ports need to have metal frames, not plastic which lacks strength and resistance to sunlight. Windows should be small in area, thickly glazed and strongly secured. Deck gear and fittings must be able to cope with storm force winds and require backing plates or other reinforcing. All deck and cockpit lockers should have seals

and reliable catches. Rigging, turnbuckles, chainplates, etc. must be robust enough to hold together in the worst of weather.

Below, the quality of the woods and workmanship are a good indication of the overall quality of the yacht. Are the handholds just decorative or will they actually hold when someone grabs them as the boat lurches? How is the wiring? What about the through-hulls and sea-cocks, the filters, pumps and engine installation?

CONSTRUCTION MATERIALS

1) Fibreglass, also known as GRP

The choice of the majority. Bear in mind that it is not just mass and thickness that makes a strong hull, but the choice of the materials, the engineering and the quality of the construction which are important. Many of the Taiwan produced vessels from the '70s were massively built but so poorly put together that they have been outlasted by racing shells built to a minimum weight.

Advantages. Volume production keeps costs down and gives consistent quality; it can be easily repaired; is non-corroding and reasonably strong; good resale value; a long service life provided the original quality is good.

Disadvantages. Looks like plastic; osmotic blistering can be an expensive problem; moderate resistance to impact and abrasion; to the inexperienced a poorly built boat looks just as good as a well made one.

2) Steel

The obvious choice for high latitude cruising where ice may be encountered, or where tidal conditions lead to drying out regularly.

Advantages. Inexpensive for custom and home building, particularly if a hard chine design; immensely strong and impact resistant; welding for repairs and additions simple, fittings do not have to be bolted so less potential for leaks.

Disadvantages. Salt water and steel are incompatible and corrosion a constant concern, particularly inside in the hidden corners which cannot be ventilated or maintained. A very heavy material (see *The Boat - Displacement*). Electrolysis problems with other metals and copper bottom paints. High heat and noise conductivity requires extensive interior insulation.

Interestingly, the most common reason given by someone wanting a steel yacht is that it will take longer to break up if driven onto a reef. This is probably correct but one's whole cruising life should not be based on this rare possibility; after all, we don't all drive Sherman tanks rather than cars on the roads in order to survive collisions better! Furthermore, it hasn't occurred to them that because steel yachts are so heavy it is far more difficult to break free after a grounding and this fact alone could lead to a permanent loss.

3) Aluminum

Commonly the choice for the more expensive custom yachts.
Advantages. Light in weight and very strong; marine grades are non-corrosive and can be left unfinished; fittings can be welded, so less leaks; reasonably easy material for builders to work with; hold their value well.
Disadvantages. Expensive; requires special welding techniques; susceptible to electrolysis and galvanic corrosion and particularly incompatible with any copper based antifouling paints; does not hold paints well; high heat and noise conductivity requires extensive interior insulation.

4) Wood, traditional plank on frame

A vanishing breed on the oceans.
Advantages. Beautiful if well kept; good heat and sound insulation; repairs can be made most places with local materials and skills; inexpensive to buy used due to their waning popularity.
Disadvantages. Continuous need for ongoing maintenance; quite heavy; less strong than fibreglass; seamed hulls prone to leaking; swelling and shrinking of above water areas with changes in humidity and temperature leads to leaking; prone to wet rot, dry rot, nail sickness, wood electrolysis, teredo and gribble attack; hard to resell.

5) Wood, cold moulded

Popular for multihulls and custom racers using thin veneers of wood impregnated with epoxy resin and built up in successive layers with the grain running in different directions.
Advantages. Strong, lightweight; an easy method using a simple frame plug for both the amateur and professional builder; can be finished

'bright', giving the appearance of a varnished wood hull; moderate maintenance requirements; seamless hull not prone to leaks; easy repairs. **Disadvantages.** Labour intensive to build; epoxy needs to be protected from degradation by the sun; moisture penetration can lead to deterioration; limited resale market.

6) Ferrocement

Once very popular with home builders but it is now largely discredited. Although there have been many good boats built, numerous amateur projects never made it to the sea and of those that did many proved a great disappointment or worse. A sales pitch that made one's cruising dreams seem easy and inexpensive to achieve led many people astray. **Advantages.** Can be built out of inexpensive materials by an amateur who really understands what he is doing; very cheap on the used boat market (but be very careful).
Disadvantages. Requires far more skill than most amateurs possess to build a strong, good-looking boat; very heavy; hard to keep a good finish; liable to unseen deterioration within the lay-up; very hard to resell; hard to insure; hard to survey.

7) Other Materials

The use of exotic resins and materials such as Kevlar, carbon fibre, and amazing modern adhesives and sealants is becoming more and more common to add integrity, strength or stiffness to fibreglass boats and rigs.

DESIGNS

Displacement

The displacement of a yacht is simply its weight. It has nothing to do with its quality of construction.

A century ago cruising yachts were built of wood, plank on frame, and they had heavy hulls to achieve the necessary strength for ocean voyaging. Early keels were long and shallow; the internal or external ballast weight had to be huge because of the short lever arm between the centre of floatation and the centre of gravity. (Double the length of this by having a deeper keel and you halve the weight needed for the same righting moment). Any weight above the centre of floatation is 'bad' weight which needs to be compensated for with weight below.

Voyagers who in the past put to sea in heavy, poorly performing vessels completed their voyages in spite of, rather than because of their boats and Slocum today would jump at the chance to trade in his *Spray* for a fibreglass performance cruiser!

Yachts no longer need to be heavy. Modern materials and building methods backed by a vast increase in design knowledge have changed this. Today, a cruising boat is far stronger, safer and lasts longer than those built decades ago. Yet as a broker, I still get requests for heavy displacement boats even when the client knows no more than "it's traditional to go offshore in heavy boats".

After considering the advantages and disadvantages of both light and heavy designs most cruisers choose a moderate displacement boat.

The following points should be considered before buying.

1) Excess weight detracts from performance which means longer passage times, poor windward ability. More water, food and other stores need to be carried, which in turn means more weight and so on. Add more sail area to compensate and a heavier rig is needed which means more weight, and being high it requires even more ballast to balance the boat.

Conversely, the very light boat has little tolerance for much additional load in the form of stores and may therefore be unsuitable for longer passages.

2) Because of greater inertia heavy boats move less in a sea and this is a benefit particularly to those prone to sickness. The converse is that if the boat won't move something has to give so the wave breaks. Therefore heavy boats are very wet boats and this is uncomfortable and debilitating. Very light boats are dry but bob around like corks which is also very wearing.

In storms, the greater inertia of heavy boats may be an advantage when broadside to a breaking wave in resisting a knockdown, but it is a definite disadvantage when running before the wind as the stern will not lift so readily to the wave and pooping is a real danger. When running down the front of a wave the bow will be slow to rise in the trough, which in really bad conditions may result in pitchpoling.

Light boats with their better performance can often outrun a wave, are more responsive to the helm and are less likely to be pooped or pitchpoled, but may capsize more readily and if beamy, may be slow to return upright.

3) In a grounding, the heavier vessel will drive on harder, will be more difficult to break free whether using a motor, kedging off or with a tow from another boat.

4) The heavier the vessel, the more expensive it will be to build and equip. Anchoring systems must be more massive, engines larger, more water must be carried for the slower passages, and so on.

Since 'heavy' is slow and unsafe and 'light' over-lively and a poor load carrier, a reasonable compromise is obviously needed to balance performance, safety and comfort. A look at recently designed monohull cruising boats which can be considered moderate displacement finds 35 footers displacing in the range of 11,000 to 16,000 lbs; 40 footers range between 15,000 and 22,000 lbs; 45 footers between 20,000 and 30,000 lbs.

Keels

Between the traditional long keel which starts at the stem and ends at the stern to the extremely efficient, very deep blade keels with bulbs of the round-the-world racers there are various compromises for the cruising yacht.

The majority of production cruising boats have some sort of fin keel and the most popular is a moderate draft fin with a chord somewhat longer than the depth. There are still many yachts built in the '50s and '60s which have 'full' keels with attached rudders. These are not at all like the long keels of traditional designs but are deep and efficient. Many were designed as racing yachts in the time of the CCA and RORC rating rules and make excellent cruising boats. Some designers have tried to improve on the old long keel by having a 'cutaway', where the keel starts abruptly some way back from the bow. By common usage any vessel with the rudder attached to the keel is called 'full keel'.

Windward sailing ability decreases as the keel gets longer and shallower. Long keels are reputed to track better off the wind, though we have sailed some which are dogs to keep on a course.

Too much directional stability brings its own problems, as when a quartering wave hits it will break if the boat doesn't move with it and many long keeled vessels have water constantly slopping on board. Ideally the boat should 'give' with the wave, resuming its assigned course as the wave passes beneath.

After a grounding a long keeled boat can have great difficulty in getting off because of the large area of contact, aggravated by the fact that such boats are usually very heavy. With a fin which is not too long it is usually possible to use the engine and full rudder to turn the boat and wriggle one's way back into deeper water. Certainly, using a kedge anchor or a pull from another boat the grounded fin keeler can nearly always be turned.

Bagheera has a keel which draws 7' and is nearly 7' long at the hull, tapering at the front to a base of about 4'. We favoured this deep keel over the shallow draft option because of our conviction that sailing efficiency is crucial to safety on the oceans. There were very few places where this draft limited our cruising.

The common metals used for external keels are lead, usually alloyed to make it less malleable, and cast iron. Lead has a greater specific gravity and so the same ballast weight can be achieved with less material, it doesn't corrode and its softness can act as a shock absorber in the event of a collision with an underwater object. It is more expensive than iron and far more easily damaged in a grounding, when bending and mushrooming of the metal can occur to the extent that windward ability may be lost.

Iron has to be protected with coal-tar epoxy or another moisture barrier to prevent corrosion. It is immensely strong and hard to damage and makes an excellent cruising keel provided the hull where it attaches has been engineered to take a lot of punishment, as all the force of a grounding will be transferred from the keel which has no 'give' at all.

Many cruising designs now have bulbs or wings at the bottom, a method of achieving shallow draft with a low centre of gravity and improved windward performance. Wings should not be over large because of the chance of damage in a grounding and should be shaped to shed kelp, plastic garbage and trap lines.

Centreboards or drop keels are found on some monohulls where both shallow draft and windward ability are required. These are usually heavy boats due to the higher placement of the ballast and the boards are vulnerable to damage and may create noise due to movement within the casing.

Internal ballast is rarely found these days except for trim purposes or with centreboard designs. Ballast encapsulated inside a fibreglass or metal keel is common and can be any mixture of lead, steel and cement. A severe grounding can result in loss of ballast, or water entry into the hull depending on the construction.

Multihulls do not need ballast weight to remain upright. Windward ability is achieved with shallow stub keels, centreboards or asymmetric hulls.

Rudders and Skegs

The rudder has to control the direction of the boat under all conditions. Light steering and instant, positive response, freedom from stalling and 'feel' are all desirable.

A skeg is principally there to give directional stability, and does in some cases allow for a lower rudder support. Both rudders and skegs are increasingly effective the further aft they are placed.

1) Attached to a Semi-skeg

The most popular configuration.

Advantages. Semi-balanced, so easy steering for the crew and self steering gear/autopilots; good directional stability; a rudder with damage to the lower part can continue to be used to get home.

Disadvantages. Not easy to remove in the water for repairs.

2) Spade Rudders

The second most favoured rudders on modern cruisers and our choice when combined with but not attached to a separate skeg or a bustle. The latter is like a long, shallow skeg which usually extends from the back of the keel to the rudder post.

Advantages. Balanced, so easy steering in all weathers; the most efficient rudder with immediate response, a godsend when running before the wind in storm conditions; easily dropped out of the boat in the water for repairs; can continue to be used to get home when much of the rudder is damaged.

Disadvantage. Supported only at the top by the rudder post so needs to be very robust in this area to minimise damage from impact or grounding.

3) Attached to the Keel

Advantages. Well protected from objects which the yacht may run over.
Disadvantages. Not balanced, so is heavy to steer; less effective than a separate rudder at the extreme aft end; cannot be removed easily for repairs in the water.

4) Attached to the transom

Advantages. Being as far aft as possible is very effective; easily removed for repairs; can be used with a trim tab self-steering vane gear.
Disadvantages. Vulnerable to other craft, sea walls etc.; may be difficult to balance depending on the design; wheel steering quadrant or tiller arm may require opening in transom.

5) Attached to a Full Skeg

Advantages. More effective than attached to the keel as it is usually further aft; good directional stability; there may be a measure of protection provided by the skeg, but see 'warning' below.
Disadvantages. Not balanced, so heavy to steer; cannot be removed easily for repairs in the water; damage to skeg can render the rudder inoperative.

Note: It is our experience that except in areas like the Pacific Northwest where huge floating logs are commonplace, or in ice packs, nearly all damage to rudders is caused by dragging at anchor and backingdown onto an obstruction. One occasionally hears of a yacht suffer ing rudder damage when lying to a sea anchor streamed from the bow due to sliding backwards down a wave. All the rudders discussed above are vulnerable in these cases.

Skegs can impart a dangerous false sense of security. Their purpose is to give directional stability and give some support to the rudder, not to protect it from impact. A collision heavy enough to severely damage a rudder can tear a skeg out, holing the hull, and creating a dangerous situation.

Beam, Freeboard and Draft

Yachts have recently been tending towards greater beam. These boats benefit from increased volume below and such a boat performs at its optimum at lower angles of heel than older designs, which greatly increases comfort. It has greater form stability due to the beam resisting heeling but if knocked down and capsized this factor can make returning to upright far slower. Some poor designs become hard to steer as the heel angle increases and can become unmanageable in heavy weather, so should be avoided.

Freeboard can't be reefed. Too much of it can be dangerous, even if it does increase internal volume, because it results in excessive windage, detracts from performance and increases vulnerability to a knockdown by a breaking sea. Furthermore, at anchor in a breeze there will be a greater tendency to sailing to and fro over a wide area, a hazard to your neighbours and a strain on the holding power of the ground tackle. Very low freeboard, on the other hand, usually means a wet boat and cramped quarters.

If you plan to do most of your cruising in areas where shallow draft is important, such as the Bahamas, Western Caribbean or the European canals, then shallow draft has to be considered and a sacrifice made in performance to windward and also, possibly, in stability. Don't do this unless absolutely necessary; in six years and 50,000 miles we were virtually never bothered by our 7 foot draft on our 40 footer and enjoyed cruising in the Bahamas. One way around this problem is to use a drop-keel or centreboard design *(see Keels)*.

Bows and Sterns

Apart from the very important aesthetic impact that the ends of a yacht have, the bow and stern also affect its sailing characteristics and the crew's comfort.

Buoyancy is needed at the bow to lift the hull over a wave and to deflect spray. Plumb bows are deficient in both respects. Clipper bows often have it to excess and tend to hobby-horse, killing performance and making life miserable for the crew. A flat underbody running back from the stem as found in so many IOR designs will pound upwind. For anchoring a reasonable amount of overhang is an advantage.

Sterns need ample reserve buoyancy to enable them to rise to following seas. Their design also affects the size and shape of the cockpit and the all-important stowage space for deck gear. Particular care must be taken if a double-ender is favoured, as many of these designs are poor in all these respects. Contrast the Valiant 40, which has plenty of volume aft and an excellent reputation as a cruising boat, with the Westsail 32 which is lacking both in buoyancy and cockpit space.

Rigs

The majority of the boats on the oceans have a single aluminum mast, masthead rigged using stainless steel 1x19 rigging, with rod rigging less desirable and unstayed rigs very rare. Keel stepped is preferred to deck stepped. Headsail furling is favoured by the majority. Mainsail furling is becoming accepted as its reliability improves.

Sails are of polyester (Dacron), the new exotics finding little favour with cruisers. Due to downwind chafe, fully battened sails are not popular. Cruising spinnakers are common *(see Sails)*.

While ketches, yawls, schooners and true cutters under 50 feet are still found with older designs, they are rare in modern fibreglass boats where simplicity and easy handling are emphasised. Fractional rigs are not really suitable for offshore cruisers as they are less well supported and need either running backstays or extreme swept back spreaders *(see Chafe)*. Backstayless rigs with exaggerated roaches on the mainsails are not suitable for offshore passages.

Aluminum spars are strong, light and low maintenance and are used on nearly all production boats.

Wooden spars are still found on older boats and some far-eastern products; they are heavy and require careful and continuous maintenance.

Carbon fibre spars are becoming more popular. They have been pioneered by the racers who are looking for strength with less weight. This also benefits cruising boats; some manufacturers are offering carbon fibre masts, booms and poles as options.

The ability to hank on a storm jib is important and requires a separate, preferably removable, forestay if headsail furling gear is used. Running backstays will usually be needed to support it; this additional rigging will reinforce the mast in tough conditions. These should be arranged so that when they are not needed they can be secured out of the way.

An extra track on the mast is recommended for a storm trysail. This mainsail replacement is an excellent sail in the worst conditions and those with mainsail furling should definitely fit a track and carry this sail. This track must be fastened to the mast extremely securely to withstand heavy weather loads.

Boom gallows or a solid vang to take the weight of the boom will protect the occupants of the cockpit in the event of a topping lift failure. A topping lift which leads to the foot of the mast or to the cockpit should be retained and will be available as a spare main halyard.

At least one pole will be needed. Modern beamy boats are stable and comfortable sailing downwind 'wing-on-wing', with the mainsail one side and the headsail poled out on the other. The pole or poles should be mounted on the mast rather than the deck so that only one end needs to be clipped on to the sheets before hoisting and adjusting.

For tropical cruising, mast steps to the lower spreaders will vastly improve visibility when threading through narrow passages and reefs. The kind which fold away against the mast have less windage (noise) and don't snag halyards. A pair a few feet down from the top of the mast facilitates repairs and inspection of mast head fittings. Anyone who has fumbled from below in a bosun's chair will particularly appreciate these.

Whether buying new or used, consider going up one size or more in rigging wire, turnbuckles and tangs. This is not very expensive, adds very little to the windage but gives a huge increase in rig strength. Just going up from 3/8" diameter 1x19 stainless wire to 7/16" increases the breaking strain from 17,500 lbs to 23,500 lbs.

Any boat over 10 years old should have all standing rigging replaced before undertaking a long ocean passage.

Running rigging favoured on cruising boats is good quality pre-stretched polyester. Wire and rope-to-wire combinations cannot be end-for-ended, are hard on sheaves and as they wear develop 'butcher's hooks' which tear both sails and fingers. Exotic fibres do provide minimal stretch for racers but this is not as significant to the cruiser as is their high cost and that they are prone to sudden failure.

Decks and Cockpits

Wide side decks with good non-skid surfaces become very important in rough weather, as does the robustness of the stanchions, lifelines and handrails. Strong attachment points are needed for life-harness jacklines which run from bow to stern on each side. Nylon netting between the lifelines and toe or cap-rail increase security and are very important when there are children on board.

Decks will normally have balsa or marine closed-cell foam coring for rigidity and insulation against both heat and cold. Avoid uncored or plywood cored decks.

On older boats be prepared to remove and re-bed all deck fittings, ports, rails etc. to ensure that the boat stays dry on passage.

Yachts with anchor lockers on the foredeck will have problems if these fill in rough seas. They must be modified so that when locked closed they are effectively sealed.

It used to be thought important to have very small cockpits in cruising boats to minimise the amount of water retained after being pooped. With heavy displacement boats and some double-enders which lack sufficient buoyancy aft this is still a consideration. Most modern designs are far less liable to being pooped and a large cockpit adds much to the pleasure of life aboard, particularly in the tropics where it is the most populated area. The cockpit must have adequate drains of large diameter which preferably lead straight out of the transom without the need for crossed over drainage tubes and seacocks.

A bridge deck or companionway board as high as the seats and locked in place when at sea is a basic safety requirement. The companionway hatch should be able to be closed up in bad weather but must allow quick passage from below or from the cockpit. Hatch boards or doors must be lockable to prevent loss in a roll over.

Several strong-points will be needed in the cockpit for the crew to attach their harnesses *(see Safety)*.

Look for cockpit seats wide and long enough to lie on with high, comfortably angled coamings, also good visibility forward from the steering position. Mainsheet travellers should be outside the cockpit. The positioning and sizing of the winches may have to be altered to allow for short handed sailing, with consideration for the different capabilities of the crew. To minimize the need to go on deck at sea, as many halyards and other sail controls as possible should be led aft to the cockpit area.

A large cockpit table which folds away when at sea is a boon as most meals are eaten there in warm weather.

Spray dodgers can greatly increase comfort in wet and cold conditions. They should be made to be easily folded away or at least have the forward panels removable to allow a through-breeze when needed.

A bimini robust enough to remain up in all but the worst conditions is the best protection against both the sun and rain, and if attached by zippers to the frame may be quickly removed and stowed. Avoid dark colours if planning to be in a hot area as the temperature in the cockpit can become uncomfortable. White PVC covered fabric reflects the sun's heat and is easily cleaned. Stainless steel frames rather than aluminum will be more secure.

If possible have a dodger which is low enough for every crew member to see over from the wheel. The bimini is higher, and should give ample headroom and good visibility forward. A removable transparent panel that joins the two in rainy weather makes life in the cockpit more comfortable. Side curtains on the lifelines adjacent to the cockpit deflect spray and flying fish and minimise sunburn from reflected rays.

Be prepared to add strong catches and seals to all cockpit and deck lockers and the companionway hatch so that in the event of a knockdown or pooping a minimum of water gets below.

Accommodations

Practical interiors have evolved which combine reasonable comfort, adequate storage and safety in most conditions at sea. Beware designs which depart radically from the norm.

Do not expect to be comfortable all the time; when the weather gets rough no one can expect to be relaxed and happy and the best you can do is to minimise the discomfort.

However attractive an interior can look at a boat show, try to imagine how practical it will be when heeled at twenty-five degrees and moving up and down thirty feet every few seconds. Check for good handholds, high fiddles, stout locker closures, secure drawers. Long-term cruisers carry huge amounts of stores, clothing and other supplies. Ample storage lockers are needed and may have to be added as many production boats are deficient in this respect.

A minimum number of sea berths would be for the whole crew less one, with canvas or plywood lee-boards fitted to keep the occupant secure regardless of the antics of the boat. They should be aft of the forward one third of the boat, as the movement further forward when in big seas would make them unusable. It is very important to fight fatigue and the crew will need all the rest they can get.

The galley and head for use at sea should be well back from the bow.

The galley needs an athwartships mounted gimballed stove, at least one large deep sink as close to the centreline as possible, very good insulation in the ice box, and ample secure storage reasonably close for provisions, cooking pans, dishes and utensils, garbage and cleaners. There is no reason to think that one has to 'rough it' except in bad weather; most of the time meals like those at home are the norm.

One head compartment must be useable in all conditions and should be reasonably compact so that you can safely wedge yourself in to answer the calls of nature.

A good navigation area has a work surface at least as big as a folded chart, be sheltered from spray, ideally face forward and with a seat which is practical in rough seas.

Seakindliness

All the pundits tell us that a cruising boat should be seakindly, but to find a definition of this is difficult. What it means to us is a combination of a comfortable motion in all points of sail, light but positive steering, easy handling and dry sailing. A seakindly boat is a joy to sail, one which harmonises with rather than fights the elements and which will stand up to the unexpected.

A yacht which is good on all points of sail, even if some sacrifices are made to gain speed and windward ability, is far more likely to be seakindly than one which can't sail out of its own way.

Those who claim that they would rather get there 'slowly and safely' are deluding themselves. Slow is not safe, quite the opposite in fact, as the longer you are on passage the more likely you are to be threatened by conditions from which you cannot escape. On those inevitable occasions when the going is really tough and you wish that you were at home in bed, the efficient vessel will get there sooner and will not only shorten the time spent in misery but probably give you a more comfortable ride.

BOATING EXPERIENCE

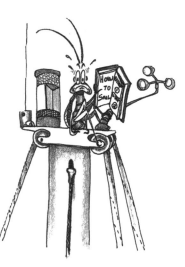

"Have I had enough experience?"
"Am I competent enough to leave?"
are typical questions and doubts of
aspiring offshore cruisers. There is
no formula for proficiency but there
are several ways to gain experience
and knowledge that will give you
diversified boating skills and the
confidence to depart.

It is important to spend as much time on the water as possible. Enjoy fine weather sailing but also seek out the bad weather so that you feel comfortable in any conditions with operations of the boat becoming automatic. Any courses that are available, from sailing skills to celestial and GPS navigation and piloting, radio operation, seamanship, first aid, engine repairs, refrigeration, weather, provisioning, etc. will not only be useful but will allay fears and put you in the cruising mode. Reading the cruising magazines will give you a feel for the life from sailors who are out there, in addition to current information on the equipment which is available. Many of the boat shows now have excellent seminars.

Although Andy and I were fortunate in that we had both grown up sailing and racing, cruising offshore does not require the sophisticated techniques that are used on the race course. Basic knowledge of the rudiments of sail trim are quite sufficient for cruising the oceans. The important aspect is competence with operations such as reefing the mainsail, setting storm sails, and gybing the spinnaker pole to wing out the genoa.

Time spent on boat handling, route planning and the running of the vessel will build courage. Thus, when adverse conditions occur, instead of causing panic, the situation can be assessed objectively and mutual decisions calmly made. 'Hands-on' courses especially can be very beneficial in building these skills. Several people have mentioned the benefits of less experienced women taking a sailing course independently to gain skills and confidence. A further offshore course taken

as a couple not only gives practise at working together but an opportunity to work out differences of opinion with an instructor.

Ideally a couple can independently handle the boat and its equipment, also share the navigation and the cooking. A practice trip with ocean experience is very useful in assessing strengths and weaknesses. Many bare-boat charters are available these days. Those in the Caribbean or Pacific, where one sails in the ocean between islands, are excellent for offshore practise, and are inexpensive, especially out of season. Who would argue with a legitimate reason to visit those warm seas and blue skies? Better still, take your own boat or crew on an excursion into the ocean for a few days. Monitor your reactions to seasickness, tiredness and areas of particular concern or incompetence. Work on these upon your return. Often modifications may be needed. For example, I frequently have to use a winch when Andy can use brute strength, so leads and possibly winch sizes have to be changed. Differences between people's abilities have to be acknowledged and accepted. If they are not, safety procedures, such as reefing, may be put off until the situation is dangerous *(see Safety - On Deck)*.

Practising docking and anchoring in a variety of situations is very important *(see Docking and Anchoring)*. Many good weather weekend cruisers are not used to approaching docks in adverse winds and tides or anchoring in anything but a light breeze. Nothing is more frustrating or demoralizing than the verbal interchange and blame that can occur with a botched job in front of a large crowd.

Knowing how to work the radio is necessary to access weather information, finding out relevant details about the next port of entry, and to cope with crisis situations, as well as for regular social contact. I was horrified, for example, by a couple on a small boat with two young children. We had talked to the husband frequently on the radio across the Pacific. On their arrival in port, emergency mail was waiting requesting he fly home immediately. The wife felt rather lost, having just arrived in a new country, so I suggested we keep in radio contact, but she declined. It transpired she had no idea how to use the radio let alone any knowledge of specific frequencies. How would she have coped if her husband had been sick or fallen overboard?

Obtaining a Ham radio license before leaving is useful *(see Communications)*, to communicate with those overseas and to keep inexpensive contact with those back home. E-mail is widely used (free but no business allowed) and phone patching' is popular; we have friends who talk to their families every night.

Understanding weather and being able to interpret weather charts is of paramount importance. Increasingly, cruisers are purchasing the software to receive weather faxes through their HF radio and regular computer.

Before doing a long trip seek out bad weather. Learn how your boat behaves when lying ahull, practice heaving-to and man overboard drills. Hoist the storm sails and make sure the sheet leads, etc. work. You will have to reef in pitch dark and driving rain, so make sure you can do it blindfolded. Go out into the ocean and experience the swells and the isolation when out of sight of land.

It's amazing how many people fight seasickness, regarding it as a weakness - particularly men! My attitude is that there is nothing to be lost by taking medication (except pride, and you don't have to tell anyone!) but a huge amount to be gained. It not only makes life far more pleasant, it is much safer, being the difference between a fully functioning crew compared to a marginally coping person *(see Seasickness* for suggestions on combatting the problem).

It should be mentioned that although sailing skills and experience are obviously desirable many start cruising cautiously and learn as they go, very successfully. They sail within their limitations, research the demands of their proposed route ahead and take the necessary precautions. They don't take risks with weather systems and have experienced crew aboard for the first long passages. After several overnight runs and varying weather and sea conditions, they soon take offshore passages in their stride. Gradually they build up experience and commonly purchase more equipment to go further afield. In time they acquire the self-sufficiency necessary to make a trip 'off the beaten track', such as *Bagheera's* 20-month meandering voyage across the Indian Ocean.

BUDGETING AND
MONEY MANAGEMENT

"How can you possibly afford it?" asked Andy's mother, never one to mince her words. "We can't," he replied. "Just as I thought," she responded and never mentioned the subject again!

It comes as a surprise to many that it is far less expensive to cruise than to live your regular lifestyle. To begin with, you have no cars, less clothing and inexpensive entertainment. Many items that you would normally run to buy, such as gifts or prepared foods, become fun projects to make on board. However, you can't live on 'peanuts'. Countless people have remarked how wonderful it must be to live on $500 a month, seemingly forgetting what they spend on food and sundries at home. Just because you are in the middle of the ocean doesn't mean the boat costs nothing to maintain or that those mouths aren't forever open!

Our main income came from the rent from our house. We also worked while living in Australia for a year. In addition, we had some funds in the bank which we felt were a necessary contingency with three young children in tow, and elderly relatives back home.

THE BUDGET

Budgeting falls into four categories: the initial budget for buying the boat and equipment, the cruising budget, the general life budget and an emergency fund.

Initial Budget

To arrive at your initial budget *see **Buying The Boat***. In addition, allow for optional extras such as electronics and general equipment.

Cruising Budget

As prices vary hugely around the world, even within areas such as the Caribbean and Mediterranean, it is hard to give a precise cruising budget. Most seem to agree that $1000-$1500 a month for a couple is adequate, but this refers only to the budget for cruising, not boat insurance, new equipment, major inland travel expenses and trips back home.

Because we picked our boat up in France we went straight into an offshore budget. We found those who leave from their home port, particularly for short periods, always claim much lower cruising costs. Not only do they have the boat organised just how they want it, gear in tip-top condition and haul-out before they leave, but they also have their lockers filled with supplies and spares that have made their way to the boat during the previous months - none of which get counted into their cruising budget!

On average, at least a third of the budget will be spent on boat-related items, but again this depends where you are cruising and how handy you are at repairs. Boat expenses include fuel, water, moorage, cruising permits and harbour dues, along with charts, pilots and guidebooks, not to mention maintenance, repairs, replacements and spares. We carried a wide variety of spares and tools and Andy was able to repair almost anything on the boat. This is an important factor when cruising 'off the beaten track'. Those who have to call in professional help for every mechanical or electrical problem, and have parts flown in, will find their budgets soaring. Knowing your boat and having basic maintenance skills before you leave can reap huge dividends.

Stocking up selectively in areas that are cheaper, both for provisions and for boat needs, such as spares and bottom paints, can also make a considerable difference to the budget. In French Polynesia, for example, a case of 24 cans of beer cost $37: fortunately we had stocked up in Venezuela at $2.95 a case!

Although there are people cruising on a wide range of incomes, from the budget cruiser in the most basic of small boats to those in mega yachts with all the 'toys' and a crew, most long distance cruisers appeared to have similar budget constraints to our own. We all enjoy eating and drinking local fare when it is inexpensive, but restaurants are given a miss where they are uneconomical, and even entertaining on board may sometimes be curtailed. In French Polynesia, for example, you were more likely to be offered tea to drink aboard *Bagheera*. Again, most cruisers want to take advantage of travel opportunities in the lands that are visited, the essence of cruising for many of us. In Europe we frequently took local buses inland as we were often anchored in tourist towns or ports and felt we were missing the true flavour of the country. Sometimes our travels needed more funds and organization, but how sad it would be to stop at Motril in Spain and not visit the Alhambra in Granada, to anchor in Mombasa in Kenya and not go on safari, or to visit Phuket in Thailand and not see the Grand Palace in Bangkok, let alone miss Patphong Road, home of the infamous go-go bars!

Most cruisers also maintain an excellent yacht and leave a good impression behind them. In the past we have known of boats that were run down and owners who left without paying their bills. This creates a negative reaction to boaters and sometimes an unwelcome reception, even additional charges, for those travelling in their wake. A clean wake policy is paramount and remember you have a wonderful asset for repaying hospitality. Being invited aboard and entertained on your boat will be a cherished memory.

General Life Budget

It is easy to forget ongoing expenses back home when estimating a cruising budget. Expenses will obviously vary hugely but we found that house and income taxes, and insurance policies - life, medical, house, university - came to a surprisingly large amount.

Emergency Fund

Hopefully you won't need to use your emergency fund but you will feel more secure if you have one. A crisis can arise back home and being able to hop onto a flight at short notice will save considerable anxiety. There may also be an accident with the boat, or a medical problem. Without an emergency fund it could be the end of your cruise.

MONEY MANAGEMENT

Credit Cards

VISA and MASTERCARD are accepted almost everywhere, less so AMERICAN EXPRESS. Most cruisers use credit cards to access money. Credit cards with a debit cash facility or direct debit cards, which can be used in many countries, overcome the interest charged with a cash withdrawal, but one has to ensure a balance is maintained in one's account back home. Be sure to keep a record of transactions.

Travellers Cheques

Carry both large and small denominations; small amounts for a quick shop in a remote area, where the exchange rate will probably be poor, and high denominations as there is often a charge per cheque. Many banks require passport identification before cashing Travellers Cheques.

Bank Transfers, Drafts and Money Orders

Even when directed to a specific bank, these can take several days to clear and can be expensive to arrange.

Cash

The U. S. dollar is the most commonly accepted foreign currency (also Sterling in many places). Cash can be useful for transactions, particularly in developing nations, but often gets a poor rate of exchange at the bank.

Eurocheques

These are accepted in Europe and many other areas of the world (not North America). They are used in conjunction with a bank account and identity card. Cheques are limited in amount but can be instantly cashed at the bank and in many shops, a real advantage over having credit cards cleared in the bank, which can take considerable time.

Watch out for **varying exchange rates**. You may be spending considerably more than you thought, and make sure you go through all your pockets for local currency before your last purchase in a country.

WORKING ALONG THE WAY

What could be more ideal than conveniently finding work when one's cruising budget is running low? But don't count on it! Unfortunately, unless one has very specific skills, work is hard to find. In our experience few have done it successfully. Dave Bonner, our sailmaker friend who made us a new mainsail in Australia and a dinghy cover in Thailand, is one of the few exceptions. The advantage of his business is that he can cruise and work simultaneously. Others we've met also work amongst the yachts by repairing engines, electrics, electronics and refrigeration. Some make T-shirts and craft items. Whatever the skill, one has to be sensitive to the local businesses.

A few cruisers manage to get jobs ashore but locals are often prejudiced against foreigners taking jobs. Doctors can sometimes find locums; others with specific skills may find piecemeal work, and some do seasonal fruit picking. English teachers may be in demand while the luxury hotels may be looking for sports instructors. Most countries have specific work permit requirements. An additional problem is that work interferes with your route planning around the world's weather systems. The time it takes to find and complete the job could put you in the middle of the hurricane season. You may also have to put the boat in a marina, spend money on smart clothing, buy a vehicle and be liable for taxation.

Writing for magazines and photography has been a viable way of making a living for some, but competition is now very stiff with staff writers often completing the major articles. Payment is generally meagre for the labour required. Some people charter successfully but standards have to be extremely high in both boat maintenance and cuisine. Bookings are unpredictable, often with more boats seeking business than charterers. Increasingly, countries are imposing qualification, ownership and safety regulations on charter yachts operating in their waters.

We were very lucky that a one-year working visa was given as a perk for being a participant in the Tall Ship's events during the Australian Bicentenary. I was able to find work as a psychologist for the Department of Health while Andy became the Winch Doctor, doing boat maintenance. He also worked for Beneteau at boat shows and painted houses for my department. We hoped this additional income would top up the cruising kitty. However, we found that once back to a regular lifestyle we needed a regular income to sustain it!

BUSINESS BACK HOME

However foot loose and fancy free they would like to be, most cruisers still have some business back home that needs attention. It could just entail forwarding mail and paying bills but may be a great deal more, such as managing your house or ordering parts for the boat. Without someone to manage these affairs you might experience considerable frustration and many expensive phone calls.

Most people find willing relatives or friends to take on this job; others employ agencies to forward the mail selectively, make sure the bank balance is topped up, pay income taxes and regular bills and be the liaison between cruisers and their friends, particularly when guests are joining the boat. As you can see, this is starting to sound like a full-time job so it is important to have everything organised in the simplest form. Try to arrange annual payments for bills and automatic transfers between bank accounts. Allocate certain schedules for sending mail. Attention to these arrangements will make life not only easier but more economical.

A problem that is familiar can be simple to solve but when details and background are lacking it can be a nightmare. We found the fax machine, and now e-mail, most useful for providing information succinctly.

Rather than asking relatives to find boat equipment, an account with a marine catalogue company works well; be sure to have their latest catalogue on hand. Have contact addresses for all the manufacturers of equipment on board. (Remember goods should always have an invoice included and be addressed to the boat; for example, *'for Canadian Yacht Bagheera in Transit'*, in the hope of avoiding any duty.)

Aside from the chores it is also important that someone knows where you are planning to be so that if there are unexpected crises, family or otherwise, you can be contacted. Regular phone calls serve this purpose, but do not schedule them so frequently that it imposes deadlines to your sailing schedule, or so rigidly that there is concern if you are a day late. An HF long distance radio can come in very useful here, with the potential to send faxes or e-mail, or use the Ham radio for phone patching, depending on your software and radio licenses *(see Communications)*. Increasingly, cell phone networks are expanding all over the world - if you want to be that contactable!

BUYING A BOAT

Before starting to look for a boat, certain basic parameters must be established.

1) The number of people who will be cruising affects the accommodations and the size of the vessel.
2) The type of cruising planned. Obviously the sailor planning to challenge the Northwest Passage will be far more particular in his needs than the one who wants to island hop in the Caribbean.
3) The kind of boat favoured *(see Designs and Construction)*.
4) The budget available for the boat and equipment, including any taxes payable.

Affordability is a major consideration and if your cruising includes ocean passages it is advisable to buy quality rather than size. A smaller but well-constructed boat is far better than a larger one built to a price for the weekend sailor.

NEW OR USED?

A new yacht comes with its gloss unmarred, gift-wrapped with a good warranty and with zero hours on the sails and machinery. Choices of hull colour, upholstery, deck gear etc. are often offered and the boat can be outfitted with the exact equipment the buyer favours. Apart from some initial teething troubles, cruising should be reasonably free of gear failure for several years.

When buying new, go to a dealer who has a good reputation for service, who can arrange to install all the extra equipment and electronics and who will stand behind his product. A yacht is highly complex and any glitches need to be sorted out promptly.

The downside to buying new is the greater cost, which can be considerable, particularly where additional taxes are levied on new vessels. Whatever the quality of the yacht purchased, depreciation will be significant in the first year, less so in the second and third years and minimal thereafter provided it is well built and maintained.

A used boat costs less and may come with extra equipment added by previous owners. Probably the best value for money is a yacht that is only a couple of years old but these are not always easy to find. The older the boat, the more wear and tear there will be in machinery, sails, equipment and cosmetics. This means more ongoing maintenance and gear replacement to budget for, but there is no reason why a vessel which is sound structurally should not give several decades of service.

MONOHULL OR MULTI?

The increasing popularity of cruising multihulls in several parts of the world shows that these can be practical offshore vessels. Catamarans are more often favoured over trimarans, and hundreds of successful ocean crossings have been made.

A monohull gets its stability from the ballast which acts like a pendulum below the centre of floatation, and even if completely rolled over can be expected to right itself. A multihull relies entirely on the floatation of widely spaced hulls and if capsized will not be able to be righted, making route planning to avoid extreme weather conditions even more important.

Advantages of multihulls. High sailing speeds (unless heavily loaded) and the ability to have tremendous interior and deck space; also light weight, shallow draft and the lack of heeling.

Disadvantages. The constant quick motion can induce sickness, the inability to carry much load without severely inhibiting performance and the high cost when properly engineered to take the enormous stresses these craft are subjected to in a big sea.

PRODUCTION YACHTS

The advent of fibreglass in the '40s has led to yachts being produced in factories on a production line, giving the consumer the benefits of huge savings in costs. The majority of yachts under 50' sailing the oceans are standard fibreglass models by a 'name' manufacturer. They vary in quality depending on the market being served by the builder; a typical example of some of the best are the Swans from Nautor of Finland. At the other end of the scale are boats built to minimum standards to sell at a low price for use only in sheltered waters. However, price alone will not guide a buyer as to the quality of construction as there are many quite expensive yachts which experienced sailors would not consider for ocean voyaging while others which are more affordable make reliable cruisers, particularly from some of the European builders.

CUSTOM YACHTS

Unfortunately the term 'custom' is used to cover the whole range of non-production yachts, from a masterpiece turned out by a fine yard to the amateur completed kit boat or the homebuilt effort which is loved only by its creator.

We would all love to have a naval architect design our 'dream' yacht and have it put together by an experienced yard. For those who can afford it this can be a very enjoyable experience. However, affordability is the key word, as costs can be double the equivalent production boat. For those who favour steel, aluminum, wood or exotic plastics, the custom route is usually the only option.

Several builders offer hulls and decks in various materials for home or yard finishing and these are sometimes referred to as 'semi-custom'.

There are usually several custom yachts available on the used market which can be an excellent buy if from a reputable designer's drawing board and a yard of repute. Unfortunately there are many with deficiencies in design, construction, layout or materials. Buyers should investigate the origins and history of the boat, particularly if home finished, ensuring that any survey be done by someone fully qualified *(see Surveys)*. Be wary of unusual interior layouts and radical rigs. So many less experienced people think that they can improve on what has evolved over the years.

PRIVATE SALES OR BROKERED SALES?

Many owners prefer to try to sell their yachts themselves. They may not wish to pay a broker a commission, or they believe that their yacht is worth more than the broker feels is its market value. If it is for the former reason then a buyer may get a better bargain; if for the latter then a buyer could well end up paying more than the boat is worth.

When buying privately, thoroughly research the true value of the yacht before committing. Consider using a lawyer to check on liens, to pay off any mortgages, to draw up a contract and bill of sale, ensuring that you get clear title. He should also hold your deposit in his escrow account and ensure that all taxes are paid. These are all services which are normally offered free by a good broker.

YACHT BROKERS

Using a broker should take away many of the worries when buying a used boat; but this is not always the case. As in most other professions there are good guys and bad guys and we are constantly surprised at the lack of knowledge combined with a ruthless urge to sell that many display. Choosing your broker is one of the most important steps in your search for a yacht.

Find one with whom you can communicate, who has been established a reasonable time, who comes recommended and whose business is not confined merely to the local scene. Ensure he is knowledgeable about cruising yachts, as a specialist in game fishing vessels or grand-prix racers is unlikely to be much help to you, and put him to work. Be loyal to your broker and keep in touch, so that he knows you are relying on him to work on your behalf. He has access to yachts offered by other brokers, very much like real estate, so boats you find advertised by another outfit can be shown by him. Brokers earn a commission from the seller once a boat is sold and there is no cost to the buyer for their services.

The broker should be given clear instructions regarding size, accommodations, budget, any special requirements and also be given examples of the types of boat favoured. Depending on your needs he will search locally, nationally or world-wide. International multiple-listing services such as the BUCNET to which major brokers subscribe have considerably simplified this process; a client who has a clear idea of what he wants can often have details of suitable boats in his hands within minutes of meeting the broker.

THE BUYING PROCESS

Having found a satisfactory boat the usual procedure is:

1) To make an offer in writing subject to certain conditions and pay a deposit. The conditions or 'subject clauses' protect buyers' positions until they are satisfied that they wish to go ahead with the purchase. Typical conditions are: 'Subject to satisfactory surveys', 'subject to satisfactory sea trial' and 'subject to satisfactory financing arrangements'. The deposit is usually 10% of the offered price and should always be held in an escrow account.

    If using a broker the documentation, etc. will be done for you, though it may be that your lawyer will also want to check. If buying privately a lawyer is strongly recommended.

2) There is usually some negotiation on both the price and the terms, with the broker acting as a go-between. When agreement is reached this conditional contract is signed by the buyers and sellers.

3) The parties will have an agreed timetable both for the removal of the subject clauses and for completing the purchase. The cost of all surveys and inspections is borne by the buyers and when all conditions are satisfied they must sign off the 'subjects'. At this time there is a firm contract. Should any of the conditions not be satisfactory and not signed off then the buyers may wish to re-negotiate or back out and recover the deposit *(see Surveys)*.

4) On the completion date the buyers should have insurance in place and have made arrangements for mooring the boat. In exchange for a bank draft for the balance owing they will receive the keys and title with a bill of sale properly executed.

5) There are different requirements in various countries for registering your ownership of a yacht. If your plan is to cruise foreign waters it is important that the correct papers are obtained. For instance, in the USA there is State Licensing or Federal Documentation. A State Licence will usually not be accepted in another country so the process of Documentation through the US Coastguard is necessary. Similarly, in the UK yachts need to be either Registered as a British vessel or be on the Small Ships Registry. In Canada buyers should get their boats Federally Registered for travel abroad; although there is also has a Provincial licensing system this is not accepted in most places overseas.

SURVEYS

The survey process is the most important step to be taken before committing to the purchase of a vessel.

The buyers must decide how many professionals they will employ as the cost of these inspections falls to them. If the boat is only a couple of years old and has obviously been well maintained a hull survey will probably suffice. The older the boat the more important it is to have the machinery and rig checked out. Sometimes the same surveyor will do all three jobs, but it is preferable that engines be checked by a specialist in the particular model and that a rigger does the spars.

The choice of a surveyor is important. In many places anyone can hang up a shingle and set up in business without qualifications, thus picking names out of the telephone directory may not be satisfactory. In the USA there are some professional bodies such as SAMS and NAMS whose members are required to be qualified.

Brokers are frequently asked to suggest surveyors and the majority will suggest a choice of good professionals. Unfortunately there are also some who are so anxious for the sale to go through that they will recommend an incompetent or dishonest one. Reputation and referrals by satisfied clients are the only sure way, so get some names and follow up references.

The one you choose should be competent in the hull material and type of construction. Most are experienced with fibreglass but wood, metals and ferrocement require special knowledge and equipment.

The hull survey will include a haul-out so that the underwater parts can be checked. It should also be a 'buyer's survey' not an insurance survey which is far less thorough. Try to be present but keep out of the way; you will be called over if anything unusual is found. At completion there will be a verbal report with a number of recommendations; some are important and may need to be done right away while others can be done during routine maintenance. A written report will follow; the insurers and any financing body will require copies.

Many surveyors will also give their estimate of market value. This may or may not be accurate since values change with the economy, the competition and locality.

All used boats will have some deficiencies and a buyer cannot expect a 'new' condition for a 'used' price. Depending on what the surveyors find and the amount of the offer, a decision has to be made as to whether to proceed, re-negotiate or withdraw. Wear and tear due to the vessel's age should be accepted, as should minor maintenance lapses. Any structural defects or damage should be assessed for the cost of putting right, unless these were known before the offer was made. If significant, the seller might be induced to adjust the price or contribute towards the repairs.

SEA TRIALS

Sea trials rarely enable a buyer to assess the sailing qualities of a vessel properly.

The main value to be derived from a sea trial is to ensure that everything works. All sails should be hoisted and inspected, the engine given a good work-out, all electronic and electrical gear must be seen to work satisfactorily. The steering gear, winches, windlass, propane and water systems, heater and pumps, should all be tested.

Ideally one would arrange for these trials to be done in a variety of wind and sea conditions so that the behaviour of the boat can be assessed. Unfortunately this is almost impossible to arrange and one has to accept the weather that prevails on the day of the trial. Unless lucky enough to have a full gale coincide with the sea trial, one has to use other criteria to establish whether the boat is going to be suitable for longterm cruising. This will normally have been done before reaching the offer to purchase stage, based on the design and the reputation of the model, designer and builder.

This is also the time to ensure that the inventory is agreed. We well remember a case where two lawyers profited substantially. When a new owner took delivery he found that the bulkhead mounted clock and barometer had been removed. The seller claimed sentimental value, a gift from a loved one. The buyer rightly claimed that they were part of the yacht. Instead of simply replacing the missing items with new ones the seller became stubborn and they ended up in court.

A list of equipment should be supplied by the owner and incorporated into a specification sheet by the broker. During sea trials all this equipment should be identified; anything on the yacht not listed should be discussed and agreement reached between the buyer, seller and broker as to what remains and what will be removed before delivery. Charts and navigation gear, galley equipment and linen, fishing tackle, dinghies and outboards, spare parts and safety equipment may all be excluded, it being gear that the sellers intend to remove for use on their next yacht.

CHAFE

*Chafe probably is the most frequent cause for repairs at sea;
chafe related breakdowns particularly occur when it really blows.
Nearly all chafe damage can be prevented by careful preparation and by choosing the right gear.*

All sails and running rigging should be checked for wear before
long passages. Go up the mast and visually check the standing rigging
and spreaders especially for chafe causing snags. If something looks,
sounds or feels different always investigate.

MAINSAILS

Mainsails are vulnerable when sailing downwind as the boat's continuous rolling in the ocean swells causes the fabric to rub constantly on the spreaders and shrouds, especially with swept-back
spreaders and with fully battened mains.

Preventive measures include
1) Having a vang or preventer which exerts downward pressure on
    the boom to remove as much belly and twist from the sail as pos-
    sible.
2) Sailing with the wind on the quarter instead of dead down wind,
    and sheeting in slightly.
3) Applying self-adhesive chafe patches where the sail touches the
    spreaders and to every seam where it touches the shrouds, not for-
    getting that when the sail is reefed these places will change.
4) With full battens, sewing thick dacron webbing patches where there
    is contact between batten pockets and shrouds, again including con-
    tact points when reefed.
5) Ensuring that spreader tips are taped and smooth.
6) Taping carpet (poor man's baggywrinkle) to the backs of spread-
    ers and at intervals on the shrouds before each long passage.
7) Triple stitching all seams of all sails is most important.
8) If a lazy jack system is fitted, every effort should be made to keep
    the lines and blocks off the sail and the latter should be padded.

HEADSAILS

These are less vulnerable. Chafe mainly occurs if there is contact between the foot of the sail and the stanchions; it may also happen if the leech contacts the spreaders and inner forestay when tacking. Self adhesive chafe patches should be applied to the sail at these chafe points.

MIZZENS

Use the same precautions as for mainsails.

RUNNING RIGGING

1) Halyards wear at the masthead sheaves and to a lesser extent at snap-shackles, turning blocks and winches. Always have excess length so that worn ends may be cut away. Use low stretch all-rope halyards unless you are an expert at wire splicing at sea!

2) Both headsail and spinnaker wear quickly when using a pole to wing out the sails. Prevent this by covering the last few inches where they pass through the jaws of the pole with soft plastic hose (use reinforced nylon, such as garden hose).

LINES

Short lengths of hose (fire hose works well and doesn't 'walk' along the lines) are also convenient for slipping over mooring lines, anchor strop or dinghy towing line to prevent chafe at the fairlead or bow roller. The same remedy will prevent chafe on stern lines ashore especially when on rocks or around trees. In heavy weather, warps or a drogue towed from the stern and sea anchors must also be protected. Anchors stowed on deck, in lockers or the bilge must be secured as any movement can cause damage.

CHAFE BELOW

As on deck, the constant motion of the boat can cause chafe to items below or in deck lockers. Goods that can slide around can rub against themselves, the hull, and the bulkheads, causing breakages and leaking.

Dishes, mugs, glasses, etc. should be secured with pegs to hold them securely in place when stacked. Use baffles in food cupboards and stuff with soft items (we use sponges) if there is still a problem. Use old socks around wine bottles! Clothes in hanging lockers can rub and wear; stop the movement by packing tightly. Protect good clothes from sailing ones that might have abrasive zippers and Velcro.

Electric cables, water hoses, etc. can be damaged by constant movement, so secure with stainless steel hose clamps and 'zap straps'. Have floorboards fastened in the cabin sole in case of a knockdown. Make sure all locker contents can be made fast so no movement occurs; not only can there be chafe but the banging will drive you crazy as you are trying to get to sleep!

CHILDREN ON BOARD

It was particularly special for us that we were able to cruise with our children. But what did they feel about our proposed new lifestyle? When we made our decision to 'blue water' cruise, Duncan was eight, Colin just six and Jamie not yet two years old. For the elder two children, going away on the boat was an exciting proposition. They had cruised most long weekends and all their summer holidays and they loved life on board. When we mentioned that it would at times be rougher than the benign waters of the Pacific Northwest, they cheered, "Better bouncing in the forward cabin." They had never had a problem with sea sickness or living in confined quarters, so we had no qualms about their adaptability on a full-time basis—so long as we could take them ashore regularly to run off their energy.

Obviously not all children have enjoyed such a fortunate initiation to sailing. Just as their parents may have anxieties about the proposed new lifestyle, so may their children. In particular, it is generally not appealing to teenagers to be hauled away from their peers; being cooped up on a small boat in the middle of the ocean probably isn't the preferred environment for either the teenagers or their parents. This isn't to say that there aren't many teenagers happily cruising but you need to be sensitive to their social and emotional needs and plan the route accordingly.

Whatever the age, cruising must be fun. If it isn't fun for some on board it won't be fun in the long run for anyone. Being transient and always leaving new friends can be hard on children, so we modified our cruising plans enormously for the boys. We soon learnt that it was also to our benefit, as their interests, activities and friends were the highlights of much of our trip. If we met another family we would stay extra time in an anchorage or plan to cruise together. Encouraged especially by Andy, the boys became intensely interested in wild life, so visiting out-of-the-way places, diving and going on safari took much of our travel time. Now their memories are often better than ours because these experiences stimulated them to read many of the reference books we had on board. When Colin became interested in gems and fossils, we went off to the mines in Sri Lanka and made these subjects much of our focus in East and South Africa. Whether shells, or fish, or coral, the boys were fascinated by the underwater and we could never have enough of the outer islands. This is in sharp contrast to many cruisers who soon profess to be 'islanded out'.

AGE

I am frequently asked the best age for children to cruise. As mentioned in *Age and Stage* I strongly believe that if the opportunity to go sailing presents itself you should take advantage of it. It is too wonderful an experience to be missed. However, the general consensus of the many boat kids we have known and their parents is that the optimum ages for children to sail extendedly are between six and twelve. At this stage they are relatively independent, readily accept change and enjoy doing activities with their parents. Children under six are no problem on board, with certain safety requirements, but they do not remember very much. The isolated incidents they can recall might have happened anywhere and the special flavours of different cultures and scenery are lost to them.

Over thirteen, children are getting into those rather frustrating teenage years. One minute they are full of enthusiasm to rush off diving, to the beach, or just to come ashore with their parents to imbibe the wondrous sights. The next moment it seems they are much too old to build dams or look for shells, and going ashore to see yet another ruin is plain boring, particularly with their parents—sound familiar? The mood and character changes associated with puberty put a strain on children and adults when confined together, 24 hours a day!

ACTIVITIES ON BOARD

We received several comments like, "Won't the boys be bored out of their minds? How will you be able to entertain them all day long?" While we were cruising the boys never once said "I'm bored" although they've said it frequently since we've been back. We never had to entertain them, but did provide quantities of materials for them to amuse themselves and took an active interest in any of their projects. Toys such as Lego, Playmobil and farm animals were used separately or in combination and frequently 'set-ups' covered the entire main cabin table. Duncan was a great motivator in getting these started and Colin was very creative with the role-playing to go with them. With the fiddles at the edges of the table in place and with the help of non-slip mats, these creations grew in the roughest of seas and when entire battalions of horses keeled over in unison it just added to the make-believe.

Art supplies—coloured paper, glue, scissors, pens, crayons and paints (in harbour!) were a great favourite with Colin, and later he spent hours making most detailed models in multi-coloured Fimo clay. I thoroughly recommend this clay; it stays malleable, the dyes do not stain and it only takes ten minutes to bake, although keeping the necessary low temperature in our oven was quite a challenge. A wide range of art supplies were used to make birthday cards; special cards can take all day and boat children become very creative.

We had many board games. They were played in the evenings when we were cruising alone and occasionally on trips but card games were played morning, noon and night. I wonder how many thousands of games of UNO I have played in the cockpit!

Reading was a number one activity and the boys never hankered after TV although I have to admit they made a beeline for the closest television set when on shore. When crossing the Indian Ocean I calculated we had about 500 books on board, a major portion being for the children. Many were reference books or children's encyclopedias that were read over and over again. I frequently read aloud on passages. Not only did it make good entertainment (we particularly enjoyed Roald Dahl) the trip passed quickly and it developed the boys' auditory skills, an area that wasn't being reinforced with school on board.

The boys also developed collections. They had bags of foreign coins and we started an album for stamps with underwater life. They had their own boxes of shells and carvings, and Colin had his huge collection of rocks, gems and fossils. "Not more rocks," Andy would moan as another bag came on board, "how does this boat keep afloat?"

There were several forms of music aboard. The boys played the keyboard and recorder and listened at length to tapes in the main cabin or latterly on their Walkmans. Besides music we had story tapes and particular ones for special occasions. Christmas tapes were special favourites but weren't allowed to be played until December 1st! Duncan taught himself the guitar as we cruised up the Australian coast as light relief from the high school curriculum and became very proficient at accompanying us at beach barbecues. When he returned to school in Canada he took up the tuba - imagine having that on a boat!

With all these activities, together with the excitements of the sea the changing routine of the daily watches, the special attention to preparing enticing culinary creations particularly when there were special celebrations and the chit-chat on the radio, far from being boring, the problem was finding time to fit everything in.

When at anchor and not ashore, the boys spent a huge amount of time in the water - swimming, snorkelling, and off in the dinghy. In the Mediterranean they found a small boat adrift and they had a great time paddling it around; in the Caribbean we purchased a windsurfer and in Singapore we bought an inflatable ring to tow. They could spend hours swinging from the bosun's chair strung up on a halyard or climbing up the mast to the spreaders. Jumping off the spinnaker pole was a very popular activity with their friends and there would often be a line of kids on the deck awaiting their turn -interspersed on occasion by a few adults.

With the advent of sailing and navigation software, the number of yachts with a computer on board is increasing dramatically and with it the enjoyment of computer games for cruising kids. The development of children's computer skills is of course very important for their future life and the boat is the perfect place to practise. Sending e-mail or faxes to friends back home is an additional attraction.

EDUCATION

Travelling itself is a wonderful education but being committed to the regular curriculum, I never considered that the children's formal schooling could be abandoned. As far as Andy and I were concerned, although we were opting out of a regular lifestyle, we did not want to compromise our children's future. I was delighted with the existence and quality of the British Columbia Correspondence Education Programme. Reactions to our taking the boys out of regular school varied. Most believed the experience of travel would compensate, while others were quite critical, although being a qualified teacher did help allay their fears. Ironically, while we were away, home-schooling became an acceptable popular alternative and I was rebuked by one woman on our return for then putting the boys back into the regular system!

Although having a Teaching Certificate gave me familiarity with the texts, goals and realistic expectations, it wasn't necessary for me to have these qualifications for the boys to complete the programme itself. Except for the younger grades each level was presented so the children could complete the work themselves. My involvement was in supervision, extra explanation, inspiration or materials and general

encouragement. School often involved family and friends. One of the disadvantages of working independently is the stimulation lost from the rest of the class so we substituted with family brainstorming. Friends also became interviewees and audiences.

There are many different educational programmes being studied by the children afloat. Some are completing Canadian programmes from other provinces while most American families subscribe to the Calvert system, with programmes such as the University of Nebraska course for the later years of high school. The Australian States with many children in the Outback also have their own well-developed systems. Our boys took the correspondence programme from New South Wales after leaving their Australian schools and before the beginning of the next Canadian school year. (The Australian school year runs with the calendar year). All these programmes appeared to work successfully, particularly because they were structured, setting out a daily routine to be followed with supervision by parents.

The systems used different teaching and marking methods. The Calvert system appeared to be run on traditional lines, was not as child oriented in instruction as the Canadian and Australian and there were complaints about the cost of the exams. The Canadian and Australian systems followed modern educational philosophies and were both experiential and creative. Both programmes charged minimal costs for supplies. They required papers be sent at regular intervals for marking. This system works well in a regular postal area. However, the nature of yachting - going off the beaten track and having to take advantage of favourable weather conditions - produces erratic itineraries. Feedback is often several months away, and the educational impact substantially reduced.

I tried to overcome this by marking the boys' work at the time and explaining their errors. However this involved hours of extra work, particularly when I had to figure out all the math problems myself!

The New South Wales system emphasized the verbal and the personal. Colin, in particular, enjoyed completing many of his lessons into the tape recorder. Feedback was also given verbally by tape. The problem with this method was that it took hours to listen to every aspect of their work and the corrections suggested, compared to speed reading the written and focusing on the pertinent comments for the subject at hand. The lessons involved several separate sheets which provided variety but were easily mislaid and made school in the cockpit impossible, as they could be whisked up by the wind and into the water in an instant.

A popular British course is the Worldwide Education Service which sets out programmes for a year. Texts have to be ordered and work sent off at the end of each semester with an evaluation of teacher and pupil. Most parents seemed to feel that this offered a flexibility that suited the cruising lifestyle but that they were very much teachers, rather than supervisors.

An alternative to following a regular system is for the parents to set school schedules daily. We met very few people who did this because of the work involved and the resentment from their children who resisted a timetable imposed by their parents. When this route was followed it was generally short term, filling in the gap between two systems, returning home, or following math and reading texts and writing a diary, if only cruising for a year.

Time spent on school varied from about two to five hours a day. For us it was generally three to four and a half hours depending on the type of assignments required. Story writing, research, science experiments and art projects often took longer but were the most fulfilling. The Canadian programme covered all regular subjects including four language arts, maths, science, social studies and art, and suggested games and drama activities as well. Those completing only the academic basics took less time to complete their courses but often, we noticed, these children complained they were bored with school. We met no one who adhered to a monday to friday routine. School fitted in around visits ashore and weather conditions on trips.

Although correspondence programmes work well for elementary school, the high school programmes were often restricted in scope, particularly in science, and much more demanding. After a year of enjoying school in Australia, Duncan found the Grade 8 correspondence programme somewhat tedious and very time consuming. He was approaching 13 and although he still enjoyed the travel, he missed the challenge of the classroom, team sports and general socialization with his mates. We met a number of teenage 'boat kids' around the world who were obviously happy with their alternate lifestyle; however, like Duncan almost all were looking forward to returning home and becoming 'regular' adolescents at the local high school.

Having been a regular programmed Mum with Duncan and Colin - planning, paying for, and helping organize their pre-school - I was fascinated to find that Jamie did 90 percent of the fine and gross motor activities spontaneously. Of course, by this time I knew what equipment to have around. Not surprisingly, water play was his favourite activity and he spent hours in 'his' swimming pool, dripping also in suntan lotion and decked in a large hat. Swinging from the rigging, or even climbing up the chart table was great fun when no playgrounds were around; and how many little boys have been able to 'help' Daddy, on a daily basis, with their own set of tools?

SAFETY

Having children on board raises the question of safety. When the boys
were small we tied the car seat to the stern pulpit. They were safe and
secure and on the leeward side they were entertained by the wake gur-
gling by.

When Duncan was a baby we had a San Juan 24 and I made him
a covered, canvas hammock that hung from the deckhead and was stead-
ied with shockcord. Much was the surprise of the customs official who
came on board as we entered the States when a small hand suddenly
pulled his hair; Andy had forgotten to mention three-month-old
Duncan on the crew list! We soon moved up in boat size and Colin and
Jamie slept in a basket, then a carry cot that was firmly wedged in the
quarter berth with cushions. As they became bigger this berth also became
a play pen with a lee cloth at the foot and the boys would spend many
a happy hour surrounded by their toys. As the movement of a boat is
so soporific, they would generally fall asleep on a passage.

When anchored we often put the boys in a jolly jumper strung
on a halyard. They loved bouncing during 'happy hour', in fact
Duncan was such an ace performer on the foredeck he used to draw
quite a crowd. Of course, we were always there with him for safety.
It is the one to three-year-old stage that is most hectic and it is common to put netting all around the lifelines during this period, indeed
we had it around *Bagheera* for our entire circumnavigation. It makes

the boat safe, stops toys going overboard and psychologically takes a load off one's mind.

Most boat children learn to swim when they are young and nothing is quite like the enthusiasm they exude when learning to snorkel in their tiny masks and flippers. Sadly, boat families have not been without their tragedies. When swimming from the boat, especially when choppy, have young children in life jackets or arm bands if there is any doubt that you may not be able to swim with them or watch at all times. Jamie always wore his and because I would also be on deck, I was able to relax.

At sea the boys were not allowed out of the cockpit except on specific supervised occasions, such as watching dolphins from the bow. Andy and I also had the same rule. If one went on deck, the other was in the cockpit observing. It would only be on a very calm day that the one on deck wouldn't wear a lifeharness. Our cockpit is roomy, feels secure and we never felt confined. Daily, until Australia, Jamie wore his comfortable lifejacket (some you can't sit down in or a neck collar is uncomfortable). Duncan and Colin wore lifejackets in cold climes but like all the kids only wore life-harnesses in the tropics when on watch alone or when it was rough. If rough and we wanted to tack or gybe or make a sail adjustment, the boys generally stayed below. Flogging lines, a swinging boom and not being able to work the cockpit freely were the hazards of having them on deck.

For ease and safety ashore a back-pack works well for babies and toddlers if the terrain is rough. We much preferred to take Jamie in the stroller if possible; it was not only more relaxing for us it was a great carrier for all the groceries on the way home. Unfortunately we overtaxed it and it finally broke down at a most inopportune moment when I was trying to escape some persistent vendors in the bazaar in Istanbul!

Transferring in and out of the dinghy can be tricky with young children (see **Dinghies and Outboards** for the safest types) as can landing on the beach on the ocean waves. Again children should always wear lifejackets. We have seen several who don't because of the problem of not wanting to carry them on land. Having a lockable pouch that is secured to the dinghy can be useful for many other items such as jackets, waterproof camera bags, anchor etc.

It is important for children to know the dangers ashore. In the tropics always wear reef shoes to protect against stonefish, cone shells and sea urchins. Make sure everyone is familiar with manchineel trees, particularly the apples *(see Dangers)*. If shell collecting, it is wise to use tongs and gloves.

All around the world people were exceptionally kind to the boys, and when school was completed they frequently went to the local villages to play for the rest of the day. However, as mentioned in *Travel*, you obviously do have to assess the situation and be careful. There are some areas children should not wander alone, nor should any tourist. This can become a particular problem with teenagers who tend to seek independence.

HEALTH

Cleanliness becomes a much bigger issue when children are around. Ashore, I was sensitive to questionable sanitation in food preparation, whether water and drinks with ice were safe, and to the state of washrooms. One of the many advantages of travelling on a boat is that you always have the option of going 'home' where you know health conditions are safe.

Boat living tends to be a very healthy lifestyle for all ages; children in particular thrive on it. In hot climates small bodies do become dehydrated quickly, however, and it is important to have beverages or water always at hand. If it can be cold it is much more appealing. Watch out for dehydration on visits ashore. Boaters tend to walk long distances and the last leg back to the boat in the heat of the day can spoil a morning of interest and fun.

Children are prone to cuts and scrapes. In the tropics these tend to fester in sea water due to the bacteria which aggravate healing rather than promote it (*see Medical*).

Sunburn is a hazard for children especially because they love to spend hours in the water. Sunscreen (at least SPF 15) should be reapplied frequently, particularly when swimming. In some areas the ozone layer is thin, such as over southern Australia. Although I had been warned and had creamed Colin up earlier in the day I was horrified at a burn he got north of Sydney after a very short time in the sun in early afternoon. Wearing a T-shirt in the middle of the day and whenever snorkelling, is wise. Hats that shade the face and head and have a flap over the back of the neck are best. On the boat a bimini cover over the cockpit is a must; we found that side curtains on the lifelines by the cockpit also stopped us burning from the reflection off the water.

Children must be kept up to date with their regular shots and enquiries should be made regarding special immunizations well in advance of arrival in a country.

Babies are easy to manage on a boat and need no special health considerations, especially when breast feeding, although as considerable time is often spent with them below it can be hard on mothers who suffer from seasickness. Sterilizing bottles, etc. can be done in the regular way on the stove. For those with enough electrical power a microwave is also handy for warming food. Disposable diapers/nappies are the most convenient although bulky to stow; remember they are plastic when disposing. In some countries they are very expensive or not readily available and cloth diapers are the only choice. Always wash these in fresh water, even the smallest amount of salt can cause diaper rash -a good argument for having a water maker! Be sure to stock up on creams and other supplies.

SOCIAL LIFE

One of the greatest concerns of kids going cruising is whether they will meet other kids. As much as your children might like to be with

you they are not going to enjoy an entirely adult world and without peer contact will find it difficult to re-immerse into school.

How many families one finds cruising depends on the area and the route. There are definite 'milk runs' that yachts follow according to the weather systems *(see Route Planning)*. We met several families in the Mediterranean, for example, that were on a similar circuit. In the Atlantic Rally for Cruisers, 21 other boats, out of 209, had children on board; we were also able to enjoy their company as we cruised up the Caribbean chain. Most of these boats were on their way back to the States, Canada and Europe. We started meeting a new group of cruising families in the Galapagos Islands and on arriving in Bora Bora in French Polynesia, the boys were invited to a birthday party of 12 cruising kids. There were several families for Christmas in Thailand, then we were on our own as we wandered slowly across the Indian Ocean. In South Africa there was a new group and many of us completed our circumnavigations together as we reached the Caribbean.

One of the problems with cruising is that you are continually saying goodbye. This can be unsettling for children. Although there is no way around this with shore-based families unless one is returning by the same route later in the season, making plans to meet other cruising kids further 'down the line' is very feasible and lends a positive side to the parting. It is even more fun and much more likely to happen if you can keep in touch by radio. With a range of 30 miles, a VHF radio is very limited. A Single Side Band or Ham radio is far more satisfactory or even a short wave receiver. Using the radio for social purposes is of course but one of its important uses *(see Communications)*.

The natural worldliness of cruising kids can be overwhelming. At Colin's eleventh birthday in Bali, I suggested to his guests that they tell a memorable story of their travels. One story sparked another until we had gone around the world and back. Just as the adults experience wonderful camaraderie, boat children also develop a strong bond. Unlike their regular life this is not burdened by age, grade or gender. They all get together enthusiastically and share activities whether school, chores or fun. As they live the same lifestyle, they understand each other and with so many common memories of far distant lands, their friendships are also long lived.

RETURNING TO THE 'REAL' WORLD

Most boat children want to return to regular school, particularly high school. They generally adapt readily and find they are equal to or ahead of their peers academically and considerably advanced in some areas of knowledge. Duncan's first social studies class, for example, was on the Galapagos Islands. After he had correctly answered all of the questions verbally, the teacher decided he would have to set him a different assignment. Cruising children also have to be cautioned about knowing more than their teachers!

Like adults, however, it does take a while to adjust. Jamie could not get over the fact that regular school took the whole day and Colin complained about the wasted time in class and imposed structure. Having been envied around the world for their lifestyle they find their peers aren't the least interested, so they make a point of not talking about the trip at all. This disinterest is particularly hard on teenagers with their need for acceptance. It was different with Jamie's younger friends; his classes have made several trips to the boat, and now Duncan's university peers ply us with questions.

There are also areas where boat children are behind that are inconsequential to adults, but are very important to the conversation and acceptance of kids. Examples are knowing what has happened on certain TV shows, seeing the latest movies, and in our case playing games like Super Nintendo or knowing how to rollerblade. These were mastered quickly but were important for the boys re-immersion.

All too soon, Duncan, Colin and Jamie were regular social kids with few outward signs they had been away. Even Jamie's English/Australian/ South African accent was beginning to fade. But then the change stopped. What they retained was a huge knowledge of the world and vivid memories of our unique experiences. Although they appreciate the western world's materialistic ways they are very aware of how most of the world's people live. Duncan and Colin, in particular, are still avid readers; they enjoy their own company and are personable conversationalists with adults. They are all focussed individuals. Colin continues with the art he started in our travels, Jamie is still a boat kid and spends most of his free time dinghy racing and travelling to regattas, while Duncan, besides being a committed rugby player, takes *Bagheera* cruising with his friends and is showing definite signs of having the wanderlust in his bones.

CLOTHING

FOUL WEATHER GEAR

Good-quality offshore wet weather gear is a necessity, even when cruising in the tropics. When squalls come through they can be cold; a lightweight jacket doesn't cut the chill. In northern climes you might need a float coat or survival suit. The gear should be comfortable and easy to put on. Zippers should run freely and the hood must secure well and give good protection. If the pants are a struggle you probably won't wear them as much as you should. Being too cold has the same effect as being seasick; you are no longer alert and may become a liability. Sailing boots are also a necessity. We prefer long ones as they are better when landing on the beach and stepping out of the dinghy.

Have warm clothing to put under the foul weather gear; a fleece or heavy track suit works well with thermal underwear for extra warmth. The polypropylene varieties are good as they wick moisture from the skin. Although close-knit and oiled wool sweaters give excellent warmth, many people are allergic to wool close to their skin, particularly if it is damp.

Having to put on several layers when the going is rough can make one feel queasy. I have a cotton padded suit that I wear under my foul weather gear that is easy to slip into and just zips up. The boys call it my 'duvet suit'! If the going is rough and to windward, a long, thin cut of towelling around the neck stops cold spray trickling down inside. Also, have warm socks, gloves and a variety of hats - cosy ones that keep your ears warm and plenty of hats for the sun (especially if you are bald!).

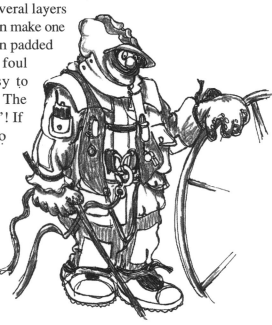

In addition, a light spray-proof jacket which is easily folded and carried is useful for going ashore in the dinghy.

EVERYDAY WEAR

It always amazes me how respectable cruisers look. How do we do it? As you need clothing for every occasion and climate but do not have a huge amount of room you have to become creative about stowage. This generally starts with the women on board claiming the largest hanging lockers!

To keep your wardrobe down to a minimum, analyze your cruising plans. Those who plan to sail in the tropics will mostly dress casually - a bunch of bikinis with coverall T-shirts, sarongs and shorts, or a skirt to go ashore. Temperate climates demand sweaters and long pants, with the occasional need for formal dress. I had three smart outfits on board, for example, and Andy could rise to grey pants, white shirt and tie, and navy blue blazer. We didn't wear these clothes often but some occasions, such as events with the Royal Naval Sailing Association in Gibraltar and being Canada's Tall Ship in the Australian Bicentennial Celebrations, warranted their space on board.

Smart attire may also be needed if you are considering working ashore at some point in your cruise.

The space required for stowage and accessibility can greatly be helped by bagging items such as socks, underwear and bathing suits; the mesh 'dryer' bags work well. T-shirts folded in half and stacked on a shelf not only take little room but their weight acts as a natural iron. Clothes in the hanging locker get squashed, but if dampened and hung out in the trade winds to dry, they quickly lose their wrinkles. Those cruisers with a generator, appropriate inverter (check the wattage of the iron carefully) or plugged into shore power may even have the luxury of using an iron.

Despite the popular trend towards 100 percent cotton clothing, it isn't necessarily the best material to have on board. Cotton items tend to be heavy in weight and are absorbent and clammy to wear. They can also take a long time to dry when laundered. Jeans are a typical example. They are hard on the hands to wash and take a huge amount of water to rinse. The thick cloth tends to absorb salt, making them feel damp to wear and abrasive on cushions. Fabrics made with some polyester content are lighter in weight, dry quicker, even from body heat, and are smarter as they lose their wrinkles more quickly. There is no ideal with zippers; nylon zippers seem to jam, while metal can rust! Try paraffin wax or greaseless, silicone spray on all nylon zippers - clothes, sailcovers etc. Coca-Cola works well on metal ones, as does WD-40.

As mentioned in *Travel,* be aware of local customs for dress. In most developing countries women in particular dress conservatively, thus the appropriate attire for shopping and sightseeing is a skirt. Even where shorts are accepted, wear a conservative length; short shorts can give the wrong impression and generate corresponding reactions. Dressing smartly, for example, in long pants, shoes and a shirt when the skipper clears in with the authorities shows respect and creates a good impression; entry procedures are likely to be quicker and more friendly!

You don't need everything before you leave. Finding bargains and buying new clothes along the way is fun and many indulge in the occasional place-named T-shirt as one of the mementoes of the many countries to which they have travelled. Watch out for sizing; the same numbers in Britain and the US, for example, indicate different clothes and shoe sizes.

Inevitably some clothing gets spoiled on a boat and there will be the occasional loss from a sudden squall when the laundry is hanging out to dry. Leave expensive outfits at home.

Lockers that can 'breathe' will help prevent mustiness. Vents at the top and bottom are usually easy to add. Giving your clothing a regular airing in the sun also helps keep it fresh. Never put an item away that has been exposed to saltwater. Mould will not only quickly develop but it will also spread through the rest of the clothing like wildfire.

SHOES

Sandals, commonly flip-flops or Teva type, are the only way to go in hot climes. Have ones that float and don't deteriorate when wet. They should be comfortable for walking long distances and they need a back strap for hiking. Most people don't wear running or tennis shoes in the tropics as both your shoes and feet rot and your body temperature goes up by several degrees. Also, shoes that have been in salt water take a long time to dry. Use 'Surf Socks' or plastic sandals for stepping out of the dinghy and wandering the beaches and reefs *(see Dangers)*.

In the tropics, bare-footed is the common way to go on board. It is considered poor form to board, particularly the larger boats, with shoes on unless the crew are wearing them. For sailing you need a deck with a good non-slip surface and as few toe-catchers as possible. In temperate climates, have deck shoes on the boat and comfortable shoes ashore as cruisers do a lot of walking.

LAUNDRY

Although doing laundry without a washing machine will be perceived as a huge task on board, it really isn't that bad. Firstly, clothing is worn much less than in one's shore life and secondly, laundry can often be fitted around other activities. I frequently got on with the laundry in the galley sink while the boys were doing school work, for example. On deck I had a large laundry tub. Most of the time Jamie claimed this as his swimming pool but when I was soaking the clothing he was quite happy to stomp or scrub it as his play.

Soaking clothing overnight using a stain removing detergent is hugely beneficial in taking much of the elbow grease out of the task, as is using only small amounts of detergent to minimize rinsing. Incidentally, cruisers tend not to wash items in salt water, finding it takes much more fresh water to rinse out the salt. Unless you have endless hot water buy washing soap for cold water, if available; it dissolves more easily. The liquid is even better but takes more room to store. As well as the soaking powders, very effective stain removing bars of soap can be found in many countries.

Clothing hung out to dry in the wind and sun has a wonderful smell and texture. Plastic clothes pegs seem to last longer than wooden ones and won't stain. Dry white items the right way out and they will be sparkling, but reverse coloured ones or they will be faded by the sun. You will find that by not using washing machines and dryers your clothes will last a remarkably long time. Even T-shirts that Duncan had started with were still respectable for Jamie six years later.

Although the life lines seem like a convenient washing line, I seldom use them (unless I am desperate, when I fill the entire deck!) as they have two disadvantages. Firstly, as they are so thin the clothes pins don't grab well and once flicked off, the garments go straight overboard; heavy towels are particularly vulnerable. Secondly, although most stanchions are stainless steel it is common for clothing to get a yellow stain from them, which is hard to remove. (Clothing also often gets yellow stains from being in lockers; small marks that are inevitably right on the front!)

I always string washing lines between the forestay and shrouds, and shrouds and mast. These hold the clothes pins well and being high the clothing quickly dries in the wind. Just remember to take the lines down with the laundry. I have been most unpopular on occasion with Andy when he has rushed up to the foredeck in the middle of a night-time rain squall to attend to the anchor and he has 'hanged' himself on the way!

In colder climes the weather might not co-operate with drying on deck. I distinctly remember laundry hanging limp in Bayona, Spain, for three days. The sun that had seemed warm and long lived when I started the job had been swallowed up by fog just as I finished. Every time we went forward these wet, clammy clothes seemed to be attracted to us like magnets! When the weather is bad I generally either wash small quantities and dry them overnight below, or look for a Laundromat. Most of the major towns in the western world have them. The trouble is, these centres are the places we try to avoid. However, occasionally it is bliss to take up the pile, often several bags full (a dock cart is useful) and load several machines simultaneously. In many places locals will do laundry for you but these laundry ladies are often a distance away and the items need to be carefully counted as there may be disputes when the laundry is returned.

SEWING

Have a good sewing kit on board with a mix of coloured threads, buttons, needles, pins etc. to extend the life of clothing. Sewing machines are useful, if there is room, with good hand crank ones available. Cruisers commonly make courtesy flags, cushion covers, instrument covers, even dodgers and the like. Make sure you get a heavy duty machine and the correct needles if considering sail repairs.

CLUB AND ASSOCIATION MEMBERSHIPS

*A worthwhile expense is membership
in a recognised yacht club. Not only
does it provide a supportive group at
home but many yacht clubs around the
world will also welcome you.
Incidentally, they often like to see a
current membership card or a letter of good standing from the
Commodore before offering the use of their facilities.*

We met interesting and helpful people at yacht/sailing clubs and
were toured around by many. In turn, they were thrilled to be introduced to a group of international yachts. We also enjoyed the facilities - hot showers, telephone access, a comfortable place in which to
relax, a mailing address and staff who were generally happy to give
information and take messages. In Fortaleza, Brazil, they kept the club
open over the Easter weekend solely for the international cruisers' benefit. How pleasant it was to come back after a hot day touring to have
the pool and bar to ourselves.

Associations such as the Ocean Cruising Club in the U.K., the
Seven Seas Cruising Association and Cruising Club of America in the
U.S. and the Bluewater Cruising Association and World Cruising Club
in Canada are invaluable sources of information for both fitting out,
route planning and local information. Many have regular newsletters
with information from offshore members, regular series of talks and
archives of other information available *(see Appendix B)*. Eligibility
for membership varies with some associations requiring a previous
qualifying offshore passage.

There are many other types of world-wide associations. Their
local members can give a varied, personal dimension to a visit and it
is worthwhile making the effort to contact them. We knew people who
were members of the Rotary Club, for example, and in the Cook Islands
when the Scoutmaster found out our boys had been Cubs in Vancouver,
he invited them to become honourary members of the local Scout group.

COMMUNICATIONS

Communications is probably the most rapidly evolving area for cruisers, and a high priority.

ON BOARD

VHF Radio

A VHF radio is one of your primary pieces of safety equipment and your main two-way communication link with anyone nearby. The range is seldom more than thirty miles and is line of sight, so reception can be poor if there is a large obstruction between you and the other party. VHF is used for calling port authorities, getting advice on harbours, picking up local weather forecasts and navigational information, as well as socializing with your friends and other boats. Generally, contact is made on Channel 16 then channels are switched for the interchange. Channel 16 is monitored internationally as a distress frequency and at sea should be used to alert ships of your presence. Ships are also an additional source for weather information.

Besides fixed units, portable handheld VHF radios are popular. How popular is evident in a busy anchorage when communication between the mother ship and the 'mobile' is often nonstop. (Instead of our call sign being "Bagheera mobile" we decided on "Rikki Tikki Tavi", the name of Kipling's mongoose, in keeping with Bagheera, his black panther!) Although the range of the portable units is considerably less than the installed units (due to small output wattage and antenna height) they are very useful for co-ordinating with people ashore, for safety when on dinghy expeditions and as a safety item to be taken in the liferaft. If it is within your budget it is worth getting a splash proof model, especially if you have children!

HF Radios - Single Sideband and Ham

An HF, SSB or Ham, radio has a transmitting and receiving range of several thousand miles depending on the frequencies used and the propagation conditions at the time.

The only difference between a marine SSB and a Ham radio is the allocation of frequency bands. (Also, marine SSB radios are more weatherproof.) To use the Ham bands you must pass tests and have a personal call sign assigned. 'Pirates' are not welcome, in fact, are illegal. A license may be taken away from a bona fide Ham operator if two way communication is made with a non-licensed person on the assigned Ham bands.

In the past, two separate radios were required (although many cruisers had their Ham radios modified). Now there are legal, weatherproof, all-band units on the market. An HF radio is extremely useful on long trips for safety, weather, medical assistance, finding out about your next destination and great for one's social life. Radio 'nets' are common between cruisers and become part of the routine of the day at sea. Many a friendship has been established on the HF radio and because anyone can listen in these 'nets' become the core of the cruising camaraderie.

Phone patching and using e-mail without a charge is an advantage of having a Ham license, as well as meeting shore-based people who enjoy communicating with offshore cruisers. Around the world there are amateur radio operators who dedicate their lives to cruisers. They have very good signals due to their elaborate antennas and give weather forecasts, check positions and relay messages. No business for profit can be done on the Ham frequencies although it seems acceptable to order parts for the boat. Increasingly VHF and SSB nets are being established in the more popular cruising areas which are also excellent sources of information and communication. *(Also see On-board 'phone, fax & e-mail.)*

The HF radio is also your link with the general news of the world. The BBC World Service can be heard almost everywhere; Voice of America, Radio Australia and Radio Moscow also entertained us royally on night watches. (We had a long cord with earphones from the radio to the cockpit.) Also, Christian Science World Radio is excellent for up-to-date news.

Not only is world news of interest but it may be pertinent, sometimes crucial, to one's travels. Sadly, paradise is often in conflict. For example, when we crossed the South Pacific in 1987 there were ugly demonstrations the day we left Panama, a bomb explosion close to the yachts in Tahiti, two political coups in Fiji and riots prior to a referendum in New Caledonia. Many cruisers crossing the Indian Ocean in '90 learned of the outbreak of the Gulf War from listening to the radio and were able to decide whether to avoid the Suez Canal and return home via South Africa instead. Often the broadcasts make local situations sound worse than they really are, but one should listen, to determine the appropriateness of a visit.

High Seas weather forecasts are broadcast by most maritime nations on the HF marine bands. Regular and weather faxes can also be received and sent through the HF radio via a computer and printed out with the appropriate hardware and software.

For those who do not have a two-way HF transceiver, a short wave radio will allow you to receive. Make sure it has the ability to pick up SSB transmissions.

(Also *see Electronics* for further equipment details)

On board 'phone, fax and e-mail

It is becoming very easy to communicate worldwide with today's rapidly evolving technologies, but cost can be high. Systems should be researched carefully both for the initial equipment costs and for user fees, activation fees, service charges and world roaming fees.

Most countries still offer telephone links through the VHF or SSB radio via a coast station operator and for occasional use from offshore this is the least expensive option for voice communications. Close to home, cell phones are ideal but problems and costs rise as you sail further afield.

For communication anywhere in the world, phones are available using the Immarsat satellite systems (Immarsat C and Mini M are suitable for smaller craft). The Skytel system is similar and at a lower cost to the user, but coverage is limited in the main to North and Central America and the Caribbean. These systems provide voice, fax and data service, email connection, weather reports, medical help as well as news and stock market reports. The Iridium World Satellite Service offers world wide voice communication using a hand-held device that is very convenient.

E-mail is becoming a popular and financially viable way of communicating for the budget cruiser who has a laptop, TNC (Terminal

Node Controller) modem and SSB/Ham radio. The cheapest TNC's are only a few hundred dollars. More expensive Pactor 11 units transfer data faster. Programmes such as SAILMAIL (SSB) and AIRMAIL (Ham) can be downloaded from the Internet.

Orbcomm is a new system using satellites to provide e-mail communications using a small hand-held transceiver, at present only made by Magellan who also integrate a GPS. Service is expected to eventually provide global coverage.

ASHORE

Telephone
Regular phone cards can increasingly be used, so check for overseas coverage and country codes, Canada Direct, AT&T Direct etc:, before leaving. Using these services will greatly reduce the cost of calls. Check charges before using a credit card. In the more remote areas don't be surprised if a phone call takes all day with your bagful of cash rapidly disappearing when you finally get through! Many countries have local phone cards that are bought in advance; often overseas rates are favourable.

Faxes and E-mail
Faxes can be sent around the world, with various charges attached. Now the world has launched into e-mail. Either send e-mail from the boat, from shore telephone lines or internet cafes, now found wherever there is tourism. Saving e-mails on a disk (using text only format) will save time and charges. The convenient, inexpensive Pocketmail units (that only have to be held to a telephone headset to send email) are also extremely popular.

Mail
Using addresses of friends, friends of friends, yacht clubs, Poste Restante, American Express and your visitors are all common ways of receiving mail. As itineraries need to be flexible it is important to choose an address at a place far enough on in your route, even though you have to wait longer to get your letters; but make sure the agency does not have an automatic return policy after a certain period (common with American Express).

Rather than 'hold for arrival' try hold until a specific date e.g.

'hold until July 1st'. If a considerable amount of mail is being sent to a remote area, sending a postcard ahead to the postmaster is always appreciated. If there is any doubt about your contact address back home get a P.O. box.

Special Deliveries

Sometimes you may need equipment in a hurry or a large item delivered. Certain world courier agencies are available for this, such as Fedex or UPS, but do not expect prompt service in outlying or third world countries, whatever their claims! Occasionally couriers are cheaper than regular mail; do your research!

The regular mail service is generally reliable for parcels. When large they may need to be sent air freight, but can often be subject to delays. All packages should contain an invoice for contents.

Note. Be sure to write 'FOR *(NATIONALITY)* YACHT *(NAME)* IN TRANSIT' in bold letters on a package to avoid duty. It works in most countries but not all. If you have some time flexibility it is worth finding out the duty imposed locally versus your next port of call. In some countries it is 100%. Items that are not obviously yacht equipment may be differently categorized; for example, wet weather gear might be called clothing.

News

Besides the local newspaper, *Time, Newsweek* and, to a lesser extent, the *Economist* have wide distribution.

DANGERS

So many dream of sailing away but seem unable to take that final step, to actually GO. Even if they have a good boat, financial security, time after time the departure date is postponed "because the boat isn't quite ready" or " my crew let me down". Others, perfectly able to do it, don't even get to the planning stage but say wistfully, "I would do what you have done but my wife (or mother, boss, doctor, guru, whatever!) won't let me." In the main, however, it is really the fear of the unknown and of being unable to cope that holds people back from cruising offshore.

Although there are dangers out there, not only physical but also health and social problems which can devastate one's plans as completely as an accident to the yacht, the majority are avoidable. Most crises are due to mistakes on board; we are all guilty of failures here. Many, such as some health hazards, can be countered by being forewarned and prepared.

Finally, there are acts of God, situations which happen through no one's fault, and problems caused by others which are beyond our control.

To put this in perspective, many of these hazards and more exist in your regular life - in the home, crossing the street, motoring on the highways, skiing or hunting - but these are familiar and don't seem a threat. With proper preparation major cruising problems are also few and far between.

PERSONAL RELATIONSHIPS

More cruising plans founder through the breakdown of relationships on board than for any other reason. That man with whom you have lived happily ashore for years may have a complete change of personality on board. Maybe he becomes an arrogant know-it-all, or so incompetent that your confidence is completely eroded. That woman who was always so quietly supportive suddenly becomes argumentative and demanding.

Those good friends who were committed to joining you for the long passages turn out to be unreliable on watch or to have unpleasant social habits, or they may be fine crew but refuse to continue due to your own shortcomings. Friends who come to join you for coastal cruising can cause resentment by treating you like a charter boat as they feel this is their holiday.

Some single-handers sail alone not from choice but simply because they cannot find a compatible sailing companion. Life in a small vessel is different, with little privacy and the overriding need for everyone to have confidence and be at ease with each other. There is no room for a person who is disruptive, macho or who doesn't contribute.

THINGS THAT GO 'BUMP' IN THE NIGHT

Ships that don't see you, containers floating barely awash, whale collisions and other hazards to a yacht on passage are of concern to all sailors. As for ships, the answer is simply good watchkeeping. Always give them a wide berth; in addition, alert them to your presence by radio.

Containers, logs, oil drums etc. and whales will not be seen at night and often not by day, but damaging collisions are rare. In our six year circumnavigation we had a couple of bumps with large turtles, an occasional brush with logs and picked up some fishing nets. None of our many cruising friends had major damage through collisions, except one single-hander who woke up to find that he had sailed into the side of a freighter in the south Atlantic! *(See Safety)*

NAVIGATION ERRORS

Probably the major cause of losses of not only yachts but also big ships is through navigation error.

Sixty years ago sailors could go for many days without a break in the clouds or with no visible horizon to use for a sextant sight. They had to rely entirely on dead reckoning ('DR'—a position derived only from course and speed). The development of electronic aids, from radio direction finding through Omega, Decca, Loran, Transit satnav and now GPS, has enabled us to know where we are with increasing accuracy. GPS now gives continuous positions to an accuracy within 6 metres worldwide, 95% of the time. Unfortunately this does not mean that a GPS receiver will solve all navigation problems.

Firstly, the GPS positions are far more accurate than many of the world's charts, which were originally produced using celestial observations and chronometers. A charted island may be more than a mile out of its true position and errors of smaller magnitude are commonplace; thus, although a GPS is far superior to former systems it cannot be used to make a night-time entry to a strange harbour or passage between two reefs. Secondly, electronics can fail, battery power may be lost or lightning could strike. Lightning is likely to fry all electronics even those not connected into the boat's power, so your backup GPS and the backup to the backup may be dead *(see Lightning)*.

It is dangerous to rely solely on electronics. A knowledge of celestial navigation and regular practice is important. The upkeep of a dead reckoning position at all times is basic seamanship. Use of depths, landmarks and compass bearings will confirm the accuracy or otherwise of an electronic landfall, which should never be taken as correct until confirmed by these 'old-fashioned' methods.

It is also dangerous if only one person on board can navigate. Something might happen to this person, so all the crew should participate in the day-to-day navigation and have the ability to get safely to port.

WEATHER - STORMS, HURRICANES, CYCLONES, TYPHOONS, MONSOONS

While weather has been dealt with extensively elsewhere *(Route Planning and Weather,* and *Safety)*, it is the subject which most concerns cruisers. Careful route planning, not having a rigid timetable and a good knowledge of meteorology will minimize the occasions when you have to deal with extremes.

A prepared vessel that is well handled will help you get through a storm that cannot be avoided. Experienced cruisers are elsewhere in the hurricane season. However, if you do get caught, it is usual to have at least a 48-hour warning of a hurricane, which generally gives time to head out of its path, or possibly to head for a hurricane hole. (An HF radio is mandatory to obtain weather forecasts if you wish to cruise in places in the 'wrong' season. Don't be lulled into a false sense of security by local radio forecasts as the government may be playing down the situation because of the threat to tourism.) Sometimes the anchorage will be less than ideal and the boat may be in jeopardy. Depending on the circumstances a decision will have to be made to move ashore. Never take the risk of staying on board; remember your lives are far more important than the yacht.

THIEVES AND PIRATES

Petty theft is a constant annoyance throughout the world, particularly in heavily populated places. Added to this annoyance is the fact that it is often your fellow yachtsmen who do the stealing, with certain nationalities having so bad a reputation that some Harbour Masters will segregate them in a marina and warn everyone else.

The most sought-after booty is an outboard motor and inflatable dinghy, both easily hidden to be sold later; deck gear, lines, electronics and even a liferaft are at risk.

Take precautions such as removing equipment from the decks; locking the dinghy or hoisting it out of the water at night; moor near friends and suggest that all the cruisers keep watch for each other. Thieves are bold. We have known couples whose boats were emptied while they were asleep when cruising alone in isolated areas such as in East Africa and South America. Anchor away from populated areas, secure hatches so that they cannot be opened sufficiently to allow anyone below, rig an alarm system if possible.

We were twice boarded by thieves. In Zanzibar we were awakened by a 'thunk' at 2:00am. Andy rushed up on deck through the forward hatch yelling, while Liza turned on deck lights and also contributed to the noise. Two intruders had been trying to remove the outboard with a crowbar from where it was chained to the pushpit. They left in such a hurry that we captured their dug-out canoe, an item of great value to the locals, which we delivered to the local police the next day for identification and destruction. When analyzing what they might have stolen from the deck we concluded that all they had got away with was a bag of garbage! After this incident we rigged an elaborate system of tripwires joined to cans and bottles which would alert us if somebody climbed on board.

The next attempt at theft was in Mtwara, Tanzania. This time we heard the burglars as they came alongside with their canoe right beside our berth, and again scared them off.

Now our secret weapon is a tape recording of a couple of Dobermans going berserk which can be switched on from our berth and it would be a brave thief who stayed around to risk confronting these dogs!

Other yachtsmen have tried using alarms connected to movement detectors in the cockpit with some success, and an Australian sheep farmer of our acquaintance swears by his electrified lifelines!

Be aware that in many countries you may be in for a double-whammy if you report stolen goods. Not only are you unlikely to ever recover them and could possibly be delayed by all the formalities and paperwork, but the missing items will be deemed to have been imported and you will be charged duty on them! In other places you may wake up to find the dinghy gone but some hours later the fisherman who 'found' it will return it. . . . for a reward, of course!

Piracy still goes on in certain parts of the world; places like Socotra (at the southern end of the Red Sea), the Malacca Strait and parts of the Philippines have a bad reputation. By avoiding these areas if possible, or travelling in daylight well offshore and in company with other boats, most yachtsmen keep out of trouble and reports of problems are rare. We had a scare in the Malacca Strait, when we broke one of our rules by setting a deadline and had to sail at night to keep it. Three times during the night on our way from Lumut to Penang, in Malaysia, we were approached by a fast vessel carrying no lights, which veered away the moment we put a searchlight on it. That the men on board were up to no good we have little doubt, but whether they were pirates or aggressive fishermen (we had run over some unlit lines) we will never know.

It is not unusual to be approached by native craft or even by modern deep sea fishing vessels who are curious and who often will want to give a gift of fish or to trade for tobacco, beer or other items. Obviously we watched these people carefully to see if there was any sign of aggression but always had rewarding and friendly experiences.

FIREARMS

We did not carry firearms aboard *Bagheera*. Although many people carry guns when they first start cruising, most of those with experience have given them up as more of a problem than a benefit.

On entering foreign countries if guns are carried they have to be declared and deposited ashore with the authorities until the yacht leaves the country; a license issued at home for a weapon has no validity in another country. This means that when you need the weapon, such as sitting at anchor or cruising the coastal waters, you don't have

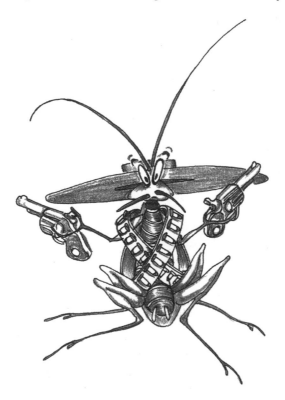

it on board. On departure you must retrieve your weapons from your port of arrival which means sailing back, often upwind (and well over two thousand miles in Indonesia), or expensive travel overland.

What if you don't declare your gun and hide it away on the boat? Unfortunately officials do regular searches, particularly if the vessel is American, as a high percentage of Americans start out armed. If firearms are found the boat is usually impounded. If the owner is lucky it might be just a large fine, if unlucky he may end up in the local prison, a horrific proposition.

If you carry a gun you have to be prepared to use it, be accurate, be lethal, and know the consequences of your action. If you shoot someone you have to be able to prove it was in self-defence - to your life, not to your property. Furthermore, we believe that using a gun against several armed boarders would be difficult, with retaliation almost certainly terminal.

However, we weren't entirely unprepared. The searchlight was effective and, once blinded, our would-be aggressors were unable to tell whether we had guns or how many people were on board. We had an antique knife in a wooden cover by the chart table and amongst our safety equipment we had a flare gun, or Very's pistol, which is lethal at close range.

Without doubt, the question of whether to carry firearms on board will be an ongoing debate amongst yachtsmen, and we were fascinated by a discussion a group of us had on our arrival in Thailand. All those who carried firearms swore they wouldn't have been alive without them. Those who didn't carry guns couldn't think of an incident when they had needed them!

HEALTH

(*See Medical* for the most common ailments of the cruiser, stocking the medical kit and being prepared en route).

Exotic places often have equally exotic diseases. Seasickness can prostrate a person, infections can be slow to clear-up, skin troubles proliferate, and water drunk by the locals may badly infect you. The sun is probably the most constant hazard to sailors in the tropics. Beware ciguatera poisoning from eating certain fish (*see Fishing*).

See *Appendix C* for books available dealing with medicine for the yachtsman. In addition take a first aid course and learn how to give injections, stitch a wound, insert a catheter and what to do in the event of a heart attack.

Cruisers planning to be away from nearby medical help will need a comprehensive medical kit. We sought the help of doctor friends who are also sailors to stock ours and also obtained local advice regarding prophylactics for malaria (the rapid increase of travel and specialized travel clinics in the western world has made this much easier), immunization against a host of tropical diseases and antibiotics to 'hold' a case of appendicitis until medical help was available. Carry prescriptions for all drugs on board, even mild ones like Codeine.

At sea, diagnostic and treatment advice can be obtained provided there is a Ham or single-sideband two-way radio on board.

BEASTIES AND BERRIES

Biting, stinging, poisoning and parasitic creatures and plants abound ashore and in the sea. The locals have learned to live with them and so must we. Australia has so many dangerous animals that it would seem an extremely hazardous place to inhabit, yet the people are highly amused if this is suggested.

Awareness of the local problems usually prepares you to avoid them. Most guide books, cruising guides and other cruisers will have the information. Use common sense, don't handle or eat anything that you can't identify, wear protective clothing where needed, don't swim in dangerous waters or pet the village animals, including monkeys (see Rabies). Some stings may result in serious allergic reactions; always have antihistamine on board.

Sharks

Although there are several dangerous sharks in tropical waters they are rarely a problem in reef areas if you are swimming or diving in daylight and in clear waters. Learn to recognize the dangerous species by reading and talking to the locals. We dive a lot and see many sharks, but only get concerned if a known problem kind such as tiger, bull or hammerhead appears, or if the behaviour of any appears excited, at which point we leave the water and move to another area. Swimming in murky water or at night in known shark areas is asking for trouble; if spearfishing get your catch out of the water as soon as possible.

Barracuda

These have been portrayed as the wolves of the sea, hunting down and tearing to pieces anyone foolish enough to be swimming in tropical waters! Nothing could be further from the truth. They are curious and do look fearsome but are not any danger to you.

Moray eels and sting rays

These will not be a problem as long as they are left alone.

Whales

There are very few authenticated records of whales attacking yachts. They are curious and intelligent animals and we always look forward to seeing them. Collisions with whales are usually because the creature is asleep on the surface. Running into a large one can cause great damage to both yacht and whale; keep a good look-out.

Jellyfish

Some tropical species are very dangerous, such as the Australian box jellyfish, whose sting can be fatal. Even the Portuguese man-o-war, encountered sailing across the surface of most oceans, can inflict agonizing stings. Being aware of the danger and avoidance is the only solution; white vinegar helps neutralize the sting.

Stonefish, cone shells, blue octopus

Any of these can inflict a fatal wound. They are found in Indo-Pacific tropical waters and should not be a problem if their presence is known and precautions taken. Stonefish conceal themselves on the bottom and reef shoes should be worn when exploring in shallow water. Learn to identify cone shells as accidents usually happen to casual uninformed shell collectors. The blue octopus may be found in tidal pools and reef areas. They are very shy and will not attack you unless handled.

Poisonous plants

Manchineel is found throughout the Caribbean, growing near beaches. The fruit of this beautiful tree looks like a crab-apple and is responsible for poisoning tourists and yachtsmen alike who cannot resist trying to eat them. Its sap can cause temporary blindness and terrible pain if it gets into the eyes, so do not handle or burn the wood as even the smoke is dangerous. Never taste any fruit, nut, berry or fungus that cannot be positively identified.

There are many plants with poisonous leaves, dangerous thorns or seeds which grip your skin with painful barbs so always take a local guide if exploring unfamiliar places. Some tropical native foods need special preparation to remove poisons. Don't buy something in the market and experiment; find out how to cook it.

Sea urchins, coral, bristle worms

All these cause painful wounds. (West Indians advocate peeing on an urchin wound as the acid dissolves the calcium spine and it works!) Coral burn often is slow to heal; the best treatment is the sap of the aloe which grows wild throughout the tropics.

Bugs

Mosquitoes *(see Pests)*, sandflies, bees and hornets, scorpions, centipedes, spiders, ticks, lice and fleas. These can be hazards ashore but rarely on board provided proper precautions are taken to keep them out. The old fashioned mosquito net is still the best defence against being tormented when ashore and is a useful item to carry with you. Lice and fleas are a problem in many places ashore, particularly in low cost accommodation. The other creatures simply have to be watched for.

Reptiles

Crocodiles are a real problem in northern Australian waters where the marine croc has made a huge comeback now that it is protected. These are aggressive and dangerous animals which inhabit both fresh and salt waters; their range includes Indonesia and parts of South-East Asia.

When in their territory one's activities are inhibited in and near the water in areas such as river estuaries and quiet bays, especially where mangroves abound. In other parts of the world, there do not appear to be any species which are likely to affect the cruiser.

Snakes

Snakes seem to be a particular fear for some. Where dangerous species are found the people seem to be able to co-exist with them without problems and no one need feel inhibited about exploring ashore provided they follow locals advice. In the Pacific and Indian Oceans sea snakes are common and one soon becomes used to swimming with them; they are poisonous but have tiny mouths and the chances of being bitten are negligible unless one handles them.

Rabies

Always assume that rabies is common and avoid contact with both domestic animals like dogs and cats and wild creatures, even harmless looking ones like bats.

THE DECISIONS ABOUT LEAVING

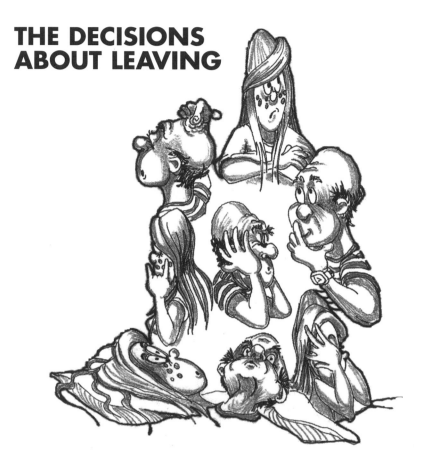

*Many of the issues that are involved in making the decision to go cruising long-term are discussed elsewhere, for example in **Anxieties About the Lifestyle, The Boat, Boating Experience, and Route Planning.** The following major life issues also may have to be addressed.*

CAREER

As cruisers come from a variety of careers there is no common denominator for opting out of employment. Some just quit their jobs, others are on sabbatical, some are laid off and looking for something else to do, some are between contract jobs and some took early retirement (surprisingly young!). A small but increasing number seem to find ways to cruise and keep companies running at the same time, although these last don't seem to be quite as relaxed as the rest!

The major concern of those quitting in mid-career is the ability to return to the 'real' world at the end of their cruise and find comparable work. Our experience has been that cruisers readily find work. The very fact that they have had the initiative to go cruising seems to give them added appeal to employers. They stand out as hard-working, self-reliant decision makers and with job security falling by the wayside, taking a period out is no longer an unusual occurrence. The popular trend of home-based businesses is an alternate avenue that has suited many of our cruising friends and acquaintances who, having had complete control of their lives, no longer find it appealing to work for someone else on their return.

FINANCES

Although cruising generally costs much less than your regular lifestyle, there may be expenses you haven't anticipated. *See Budgeting* for an overall picture of costs regarding the boat, cruising, the general life budget and an emergency fund. Also *see Business Back Home* for the importance of having someone at home to manage your affairs.

YOUR HOME

Cruisers' opinions are divided about whether to keep or sell their own homes. "The only way is to be rid of responsibilities and to cut all the ties,"declares one group, while others feel they need the security of a house to return to and, with spiralling real estate values, are worried about buying back later if they sell now.

We belonged to the latter group. "After all, we are only going for two years," (famous last words!) I argued to Andy, who wanted to sell. "We've done so much to the house and its location is ideal (just nine blocks from the boat!). What if something should happen and we have to return early; finding accommodation with three children would really compound the situation." We rented very successfully and had only two sets of tenants; the house doubled in value in the six years we were away. BUT - we were very fortunate in not only having excellent tenants but also having my step-daughter, Alison, overseeing that all was well with the house, and that the rent cheques cleared.

Most of the cruisers who rented had some concerned party minding their interests, or employed an agency to do so. To overcome this management problem and combat inflation some bought land with no encumbrances.

As increasing numbers go cruising long term, more compromises are being made. To be able to afford both a house and a boat, the family home may be sold and a smaller house, condominium or apartment purchased in its place for a shore base. These have the added advantage of lower maintenance and if in a development are more secure to leave for long periods.

If the only way cruising can be afforded is by selling your home to buy the boat, both parties must be absolutely convinced that the lifestyle is for both of them. Cruising will not be a success if one of a couple feels 'chained' to the boat because all other options have been closed.

FAMILY

Leaving relatives can be hard, whether it be the elderly, children or grandchildren. Many cruisers build into their budgets the cost of flights back home and the extra phone calls needed to keep in contact. Others plan their routes so that they stay closer to home rather than crossing the oceans. Although it may be difficult to be apart, there is the positive side that your trip will also add an excitement and a highlight in their lives. It gives them something to talk about, especially the elderly. I will never forget going to see my old nanny in Devon at the start of our trip in England. The elderly ladies around her were positively beaming and full of questions about the our travels. "We've heard all about it," they told us, "now, you will be writing lots of letters, won't you?"

Other family members put maps of the areas in their kitchens and mark in your route as you progress. Photos sent back can provide display materials for grandchildren's assignments. Also, instead of going home for a visit, you can have the family stay on the boat and provide them with a unique holiday they could never have otherwise afforded.

Those who have young children of your own should not hesitate in taking them with you *(see Children on Board)*. When they take a formal education programme, school is not compromised, indeed their all round education is substantially advanced. Children generally take to the lifestyle like 'ducks to water', so long as their parents are positive!

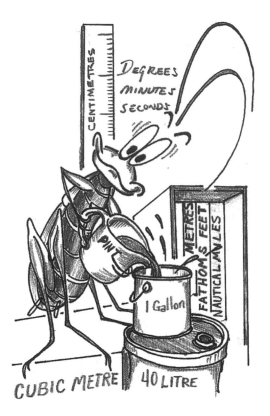

THE DIFFERENT SYSTEMS
AROUND THE WORLD

We all expect some differences when we travel, such as in language, money, dress and cuisine, but while on our six-year circumnavigating we frequently observed the confusion of North Americans on finding that many systems and procedures commonly used by the rest of the world differed from those used at home. Similar frustrations are experienced by those visiting the United States, Canada, Mexico and much of the Caribbean.

Significant differences include the buoyage systems where channel markers, for instance, are red to starboard in the US, green internationally; chart depths are a mix of metres and fathoms, and varying symbols, chart datums, etc. are used. There are different meteorological terms; wind strengths may be given in metres per second, miles per hour, knots, or in the Beaufort Scale. Metric instead of imperial measurement is the world's standard; diesel etc. is sold in litres, not gallons (and the American gallon is smaller than the imperial). Standard sizes for sailcloth, rope and rigging will probably not match your own. Particularly significant is that tools and spares will not be available to match your yacht's equipment. There are different standards and ratings for fuels, lubricants, cooking gas and fittings; 220 volt 50 cycle AC power is common rather than 110 volts 60 cycle electricity so you cannot plug directly into shore power or use any of your power tools without a transformer. There is a variety of TV systems, but most of the English speaking world uses PAL, not the American NTSC. Often, familiar name-brands in food products, medications, adhesives and cleaners are not to be found and there is an absence of the kind of yachting facilities and rescue services common at home.

Banking procedures and telephone facilities can also be markedly dissimilar. Office paper sizes are different and may not suit your computer printer. Even paper towels won't fit your regular holder.

Finally, the English language varies significantly around the world. Do cars have hoods and trunks, or bonnets and boots? Are we going for a barbecue, barbie or brai and should we put the rubbish in the dustbin, garbage in the garbage can or is it trash?

In each category throughout this book the different systems are mentioned; conversion tables are included in *Appendix A*.

DINGHIES
and OUTBOARDS

*Inflatables are overwhelmingly the choice of
offshore cruisers. Many coastal cruisers still
prefer the 'hard' dinghy.*

Your tender is your vehicle, your link with the shore and neighbours, your means of exploration and diving. In an emergency it may
be needed to take out a kedge anchor, to tow the yacht, to rescue a swimmer in trouble or even act as a liferaft.

Take into account the size of the crew, the recreational as well
as the cargo carrying needs, the cruising grounds, stowage on board
and budget. The choice of a tender can greatly affect the cruising family's life and should not be made lightly. The first choice is between
a 'hard' dinghy or an inflatable and then to choose between a bewil-
dering number of options for the best combination of dinghy and outboard.

INFLATABLES

Come in all sizes, colours and designs. Several different fabrics may be used.

Advantages

1) Very stable and can be overloaded, boarded by standing on the side without capsizing and climbed into easily from the water.
2) Can be stowed in a locker on passages or take less room on deck.
3) Can be used as an auxiliary liferaft and remain stable and afloat even when swamped.
4) Fast and safe with larger outboards.
5) Does not damage the topsides when alongside.
6) Minor damage is easy to repair and worn areas are easily reinforced.

Disadvantages

1) Difficult or impossible to row into wind and sea, so a motor is needed for setting a kedge, etc.
2) Vulnerable to damage from sharp objects, particularly coral, oysters and rocks.

In the last few years inflatables with roll-up bottoms, of metal or wood, have been developed specifically for the cruising sailor who wants a boat which can be inflated for use without any assembly, then deflated and rolled up for stowage. These boats usually have an inflatable keel which also enhances their performance under power and when being rowed.

Increasing in popularity are rigid bottom inflatables. The rigid bottom is durable for going ashore (aluminum in particular is indestructible and light) but the boat is still kind to your topsides. These give excellent performance under power and row quite well, but they are hard to stow on a passage.

Some dinghies have inflatable bottoms which are simple to use but even when properly inflated may give a wobbly ride: the newer models however, are far more rigid. The commonest dinghies have removable wood or metal floorboards which are a chore to insert and remove, particularly on the curved and obstructed deck of a sailboat.

The most common fabrics for inflatables are reinforced neoprene, hypalon and PVC, sometimes in combination. Hypalon probably has the best weathering properties and abrasion resistance, while neoprene is the best at holding pressure. PVC cannot match these fabrics but has the advantage of being less expensive and holds up quite well when used in temperate climates. For the tropics the material is badly softened by heat and the dinghies don't last. Some manufacturers give their PVC fabrics trade names. If they are not specifically labeled hypalon or neoprene, assume they are PVC.

The warranty offered by the manufacturer gives an indication of the life expectancy. The best give 10 years' warranty but there are many 20-year-old Avons, for instance, still in use.

A light colour is preferred as dark fabric can get hot enough to burn you when you sit down. The heat will also increase the pressure inside the dinghy, possibly to beyond its safe maximum. Most long distance cruisers have light coloured dinghy covers made to save wear and tear at the dock, reflect heat and prevent or slow deterioration from the weather.

Buy a dinghy which can handle the motor size required to satisfy your needs. A 10' dinghy with 8 hp will usually plane with three people. For five, 11' and 15 hp will be needed.

HARD DINGHIES

These are usually fibreglass or wood, occasionally polyethylene or aluminum, and come in a variety of shapes and sizes. One which rows well, is a stable load carrier and which can take an outboard motor is not always easy to find.

Advantages
1) They are efficient and a pleasure when rowed and are far better than an inflatable without a motor if a kedge has to be rowed out against wind and sea.

2) They can be launched more quickly in an emergency than a deflated inflatable.

3) Many models can also be used for sailing.

Disadvantages

1) Stowage. There are some which can be stowed in two halves and others which fold up but they give up a lot of the advantages to do this. Finding room on deck and stowing securely enough for the harshest of conditions is difficult on a small cruiser. Proper chocks and tiedowns must be installed; the dinghy can otherwise become a dangerous object when seas sweep the deck in a storm.

2) Lack of stability. Unsafe when heavily loaded, difficult to board from the water, difficult to land in surf without capsizing.

3) Few can take a motor large enough to transport a load at a planing speed which limits the exploring, diving and restocking range.

4) Can not be used as a liferaft as it fills too easily and becomes unstable.

OUTBOARDS

Choose these in combination with your dinghy. Consider stowage on passages when choosing horsepower and model.

Bagheera's dinghy was 10.5' and we used an 8 hp Yamaha outboard for most of the six-year circumnavigation. This motor was quiet and completely reliable, and when our three sons were small would take us all on the plane. As the boys grew, we moved up to a Mariner 9.9 hp (which were being sold for a bargain in Singapore) to keep up our speed and, in exchange for our Yamaha, we received some cash and a small Mercury 3.2. This became our commuter engine; it was economical, with its internal fuel tank it gave us more room in the dinghy for loading and it was not nearly so desirable to steal. As well the children could use it without creating undue parental anxiety!

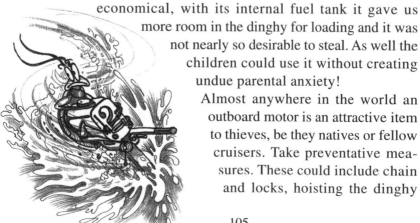

Almost anywhere in the world an outboard motor is an attractive item to thieves, be they natives or fellow cruisers. Take preventative measures. These could include chain and locks, hoisting the dinghy and outboard out of the water at night and possibly making it less attractive. On *Bagheera* we painted the motor with fluorescent paint to make it a chore for the thief to repaint before it could be used or sold.

Hydrofoil fins on the engine work well, keeping the dinghy flat when only one person is on board. Particularly consider these if you have children who will be operating the dinghy.

Outboards are heavy and awkward to get on board. We rigged a pulley system on the pole of the wind generator on our starboard quarter which easily brings the engine up to its permanent position on the aft pulpit. Commercial systems are available. Make sure the pulpit is strong enough if stowing the outboard this way; the weight of an outboard can be considerable and puts extra strain on the pulpit in rough conditions.

Dinghies and outboards are also heavy to lift up the beach. Dinghy wheels that attach to the transom greatly facilitate manoeuvrability when you are short on muscle power. The small, solid wheel varieties only work well on a hard, flat surface. To pull on soft sand, the large, inflated tires work best.

DOCKING (BERTHING), MOORING LINES, FENDERS, BOARDING LADDERS AND KNOTS

DOCKING
Alongside

*Like anchoring, docking your vessel is something to practise;
no end of obstacles can present themselves in a busy marina,
particularly when there's a crowd looking on.*

While a teenager I went on a boating trip on the Norfolk Broads. I remember it with pleasure, sailing through meadows, shooting the bridges (getting your mast down and going through the bridges without stopping) and quanting (punting) many a mile when the wind died, but I particularly remember docking. The leader of our group of teenage girls was a gung-ho intrepid sort but she had no confidence in her protégées' abilities in berthing. Every time a vessel approached a dock she would shout in her commanding voice, "Jump, jump or you will hit!" On our final day she was on board the last boat to arrive and the rest of us were ready waiting. "Jump, jump," we called to her in unison. "Yes, jump," called some other boaters who had heard her before. Jump she did, quite gutsy really, missing the dock by at least a metre and disappearing most unceremoniously into the drink!

Needless to say, this scenario is neither desirable nor safe. Manoeuvring the boat alongside is a skill that needs practise. It requires not only knowing how the boat behaves but being able to compensate for tides and wind. There should never be a need to jump across wide expanses of water but it is not uncommon to hear the person at the helm blaming the 'crew' for being too slow getting ashore as the reason for a botched docking job.

Practise turning your boat in a small space by using small bursts on the throttle forward and in reverse. Analyze the different effects of using the rudder and establish the boat's pivot point. Know how your boat behaves in reverse, which way it swings and how to use that to your advantage. *Bagheera's* stern swings to port in reverse, for example, so it is easier to dock port side to. When docking it is preferable to enter the slip bow first; but you should also be able to dock in reverse.

Practise docking procedures, especially those needed when being blown off or onto the dock, or manoeuvring in a strong current. Always use three fenders and have a spare one at hand. A gate in the lifelines helps facilitate getting ashore (also climbing on board from the dinghy). Never snub the bow line too tight in the middle of the procedure.

If any difficulty is expected rig a spring line from amidships. This should be secured as soon as possible on the dock as far back in the direction from which you have approached as you can. Gentle forward throttle will then ease the boat alongside, even if the wind is blowing you off.

Although it is very helpful to have people on the dock take your lines, always secure them yourself. If moored to a fixed object, as opposed to a floating one, such as a sea wall or pile, allowance must be made for the tidal range, with possibly someone left on board to adjust mooring lines regularly.

When fending off from the dock be sure to push on the hull; pushing on the lifelines or stanchions may bend or break them and may cause weakness in the stanchion bases and eventual leaking.

Med Moor

In many places, particularly in the Mediterranean, the common procedure is to come into the dock bow or stern to with an anchor holding the other end out to sea. After finding a space on the sea wall (make sure it isn't the ferry dock or such like), the procedure is to lower the anchor and come in slowly making sure no other anchors are fouled. Most come stern-to a sea wall, as it is convenient to let the anchor out over the bow and easy to attach a boarding plank to the stern. Bows-to gives more privacy below on aft cockpit boats but less manoeuvrability if it is necessary to leave in a hurry. Two lines are needed to attach to the shore, and fenders are necessary on both sides of the boat. Generally there are people on the dock willing to take your lines, which is fortunate, as it is often difficult to clamber ashore from either the bow or stern until secured.

If coming stern-to, confidence in steering astern is a necessity, particularly when there is a cross wind, so practise beforehand. The placement of the anchor with respect to wind, current and other anchors is also critical and it must be firmly dug in early. Tension should be kept on the anchor so that approximately the correct amount of rode is let out to avoid either the stern hitting the wharf, or conversely, the boat springing back out to sea before the lines are secured ashore.

Just as when rafting at anchor, always make sure your mast is not aligned with the boats beside you, so that if the boat is rocked by wake the masts or spreaders will not touch or tangle.

Other Types of Moorings

Instead of docks, some marinas have either buoyed mooring chains that are picked up fore and aft, or piles to secure between. Often these situations are tricky and it is worthwhile spending some time figuring out the system. The approach should always be made up-wind or up-current, depending on which is the most influential. Secure the bow line, then pay out enough to get a stern line on to the buoy or pile astern, then middle-up. Hopefully there will be someone just ahead of you that you can watch! Practise with the boat hook is useful for these manoeuvres, and essential for picking up mooring buoys.

In some anchorages that are small or crowded, the practice is to drop an anchor and then take a long stern line ashore by dinghy. Our boys became very adept at this and, by offering to take their lines, made friends with many new people.

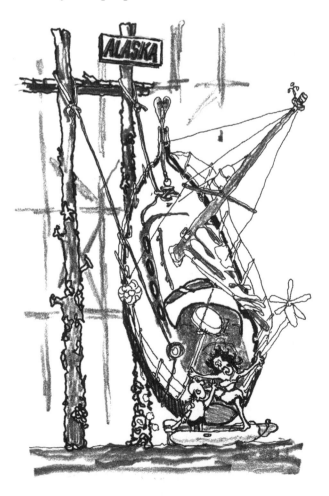

MOORING LINES

Have a variety of tie-up lines on board, particularly when going far afield where there are not standard docks. You may be at a wharf with large rises and falls in tide or there may be very few objects to which you can tie. Transitting through the Panama Canal you will need four lines of at least 125 feet each (many yachts share these).

The following is the minimum number of lines required for the various mooring scenarios discussed above.

Alongside
Nylon is good for mooring lines as it is inexpensive, has lots of stretch, resists chafe, and has reasonable resistance to ultraviolet light. You should have six lines available for going alongside although only four will probably be used (note: in some places rope sizes are measured by circumference). Nylon braided rope, 3/4" diameter, is great on the hands and easy to tie. We use two 40' lengths for bow and stern lines and two 35' lengths for the springs (and two spares) and this works well. All have spliced eyes at one end.

Stern-to
Generally only two stern lines are needed; the same lines that are used for going alongside are adequate. Other lines may be needed to secure to boats alongside. Have hosing available to go on the lines to prevent chafe on rocks ashore, and at the fairleads. Rubber snubbers on stern lines, to dampen jerking from surge or a ship's wake, work well. (We also use one on the dinghy towline).

Tying to the Shore
Long mooring lines are needed for this; we carry two 300' lengths. Being able to loop around an object and bring the line back to the boat has the advantage that one does not have to go ashore to untie the line before leaving. These lines can be polypropylene or nylon, sufficient in size to hold the boat steady in a wind. The advantage of polypropylene is that it floats but it breaks down rapidly in the sun and is also scratchy and hard to coil. We prefer nylon as it can also be used as a tow rope or for additional scope on the kedge anchor. Some cruisers have permanently mounted spools on deck to facilitate stowage of the long lengths. All lines must be easily accessible.

Throwing Mooring Lines

It's very embarrassing when coming alongside the dock to heave a line with gusto only to find it goes plop into the water, or falls at your feet. It is also inefficient; you may only have that one chance. Lines should always be coiled clockwise using a clockwise twist of the wrist in making the coil to avoid twist. To heave the coil, divide it evenly between both hands and throw, letting go of the far end, held in the hand closest to the shore, slightly before the second. It does take some practise to throw the long distances sometimes required. I spent an afternoon on the dock in Fethiye, Turkey heaving lines with the boys after a somewhat tense first attempt to go stern-to. It was amazing how many people came to join us, all welcoming an opportunity to practise without embarrassment!

Always coil the mooring lines on deck after attaching them to the cleat - something that we have all forgotten on occasion! It is far easier to lead the loop from outside the lifelines onto the cleat than to feed all the line under the lifelines and back over them again.

Lines should be washed regularly in fresh water as they become salt encrusted which makes them hard to throw and to knot.

FENDERS

Fenders come in a variety of shapes, sizes and now colours. What with coloured awnings, coloured lines, coloured fenders, even coloured fender covers and coloured cockpit cushions, boats can look exceedingly smart. Most people use the tubular varieties; buy heavy-duty ones as they will have considerable wear. Cloth fender covers protect the boat and the fender and are easily washable.

Fenders for both sides of the boat are needed, preferably three per side, totalling six. Two of ours are the fat round variety which are useful when rafting up or when lying alongside a rough wall. In many remote areas our topsides were getting scarred by the local craft that so often swarmed around us so we made up fender mats made from canvas-covered foam, the type used as camping bedrolls. Fenders can drag down the lifelines so try to have them at stanchions, or tie them to the toe rail after docking.

In certain situations, fender boards are useful. Made from 2" x 6" timber and about six feet long, they enable a boat to lie against piles. They also protect fenders when against a rough sea wall or in a canal lock. They can double as bulwarks in heavy weather and as lashing planks for extra jerry cans of fuel or water on deck.

At sea, fenders and boards should be stowed away in lockers or lashed across the stern so they do not block visibility.

BOARDING LADDERS

When stern-to the dock, a boarding ramp (sometimes called a passerelle) is needed. These can be bought or you can make one yourself. Andy made ours from an aluminum ladder and put plywood over the top. Wheels, preferably caster type, are fastened at the shore end to run over the dock. We also had lifting lines so that the boarding ladder could be raised off the ground, to stop noise and banging, as well as cockroaches and rats from climbing on board! It was fastened to the transom with a swivelling pin which fitted into a socket. When sailing, it fitted athwartships, exactly inside the stern rails.

All cruisers also have some form of boarding ladder which hangs either from the sides or the stern, the latter type often permanently mounted and lowered for use in the water. Some modern yacht designs feature convenient swim platforms, or 'sugar scoops', on their transoms which can also facilitate climbing on board when moored stern-to or boarding from the dinghy.

KNOTS

There are wonderful books on knots. Ashley's *Book of Knots* is the classic but there are just a few essential knots you need to know. Descriptions are particularly related to uses on the boat.

Bowlines

One of the most useful knots on a boat, as they make eyes and have the advantage that they never slip or jam, so can always be undone. They are used for docking, joining lines eye-to-eye and attaching jib sheets.

Clove hitches

Used when a line has to be made fast

quickly, for example to a pile. As tension
increases on the line the knot gets tighter.
We use them over the life lines for fenders, generally adding a half hitch in addition.

Half hitches
The common knot for tying mooring
lines to the dock. Depending on the situation, they may be used with a round turn.
Especially useful when there is a strain
on the line as you can hold the line with
one hand and tie the knot with the other.
Two half hitches look like a clove hitch.

Figure of eight
Used as stop knots on the end of lines such
as the genoa sheets to prevent them running out through the block.

Reef/Square Knots
Used to join ropes of equal thickness, such
as reef points.

Sheetbend
Used to join ropes of unequal thickness.

Rolling hitches
Similar to clove hitches with an extra turn
so they will not slip. I use a rolling hitch
when tying a line to the shrouds for laundry for example, so that it will not slip
down. The extra hitch goes on the side of
the pull (e.g. below, to prevent slipping
down). This is the only knot which can
be used to take the strain on a line so that
the secured end can be freed, for instance
when a genoa sheet has a riding turn on
the winch.

Belaying
To hold on a cleat, the line must go once around the base before being criss-crossed diagonally with the bitter end secured by tucking it under the last cross-over.

Splicing
Most ropes on board need splicing in some fashion whether it's to make eyes for mooring lines or to attach fittings to halyards. Proficiency with both braided and three-strand rope is necessary. Although traditionally the ends of lines were whipped to prevent fraying, nylon and polyester can be taped, then fused by heat.

Harold's "Oh Hell!" Knot
Most easily done when you're tired or feeling the motion of the boat. Comes in a variety of types, every one correct and custom-made and is certainly the simplest to do in the dark. (Ed. note: Don't use it!)

ELECTRICAL SYSTEMS

DIRECT CURRENT

The 12-volt DC system is used by nearly all cruising yachts as it is easy to service and expand. It is more practical than the 24-volt systems found on larger yachts as components are relatively inexpensive. There are still some sailors who eschew electrics and electronics, relying on kerosene lamps and a lead line instead. The majority, however, enjoy the comforts and convenience of modern equipment which has large electrical demands and requires a good DC system to run it. If cruising away from technical assistance do as much of the installation of electrical equipment as you can yourself. Thus, when repairs are needed, you will be thoroughly familiar with the systems.

The typical yacht's DC system consists of an engine-driven alternator which produces a charge to the batteries, controlled within tolerable limits by a regulator. *Bagheera,* for example, has a 115-amp engine driven alternator with a three stage 'smart' regulator. Other power sources, such as solar panels or AC to DC chargers, connected to the batteries are controlled manually or through their own dedicated regulators.

Power is drawn from the batteries, usually through a selector switch that enables one to choose the battery bank to be used and which also can combine the banks for extra power. From this switch power is made available at the starter motor, the main accessory panel, the windlass, etc.

The accessary panel should not only have circuit breakers or fuses to protect each circuit but should have instrumentation to help monitor the whole system. Two ammeters, one to display the alternator charge rate, the other to indicate current being drawn from the batteries, together with an accurate voltmeter to indicate battery charge state will give the essential information needed.

BATTERIES

The heart of the DC system is the battery. Have good quality deep-cycle lead/acid batteries or gel batteries with a capacity which far exceeds your expected power consumption. They should be securely installed in two separate banks. Batteries deteriorate and loads increase due to corroding terminals, aging motors and extra equipment. Carry the largest battery capacity you can without overloading or spoiling the boat's trim.

The most efficient and long lasting set-ups are 12-volt banks made up from 2-volt cells connected in series. The advantage of these is that a single-cell can be replaced at sea. (Replacing multi-cell batteries is rarely practicable or cost effective.) However, they are tall and need deep storage boxes. Two 6-volt batteries in series are next best but if height is a problem, the lower 12-volt single unit batteries will have to do. Be warned that the standard 8-D 12-volt battery is a back-breaker to lift on or off the boat.

The life of your batteries will depend on original quality to a certain extent but far more on the way they are treated. If they have deteriorated to the extent that they cannot be relied upon to run all the equipment needed, replace them. We are not impressed by the number of yachts we have encountered which don't use navigation lights at sea due to lack of battery power.

Many yachts (particularly those over 40 feet) have, in addition to two house battery banks, a dedicated engine starting battery. A dry-charged battery and electrolyte in a secure plastic container is carried by some yachts. In the event of loss of all battery charge, this battery can be filled and will provide enough power to start the engine.

Many cruisers now use gel batteries instead of good quality flooded deep-cycle lead-acid batteries. The advantages of gel batteries are that they are maintenance free, can be capsized or briefly immersed without damage, are very tolerant of deep cycling and vibration and have quick charging abilities with little hydrogen produced. Disadvantages are their cost (two to three times higher than their lead-acid units) a shorter life with a tendency to fail without warning, and a need for a precise charging voltage of 14 to 14.1 volts which requires the adjustment of the output of alternators and other chargers. Gel and lead-acid batteries should not be mixed in banks; use one type or the other exclusively.

Batteries have to be securely tied down so that even in a knock-down or capsize they cannot come loose. They can give out explosive hydrogen gases and heat when being charged, so good ventilation of the battery compartment is needed. The availability of 12-volt brush-less computer fans makes this easy. Keep batteries out of the bilge or any other area where they might be contaminated with sea water, as poisonous chlorine gas can result. Avoid installation in a hot engine compartment.

THE CARE AND FEEDING OF THE BATTERIES

Maintenance
Batteries will give long and faithful service if regularly charged and are never run down below 12.2 volts which is about 50% discharged. Even deep-cycle batteries deteriorate when discharged too much and a regular battery such as those used in cars can lose 10% of its capacity every time it is run completely flat. Damage also occurs with over-charging and with long storage periods. A voltmeter, either digital or analog, with an expanded display that gives accurate readings from 10 to 16 volts is a 'must'. Alarms to alert you when a pre-set voltage is reached are inexpensive and easy to install.

Lead-acid battery cells must be kept topped up with distilled water to replace what is lost during charging. 'Low maintenance' and 'maintenance-free' batteries are for cars and have no place on a boat. Tap or lake water should not be used, although rain water caught in a clean receptacle is acceptable. Keep terminals clean and tight; poor contact between leads and terminals will reduce voltage drastically.

Charging
Engine-driven alternators
Although an engine-driven alternator is the principal method of charging the batteries at sea, most yachts have inadequate systems based on automotive alternators and regulators. These may satisfy the weekend sailor but are no good for long-term cruising. When the car battery is in use, the engine is running and the small alternator continually tops up the charge. Boats require a system which rapidly and efficiently replenishes to full capacity batteries which have been considerably depleted by steady use between charges.

One of the most important and cost-effective modifications is to upgrade the standard system. By installing the largest output alternator the battery banks and engine can handle, combined with a 'smart' regulator, the batteries can be recharged safely in the shortest possible time. This expense will soon be recovered. Engines suffer when running under light load for long periods such as when being used just for battery charging. The heavier engine load and shorter charging times resulting from this installation will reduce engine wear and, at the same time, efficient re-charging will considerably prolong the batteries' life.

Solar Panels

Truly worthwhile, solar panels produce silent, free power during daylights hours. To get good charging power fairly large panels are needed; aboard *Bagheera* we have two 55-watt and two 90-watt units which together can produce up to 20 amps. They are mounted on a gimballed support above the transom and can be swivelled to point directly into the sun. In the tropics they start pouring in power as soon as the sun is over the horizon and even at 50 degrees north with grey skies there is a measurable output.

Ideally, panels should be mounted permanently and as high as possible as shade markedly reduces output. An antenna arch over the cockpit area is an ideal location. If this is not practical, portable panels which can be placed on the coachroof or bimini or even hung from the lifelines still work well.

With the aid of a voltmeter, which gives the state of the battery charge, the panel's output can be controlled manually or with a built-in regulator. For example, our friends the Sellers on Nimbus, with whom we crossed the South Pacific, are very pleased with their unit by Trace Engineering. Theirs is a 4-stage regulator with charge, absorption, float and equalization modes. In the charge mode the charge is up to14.5 volts with the full current flow from their four solar panels. In the absorption mode the voltage is held at $\pm$ 14.5. and the current flow gradually drops down. In the float mode the voltage drops to $\pm$ 13.4 and the current flow is as required to maintain voltage i.e. 1-3 amps. In equalization mode the voltage is up to $\pm$ 15.5-16.0 volts; this is used occasionally to 'condition' the batteries. (This regulator can also be used with wind generators.) Thus the regulator maximizes charging capabilities in keeping the batteries topped up automatically.

Wind generators

These vary in cost, output, noise generation and service life. Particularly in the trade winds, they can be very useful, but if sailing downwind or in areas where the wind speed averages less than 10 knots, their output can be a disappointment.

The units with the highest outputs are large and noisy, both to you and to anyone within several hundred yards. Because blade diameter has a direct effect on output, powerful wind generators are also difficult to mount permanently because they must weathercock through 360 degrees and must be high enough not to endanger the crew. Many owners resort to using them only when at anchor, dismantling them to go to sea.

There are many manufacturers offering wind generators. Before buying, try to find owners who will be able to confirm the maker's claims. Enquire particularly about the noise factor. We have come to the conclusion that wind generators with moderate output, say 6 to 10 amps in 15 knots of wind, are excellent for augmenting other systems. Trying to satisfy all one's power needs with larger models involves unacceptable discomfort.

Diesel or gasoline generators

Not many yachts under 45 feet have built-in generators. Those that do can use them for recharging rather than using the main engine for this purpose. Battery charging can often be combined with cooling down the freezer holding plates and running a watermaker.

Far more common than built-ins are small portable generators carried for emergency charging and the occasional demand for AC power, such as for power tools. (Incidentally, these should be run once a month with a load on them, because the magnetic field can be lost with non-use).

Propeller shaft-driven alternators

To have the batteries charged constantly while sailing seems too good to be true. Propeller shaft alternators work, but there are two serious side effects. The first is the considerable wear on the gearbox bearings, the stern gland and the cutlass bearing; the second is the noise generated by the rapidly rotating shaft.

Another consideration is that one has to stick with a fixed propeller rather than folding or feathering one, which badly affects light air performance and extends passage times.

Water generators

Water generators are quite large, heavy propellers on a shaft and cable which are streamed behind the boat, the cable being connected to and rotating the shaft of a generator mounted at the transom. They have a good charging rate, are quite quiet and are useful on a long passage - although a friend lost two of the propellers to sharks which must have caused considerable rearrangement of their teeth! Recovering the gear is a problem as the yacht must be brought to dead slow before propeller and cable can be hauled aboard hand over hand. This takes time and can be difficult in rough weather. Recovery can be helped by using a split styrofoam 'bullet-nosed' cone. When streamed aft on the rotating cable, the cone covers the prop which, when stopped, then floats to the surface and is much easier to pull aboard.

Battery chargers

For the times when you are tied alongside a dock with AC power available, a good quality, high output and fully automatic charger keeps batteries up without overcharging. Dual voltage (110/220 volt) units are available and are highly recommended for anyone cruising offshore.

ALTERNATING CURRENT

It is common for yachts to be wired for AC current as well as DC to allow them to take advantage of dockside power and use the output from a built-in generator if they have one. This is a completely separate system to the DC. (A cruising yacht cannot expect to be able to 'plug-in' once away from home waters and should be able to operate on a continuous basis without access to shore power.)

AC may also be obtained from the DC system through inverters, which come in various sizes. Small ones suitable for charging dry cell batteries and rechargeable tools or for running laptop computers are very inexpensive, whereas ones which can run a microwave cost considerably more and put a large load on the batteries.

Warning. Most of the world has standardised on 220-240 volt 50-cycle AC power, while North America and some of the Caribbean and South America use 110-120 volt 60-cycle AC power. The two are not compatible except through a transformer

121

which will then enable the operation of any AC equipment which is not cycle sensitive. These transformers are heavy if they are to have reasonable output and should be purchased and wired in as part of the preparations for a cruise.

As one cruises from country to country a large variety of plugs are needed to connect to shore power. A 'pigtail' with one end adapted to your shore power cord and the other prepared for quick connection to a new plug is recommended.

DRY-CELL ELECTRICS

A supply of alkaline, mercury and lithium batteries should be carried to keep flashlights, strobes, calculators, chronometers, portable electronics, cameras etc. working for long periods as the correct ones may not be found overseas. Rechargeable batteries are very useful.

ELECTRICAL MAINTENANCE

Tool kits should include a digital multimeter, AC and 12-volt DC soldering irons, wire stripper, terminals and crimper, needle-nosed pliers and a miniature screwdriver set, as well as electrical tape, cable ties and clamps. Spares should include bulbs for all navigation, anchor and deck lights, flashlights and cabin lights. Don't forget panel indicator lights and instrument lights, plus plenty of fuses in correct sizes.

After acquiring a yacht, check the wiring completely. Even on good quality boats, terminals are frequently only crimped. They should be soldered as well. If this isn't done, particularly in the tropics where there is high temperature, high salinity and high humidity, corrosion will quickly start to create problems. Moisture barriers such as Corrosion Block, Boeshield, or WD-40 should be used on terminal blocks, fuse holders, bulb sockets and switches.

Note. Making a circuit diagram of the system is helpful and remember to update it when adding new equipment.

ELECTRONICS and INSTRUMENTS

The last 10 years have seen an explosion of marine electronics which all talk to each other, are at last being built to resist moisture and which do magic things for you once you have mastered the voluminous manuals. It would be impossible for us to describe of recommend particular ones as new models appear all the time, but hopefully the following information is useful.

NECESSITIES AND DESIRABLES

My (Andy) first cruising boat was an elderly, lapstrake, engineless 26 footer with a long keel, spruce spar and cotton sails. I loved her dearly in spite of her ailments and undertook passages which in hindsight were hazardous, to say the least. In those days the only electronics commonly found were very basic 'flashing' depth sounders. These were not within my budget, so a lead line or the long oar which was my auxiliary power sufficed for depth analysis unless my keel beat them to it. The most important piece of equipment was the large bilge pump which kept me fit and alert on those long night watches.

Since then I have owned a number of yachts and with each one the number of electronics seem to proliferate. I have to admit to enjoying them immensely in spite of the fact that many are not strictly necessary. If your budget is limited then stick to the basic instruments such as a compass, depth sounder, VHF radio, barograph, and log. Most long-term cruisers, however, have an HF radio, radar, GPS, self-steering, an EPIRB and increasingly the software for weatherfax. But remember all these can go wrong so there is still a need for old-fashioned seamanship, navigation skills and common sense.

Warning. Some cruisers are navigating without bothering to acquire basic piloting or celestial navigation skills, relying instead on electronics. No matter how many GPS units are on board they can all be rendered useless by a lightning strike, including portable ones *(see Lightning).*

Also significant is that in many places around the world the information on the charts isn't nearly as accurate as the GPS reading, thus it is impossible to navigate only by your GPS position. Cruisers who have basic piloting skills will have the 'common sense' to determine whether electronic read-outs make sense.

RADIOS
(See Communications)

A VHF radiotelephone is now considered a safety necessity. We always call ships mid-ocean to make sure that they are aware of our presence, carry a portable VHF in the dinghy when on diving or exploration trips (it would also be carried in a liferaft) and report our cruising timetable to the coastguard where this was recommended, such as in the UK, Australia and South Africa. Our children were taught to use the radio correctly and were encouraged to make these calls to familiarize themselves with its use.

A VHF radio has a limited range of from 10 to 35 miles depending on power output and the height of the antenna which should be at the masthead. This estimation of distance can be useful in determining a rough position. When we picked up a Mayday call north of Haiti, we were able to tell a US Coastguard aircraft where to look based on our own position.

Another incident, this time in the first Atlantic Rally for Cruisers in 1986, saw a new cruising sailor lost and in a panic. He had decided that with two satellite navigators, he would not need to learn celestial navigation. Indeed, he didn't even keep a DR (dead reckoning position) when he set out with over two hundred other yachts from the Canaries for a passage to Barbados. The Transit Satnavs which were then available required the manual input of both heading and speed. Our intrepid mariner managed to feed both his instruments with 700 knots instead of 7, and some hours later was frantically calling for help as he appeared to be nearing the Japanese coast. Luckily for him he was heard by two other yachts on the VHF and they were able to fix his position reasonably by virtue of their own positions and the known range of their radios.

North American VHF radios carry some channels which differ in frequency from the international ones and when purchasing ensure that the radio is switchable between the international and US modes. Most units available in Europe do not have this function. Particularly significant, if cruising in North America or parts of the Caribbean, are the continuous broadcasts which can be picked up on the dedicated weather channels. Carry an emergency antenna which can easily be hooked up in the event of problems with the masthead unit.

For longer range communications most cruisers have either single-sideband and/or ham radios. A marine SSB and a Ham radio will transmit on each others frequencies with a small modification. Marinised units are now available that offer all frequencies as standard. Except in an emergency those without Ham licenses should stick to the marine bands only to adhere to the legal requirement. Correct installation of these radios is important. The novice will probably require technical help, particularly in the provision of an adequate ground plane. The combination of an insulated backstay and automatic tuner is commonly used as the antenna.

For those boats without these two-way radios, a good short wave receiver with the ability to pick up single sideband transmissions will enable you to receive high-seas weather bulletins. It will also let you listen in to Ham network to pick up useful information, plus the pleasure on long night watches to tune into the world broadcasting systems.

COMPASSES
(See Navigation and Piloting)

DEPTH SOUNDERS
Depth sounders are a necessity for exploring anchorages, gunkholing and all coastal cruising. They are a great navigation aid, particularly in poor visibility. We followed the contour lines of the ocean bed to navigate down most of the Portuguese coast when in dense fog. Best of all, they are really affordable. Depth sounders vary greatly in performance with the common ones rarely reading beyond 300 feet. Most give a digital reading of the depth; the older flashers and ana-

logue units are now rarely found, and nearly all have shallow and deep alarms which can be set.

A sounder will read the depth below the transducer, or can be programmed to give the depth below the keel or the depth from the surface. An advantage of the latter is that it gives a direct comparison with charted depths. Remember that a sounder will not warn you of an obstruction ahead, only what is directly below; although there are forward-looking sonars available, these are expensive and of limited performance.

Fishfinders are powerful and highly discriminating sounders which display a picture of the bottom as you pass over and can identify fish, etc.

Many cruisers consider that a depth sounder is the most important instrument to duplicate. The readout should be clearly visible to the person at the helm so a weatherproof display is essential. There is still a place for the old-fashioned lead line on board; its batteries never fail!

LOGS AND WATER SPEED

An accurate DR requires that the distance travelled be known. We carry old-fashioned trailing log as a spare. However, we rely on our electronic unit which gives not only total miles, but also trip miles, speed through the water and trip average. By comparing speed and the GPS speed over ground reading, the current can also be calculated accurately.

The impeller transducer should be mounted ahead of the keel and on the centreline if possible; long keel boats unable to do this may suffer inaccuracies. It would also be of the kind which is removable when under way for cleaning and repair. Carry spare impellers.

SATELLITE AND RADIO NAVIGATION

GPS has made all the older systems obsolete as it gives accurate, continuous readouts worldwide. It will also give speed and course over the ground, direction and distance to the next waypoint and will interface with plotters, computers and autopilots etc. Transit, Omega, Loran, Decca and Radio Direction Finders have all been superseded, except as back-up systems, and many transmitting stations are being phased out. Prices have come down so far that virtually everyone has a GPS. Many cruisers have two.

AUTOPILOTS

(See Steering)
Virtually all cruising yachts have self-steering, a high percentage have autopilots.

WIND SPEED AND DIRECTION

Wind speed and direction instruments are nice to have but not strictly necessary. Basic experience will tell you when to reduce sail, and a masthead fly or Windex will give you relative wind direction.

Electronic units which can be connected to the autopilot allow steering to a constant wind direction rather than a magnetic heading. This can be very useful going to windward.

RADAR

Radar is one of those toys you could always manage without until you have one, when it becomes indispensable. At night, in fog and rain, this aid inspires confidence and helps monitor other traffic movements. For landfalls on unlit coasts and transitting passages between islands or entering harbour in poor visibility, we use our eight-mile LCD radar constantly. Radar bearings and distances are true and do not rely on the accuracy of charted positions. We could even gauge the severity of tropical line-squalls coming up to us and, in areas such as Indonesia and the Malacca Strait, we used it to warn us of the approach of unlit and possibly hostile craft.

Because of the blind spot astern created when the rotating antenna is mounted against the mast, we recommend that it be mounted aft on top of a securely braced spar, as high as is practical (ours is 12' above the waterline on a 40' LOA hull). This will also make tuning and servicing easier, particularly if, when installing, enough cable is coiled below to enable the antennae to be lowered to the deck without detaching it.

As definition can be lost abeam when heeled, is it advantageous for the antenna to be mounted on a platform which can be tilted up to 20 degrees from the horizontal, and locked in position. There are units advertised which gimbal automatically. These work well, provided installation is carried out correctly to ensure there is no chafe in the wiring harness.

For small yachts the LCD radars available from Furuno, Autohelm and Raytheon are weatherproof for cockpit mounting, have lower power requirements and are considerably less bulky than the units using CRT displays.

Have a good radar reflector and check that it works. We found a blind spot with ours, which is mounted on the forward side of the mast, as ships that were dead astern were unable to pick us up.

CHART PLOTTERS
AND COMPUTER CHART DISPLAYS

These are not a substitute for real charts as electronics can fail when you most need them. Basic seamanship dictates that charts be carried not only for your planned routes, but also to cover any possible diversions made necessary by weather, emergency or plan changes.

Combined with the GPS, these units give a continuous graphic indication of your position. Good worldwide coverage is still not available and remember that chart positions are not universally accurate in many parts of the world. While your GPS will tell you where you are within a few metres, it doesn't confirm the true position of the charted features you may be sailing past.

Early chart cartridges for plotters lacked detail but there has been great improvement in this. Most chart plotters are now available weatherproofed for cockpit display.

Computer displays using compact discs are exact video pictures of paper charts. There are weatherproof laptop computers available at considerable cost but most cruisers will opt to use a regular laptop, kept safely below, only usable in the cockpit in fine weather.

CELESTIAL CALCULATORS

Celestial calculators are indispensable, although sight reduction tables and current almanac should also be carried. Good units like the Tamaya and Merlin make light work of the calculations and an LOP can be plotted within seconds. For those with a computer on board, inexpensive Astro Nav software is available which does the same job.

WEATHERFAX

Performance cruising yachts with reasonable warning of dangerous weather can decide on a course to take them out of trouble.

When cruising in areas where good forecasts for your route can be picked up in a language which you can understand, a weatherfax is not necessary. Elsewhere, for safety and peace of mind, it is worthwhile investing money and time to learn to interpret weather charts. Some units have built-in receivers, while others require a separate single-sideband receiver. Software to enable one to use a computer for weather map display is very reasonable. One can also save pictures on the computer, rather than having to print; some programmes will arrange these in a 'slide show'.

In 1996, the USA decided to reduce weatherfax broadcasts, to the dismay of yachtsmen, fishermen and merchant seamen. Luckily, most other maritime nations continue this service and a comprehensive list of stations and frequencies on board is important.

Be aware that the charts transmitted are the results of individual weather service interpretations and that these may vary. On a passage from Chagos to the Seychelles in the Western Indian Ocean, we were able to receive Australian, French and US charts. The first two showed a tropical low some 500 miles astern; the US did not show it until two days later by which time it was turning into a full cyclone. By monitoring its passage we knew we were staying well ahead of it and were safely in shelter when it caught up with us.

EPIRBS

The advantage of the 406 beacon over the others is that the COSPAS/SARSAT satellite stores the information and then rebroadcasts when within range of a receiving station. when the signal is transmitted to a receiver it in turn notifies the rescue service of the nearest country. Your personal identity code is also transmitted along with your position within a one-mile radius. (To save confusion with this coding and subsequent rescue operation, we have heard that it is important to buy your EPIRB in your home country.) This system has worldwide coverage, ten times the position accuracy, a more powerful signal and gets much faster response than the 121.5. The 121.5 relies on an earth station being within range of the COSPAS/SARSAT satellite at the time of your distress signal, which is then simultaneously relayed. although there are many of these receiving stations in the northern hemisphere, this is not so in the southern. Commercial and military aircraft are required to keep a listening watch on 121.5 Mhz and will also relay any distress signal received.

The disadvantage of the 406 is cost; however, they continue to come down in price.

EPRIBs should be stowed where they can be activated quickly and they should be taken into a liferaft when abandoning ship.

ENGINES and PROPELLERS

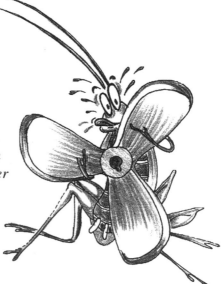

Lucky is the sailor who buys a boat with a diesel engine which is reliable, easy to service, with spare parts availability all over the world. In our experience, only Perkins, Yanmar and Isuzu come out tops in all three counts.

Fellow Vancouverites Lin and Larry Pardey have wandered the oceans of the world for 20 odd years without an engine. In the sixties our old friend Don Street dropped *Iolaire's* over the side in Grenada when it refused to co-operate, and has since sailed many thousands of miles. This sort of cruising demands high standards of skill and seamanship, and a great deal of patience. These famous authors would be the first to admit that there are many parts of the world where exploring in an engineless boat is impractical, even impossible, due to light winds and strong currents.

As well as giving power in non-sailing conditions and greatly extending the opportunities for exploration, an engine adds both comfort and safety. Comfort comes from the hot running water, fans, illumination, music and appliances which are available with electricity. An engine provides safety not only because the motor can help get you out of tricky situations, it can reduce fatigue by shortening passages, and help steady a boat for reefing or streaming a sea anchor. It also gives power for the electric and mechanically driven pumps that have huge capacities and the electronics that make navigation far more precise. For all this we give up space for the engine and tanks, carry the weight and have the aggravation and expense of the maintenance required.

A diesel engine is the preferred choice for the majority of cruising boats for its safety, reliability and low fuel consumption. Very small monohulls and many multihulls use outboard motors to save space and weight; these are vulnerable to theft in many places.

The engine size should be sufficient to enable the boat to punch through rough seas and handle without strain the charging and refrigeration loads (also watermaker if you have one). Remember it is much better for the engine to charge under load. Engine access is frequently a problem, so check that you can get to all parts which require servicing including the gear box and stern gland. Also ensure that the engine can be removed from the boat without using a chain saw!

The amount of fuel carried has to be a balance between excessive weight and a reasonable range under power. In *Bagheera* we have 125 litres (33 US gallons) which with the Perkins 4-108 diesel gives about 35 hours at 7 knots with 2,400 rpm, but far more at four knots and 1,000 rpm, the speed we used mid-ocean when we went looking for wind. We once motored in the Mediterranean for four days in windless conditions, although we did top up from the two jerry-cans which we carry on longer passages *(see Fuels)*. Midway between Sardinia and Menorca we met another yacht powering. They had plenty of fuel but were short of lube-oil. We gave them oil and they stayed in company in case we ran out of fuel. To our surprise we easily made it, in fact still had enough to power around the harbour for a couple of days after arrival!

When fitting out ensure that all tanks are well secured so that they will not break away in a knockdown or grounding. If in doubt, reinforce. A small fuel 'pickup' sump to prevent picking up an air bubble when motoring into heavy head seas is an asset. Particularly consider if having a new tank made.

Make a record of the shaft dimensions, particularly the taper, keyway and propeller nut thread, the cutlass bearing and propeller size in case replacements are needed. In many countries only metric, in others only imperial sizes will be available, so carry spare zincs and cutlass bearings.

Many favour dripless stern glands which require very little maintenance, as the constant ingress of salt water through the old fashioned stern glands is avoided. The most important thing to remember with these dripless units is to wash the contact surfaces between the carbon or plastic stationary disc and the rotating stainless disk if the boat is stored ashore, to get rid of any salt. If this is not done, pitting may result on the stainless steel polished face with wear and possible failure. On launching, the bellows should be compressed slightly by hand to allow any air to escape and ensure water reaches the contact surfaces.

A folding or feathering propeller makes a huge difference to pleasurable cruising and we would always advocate that the fixed prop be carried as a spare. Not only will the passage times be shorter but you can continue sailing in far lighter winds. We calculated that we sailed ten to fifteen miles further each day with our folding prop, enough to cut nearly two days off a 3,000 mile passage; we were particularly thankful not to have the drag of a fixed one hampering us when hurrying away from developing bad weather. With folding or feathering propellers, boats with hydraulic gearboxes do not need a shaft brake.

Having used both feathering and folding propellers, we prefer the latter, provided it is a variety where the blades are geared together, and not only because they cost less. Featherers are a bit better in reverse but lose much thrust forward due to the blades being flat. They will also pick up weed, plastic garbage and crab-trap lines as easily as fixed props. and are more vulnerable to damage.

(*Cruising World* magazine, June 1996 issue has an excellent analysis of the performance of fixed, folding and feathering propellers.)

(Also *see Dinghies and Outboards* for information on outboard engines.)

FISHING and DIVING

For those who enjoy fish, the oceans can supply wonderful fresh protein, sometimes in too great an abundance as there are real monsters out there. We carry a large game-fishing reel mounted on our stern pulpit with 100-lb test line and use tiny plastic salmon lures on a steel leader to try to keep the size of fish to manageable proportions, but we have still lost a lot of tackle to big ones. The loud scream of the reel announcing the arrival of dinner never ceased to excite our boys.

Tropical seas offer up a variety of species including various tunas, dolphin fish or mahi-mahi, wahoo and mackerel which are all good eating, plus various exotic species which we did not recognize and so released. Sharks can be a nuisance, sometimes neatly removing all but the head from the line.

The arrival of a large, angry fish on board used to mean that the family evacuated the cockpit and it became a battle between the creature and Andy, armed with a bludgeon (winch handle). Andy usually won, but it took the rest of the day to clean up and that was a real discouragement to everyone else, especially me. Then we learned the 'secret' and our problems were resolved. Alcohol, in the form of rum, rubbing or stove, squirted from a squeezy bottle into the mouth and gills, instantly makes the fish stop struggling. We do this as soon as we get the head out of the water and it can then be lifted straight into a bucket. No blood, no scales and slime, no clean-up. Magic! If the fish does wake up after a few minutes another squirt soon puts him to sleep again. This works on all fish, be it a tuna in Tonga or a salmon in Puget Sound, and leaves both parties involved in the contest a lot happier.

After a tropical night at sea, the deck will often yield a delicious meal of flying fish and sometimes even a large squid, though more often these have managed to slither back overboard leaving an indelible black smear behind them.

Fishing with a spear gun or Hawaiian sling is another source of dinner, but ensure that you kill only what is good to eat. Learn about the reef fish; many are not very good and are destroyed needlessly. Be certain that this kind of fishing is permitted, as enlightened islanders are setting aside preserves to ensure the survival of local fish populations.

Ciguatera poisoning is a common hazard in many tropical reefs. This is a toxin which originates on dead coral and travels up the food chain. It accumulates in fish without affecting them but can make people very ill. It is a nerve toxin with effects similar to those caused by 'red tide', or paralytic shellfish poisoning: numbness of lips and extremities, tingling, itching, pain in the joints, vomiting, occasionally coma and death. Reef predators such as barracuda, snapper, jacks and grouper are particularly affected. This problem appears to be very much associated with human destruction of reefs. Bermuda became affected after extensive harbour works; Raratonga harbour reopened after enlarging the channel through the coral and experienced ciguatera in fish within a mile either side of the works.

The Tuomotus in French Polynesia are particularly sad as the natives' staple diet is the coconut and fish. The atomic testing ground at the south end of the chain had a huge establishment built, including docks, sea walls, etc. which meant a lot of the reefs were destroyed. Ciguatera was soon found locally and since then has travelled right up the chain and has infected every island, to such an extent that the French government now has paramedics in virtually all the communities. One of them told us that 80% of his work is dealing with ciguatera poisoning.

Don't rely on the locals to identify which fish may be affected. Where ciguatera is found, stay away from reef fish entirely, and stick with crabs, lobster, clams and squid, which are safe.

Unless we know with certainty that the area is free of ciguatera we avoid eating any reef fish and do not put out a line unless at least 50 miles from the nearest 100-fathom line. Pelagic fish, those that live and hunt only in the deep oceans, such as mahi-mahi and tuna, are not affected.

Having caught a good fish, or maybe a lobster or squid, you will probably join with a group of cruisers for a barbecue on the beach. Often there are several nationalities getting together. This is the magic of the cruising lifestyle, collecting coconut husks and wood, then relaxing by the fire to watch the deep glow of the setting sun silhouetting the yachts at anchor. As it finally disappears over the horizon, you might have a glimpse of that elusive green flash - that is if you don't blink at the wrong moment! After a sumptuous dinner it is time for camp-fire songs and crab races, a fitting finale for yet another perfect day in paradise.

DIVING

For those who haven't dived before, looking underwater opens up a whole world of magic. However many documentaries one has seen of reef life, experiencing it oneself is enchanting. We will never forget Jamie's excitement when he went diving on Lady Musgrave Atoll, at the southern end of the Great Barrier Reef. He was six, and although he had a mask and snorkel in the South Pacific he was too young at that time to appreciate the wonders of the reef. Later, while in the Maldives, we had the unforgettable experience of swimming close, in fact holding hands, and not being able to see each other for fish.

Most cruisers just snorkel. A good quality mask is important, otherwise it will perish and leak. If possible always rinse it out after use in fresh water. If near-sighted, masks with corrective lenses are available; speaking from personal experience they make an enormous difference to one's enjoyment. Always spit into your mask and wipe it around until the glass is covered, before putting into the ocean. This will keep it from misting up.

Flippers should be snug, otherwise they will chafe, but not so tight that your feet become numb. As most reefs come close to the surface in the tropics, one needs only to dive down a few feet to enjoy them; 20 to 25 feet is a common accomplishment and in time one may be able to go deeper. Both Andy and Duncan can free dive to 40 feet with no difficulty; this has been very useful when we have dropped items overboard, including my watch. To prevent sunburn, also to keep warm, we wear T-shirts if diving for long periods. Those who dive frequently often get 'swimmer's ear' (*see Medical* for Andy's healing recipe).

You should be aware of the few dangers that exist while diving, or walking the intertidal zone. Sharks, cone shells, sea urchins etc. are documented in *Dangers*. Always keep a good look-out when in the water and be aware of what is going on around you.

Cruisers have become far more conservationist about shell

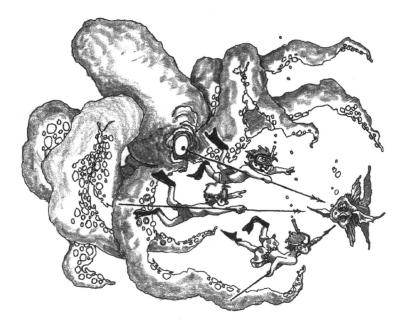

collecting. Although we spent many hours walking the intertidal zone, looking for shells in the sand and on the reefs, we only took a specimen if there were several other shells of the same species and preferred to find 'dead' shells on the beach. Any shells where the mollusc was alive, that weren't chosen for our collection, were always returned to the correct habitat, whether under the sand or on the reef. Incidentally, if you wipe your shells with a mixture of baby oil and alcohol (we find gin works best!) it brings out the depth of their colours without appearing artificially shiny.

It is always fun to turn over rocks, and discover a new colony but make sure the rocks are turned back as the creatures who live there will not thrive in the heat of the sun if the tide goes out and leaves them exposed.

Few yachtsmen carry scuba tanks because of the problem of stowing the equipment, the awkwardness of having a compressor on board or the cost of having tanks filled ashore. Hooka, however, is becoming popular. This system, whereby air is pumped at low pressure through a length of hose, allows the diver to stay down longer. It requires a portable generator, but many boats already have one on board. Hooka is not only fun for exploring further afield, but facilitates cleaning or working on the boat underwater. Also useful for the latter is Snuba, which providesa long hose to go between a scuba tank and the mouthpiece. When using this system you don't have be encumbered by the tank itself as this stays on board or in the dinghy.

FUELS and LUBRICANTS

ENGINE

DIESEL

Most cruising boats are diesel powered because of greater safety, reliability and efficiency.

Don't take the quality of fuels for granted, even in first-world countries. Contaminants such as water, rust and other solids demand a good filtering system. Fuel tanks should have access over the deepest part so that build-up can be checked with a small hand pump periodically.

Whenever possible, keep the tank full. In cooler climes condensation will develop on the inside, above the fuel level, and water will accumulate.

The primary fuel filter should ideally be duplicated. In the event of a loss in power, one filter can then be switched to the other without the mess and delay of changing cartridges and bleeding the system. *Bagheera's* primaries are a water separators and particulate filter, the secondary and tertiary are finer particulate filters.

Many boats have an electric fuel pump fitted in the fuel line. This inexpensive addition can save considerable frustration when bleeding the system after servicing.

Precautions start at the filling stage.
1) Use a fine mesh filter in a funnel (pantyhose work well or West Marine offer the Baja fuel filter funnel which employs three screens: coarse, fine and water).
2) When filling from drums or jerry cans allow to settle overnight. Drums are always suspect and we recommend you do not use the bottom six inches of fuel.

3) Add biocide at each fill. Microbes thrive in any moisture in the tank, feeding on the hydrocarbons. A black sludge builds up which will clog your filters as soon as the weather shakes it up. Once you have this contamination the tanks have to be completely purged, so avoid the problem from the outset.

GASOLINE

Although it is rare to find cruising yachts using gasoline fuel for their main engines, it is commonly used for dinghy and other motors.

Gasoline can be found virtually anywhere there is human habitation. Oil for two-cycle engines (most outboards, portable generators and portable pumps) may not be so readily available. Regular lube oils sometimes have to be substituted, often leading to increased plug fouling. Carry two-cycle oil and spare plugs.

LUBRICANTS

Good quality engine lube-oils are often hard to find in less developed parts of the world, so stock up with enough for at least three oil changes, together with the filters. Gearbox lubricants, waterproof greases and moisture repellents should also be carried.

COOKING FUELS

PROPANE AND BUTANE (LPG)

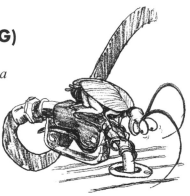

Unlike the past, when cooking on a boat was like camping, most cruisers have a stove with an oven. Almost everyone uses gas for cooking. Having discovered the ease and efficiency of cooking with gas, you will never go back to alcohol or kerosene.

However, there are several safety requirements. The gas installation has to be done correctly by qualified persons; there are national regulations covering this. An alarm which alerts you to gas and other possibly dangerous airborne substances should be part of every installation;

some of these are highly sensitive. They will operate if the batteries start to produce hydrogen, for example, and a friend was most embarrassed because the alarm on his boat always announced his visit to the heads!

In much of the world, rather than the propane that is the norm in North America, the more efficient butane is used. Butane can be put in a propane bottle but not the other way round, as butane is stored at a lower pressure. We find that both gases work equally well in our stove without modification. Some countries will require high-pressure (hydro) testing of your bottles at yearly intervals.

We carry a three-month supply using large (20-lb and 30-lb) aluminum bottles. There was never any trouble finding gas, but different national fittings are used and a series of adaptors is useful on board. In many places there is a system of exchanging bottles rather than filling privately owned ones. You hand in an empty bottle and take away a full one. Unfortunately one has to put up a large deposit to get your first bottle, but it is possible to transfer the liquid from their bottle to your bottle if you make an adaptor. It goes without saying that this is to be done with great care, but sometimes it is the only way of filling your own bottles .

In Europe, Camping Gaz bottles and regulators are available everywhere and easy to use.

Compressed natural gas (CNG) is not commonly found and a three month's supply would fill the boat.

KEROSENE

To find good quality kerosene for smell-free cooking and lighting is becoming extremely difficult. Most areas of the world now have bottled gas available for the local populations. We strongly recommend that you do not rely on this fuel except for emergency lighting.

ALCOHOL

For many years gas was not approved by the US Coastguard and alcohol cooking stoves were common. The only advantage is that an alcohol fire can be doused with water. One disadvantage is the difficulty of seeing an alcohol fire in bright light until something else is ignited. Alcohol stoves are also smelly and slow, the pressure models require pre-heating (use the priming paste to avoid spills and flare-ups), and suitable grades of cooking alcohol are not readily available outside the USA.

ELECTRIC COOKING

Electric stoves are rarely found on small cruising boats and not recommended due to the large generator required with attendant servicing demands. They are also noisy for you and your neighbours.

Microwaves, however, are becoming popular. Although there are 12-volt brands, these are expensive. Small AC units can be run from an inverter and a good bank of batteries, or a small generator.

GARBAGE DISPOSAL

Garbage is becoming a distressing eyesore all around the world. Even in remote Chagos in the Indian Ocean, 1000 miles from anywhere, there were rubber thongs, light bulbs and plastic containers all over the beaches. Plastic in particular is a worldwide problem.

Garbage amasses with horrifying speed on a boat and needs careful management (see our article in SAIL magazine May 1996). It is all too easy to toss garbage over the side and as far apart as Madeira, the British Columbian Gulf Islands and the Maldives we have come across bags of trash hidden by cruisers. While we were in Turkey the local sailors organised a clean-up of the entire coast to remove these eyesores from so many otherwise idyllic spots and made a plea to the yachting community to keep the anchorages pristine.

Before leaving on a passage dispose of all unnecessary packaging. With the common practise of double, even triple wrapping, hermetically sealing and display boxing this can come to a considerable amount. Put dry goods into reusable containers which also keep the goods fresh and free from weevils. For easier disposal try to buy liquids in glass rather than plastic.

If you are organized about sorting your garbage it is not only easier to dispose of, you can reduce the amount that accrues. During a passage we divide the garbage into 4 categories -

a) biodegradables   c) plastics
b) metal and glass containers   d) chemical materials

Biodegradeables and glass (both cut or broken into small pieces) and metal cans (pierced and crushed) can be put over the side when in at least 100 fathoms of water and several miles from land. Even fruit peel, particularly oranges and bananas, takes a while to break up.

Plastics are the real problem because they virtually last forever. Avoid the long accepted sailor's method of cutting plastic into small pieces and putting it over the side. This must not be done: both birds and turtles have been found dead after ingesting these small pieces. Plastic should be washed and stored on board. If disposal facilities are many days or weeks away, as a last resort, plastics can be burnt ashore and all solids buried deeply where they will not be washed out or dug up by animals. Extreme care must be taken of the environment: if you burn or bury remove all traces of the garbage.

Chemical items such as batteries, medications and cleaners must be stored until they can be deposited in appropriate garbage facilities. Schedule oil changes in ports.

In several countries the marine authorities give guidelines for dumping at sea which conform to the international Marpol Treaty. Of particular significance is that dumping should not occur within 3 miles off shore, and outside this limit only if pieces are less than an inch (2.5 cm), and that plastic must never be dumped.

Always check local disposal facilities before taking garbage ashore. In some places it is thrown over a convenient cliff straight into the ocean!

Also remember that one man's garbage can be another man's treasure and leave 'good' garbage in full view beside the disposal bins. This isn't something just practised in third world countries by the way. While we were in Gibraltar many a yacht benefitted from the charts, cruising guides and sundries thrown out by the charter yachts!

As cruising sailors we are privileged in being able to visit some of the most beautiful and most remote places in the world. With planning and sensitivity towards the environment we can all help to preserve these places for future generations.

INSURANCE

BOAT

Although it used to be rare for offshore cruisers to have insurance, particularly in the more remote areas, this seems to be gradually changing. One reason is that some insurance companies will now insure with just two crew on board; previously three people were always required for offshore passages. Secondly more people are making a lifestyle of cruising, with their assets tied up in their vessel.

Like many, we arranged for coverage through Lloyds of London. Rates varied considerably depending on our proposed routes which we submitted annually. In the crowded Mediterranean, rates were less than 1% per annum of the boat's value. There was a surcharge for crossing the Atlantic, with an additional crew requirement imposed, but the Caribbean was hardly more expensive. In Antigua, our policy had to be renewed to take us through the Panama Canal and across the South Pacific to Australia. It was at this point the complications began, as we were informed that we had to have a third crew member if we made a voyage. "But what is a voyage?" we asked. "A voyage is going to sea," came the reply. "But what is going to sea?" we faxed back. We wanted to be sure that a dragged anchor was not considered 'going to sea' as that would have meant having another person all the time, which would have been too much of an invasion of family privacy. We were finally told that we had to have three crew for trips over a thousand miles. There was only one of these, the 3,000-mile run from Galapagos to the Marquesas, which was acceptable. The cost was 2% in the Pacific with the rates increasing to 2.5% in the Indian Ocean. Only about 10% of the international yachts in South Africa were insured; our rate was up to 3% as this is considered a risky area. Fortunately, after Australia, our children were considered experienced and old enough to be our 'third' crew member.

Insurance is often cheaper when purchased in the area it covers. With insurance from England we were given a huge surcharge for entering Australian waters, for example, only to find Australian rates very reasonable. Having informed Lloyds of local examples they gave us a refund. Insurance is also available now for couples. For example Blue Water Insurance (see p. 261).

The reason we and others persisted with the expense of insurance was as much psychological as financial. As we had bought the boat from the proceeds of Andy's business it represented our ability to get re-established into the business world on our return. People without insurance had either come to terms with the possible financial loss or felt that with their boat handling skills the odds were against any major damage occurring. Unfortunately, it is frequently a second party that causes accidents when you may not be around, or an unpredictable weather situation.

We still can't believe our Australian incident. A thirteen-year-old lad, to whom Duncan had been talking at school some half an hour earlier, managed to run into *Bagheera* amidships. He was in an aluminum runabout, going at high speed. The trip from A to B was about half a mile and we were the only obstacle en route. Our hull was damaged from the toe rail to waterline, with the interior stove in on the starboard side. Fortunately we were not on board, the impact was just where the boys did their homework. The dinghy belonged to a local boatyard which unfortunately had just gone into receivership. After much ado, their insurance paid the $10,000 cost and *Bagheera* was superbly repaired under the supervision of a Lloyds surveyor.

Our only claim was a large one after we had been struck by lightning, when all our electrics and electronics were fried *(see Lightning)*. The claim was handled quickly and courteously by our broker in London and Lloyds agents in South Africa. It was fortunate that we were struck in South Africa as everything was easily replaced.

A few days later while a friend was commenting in a blasé

tone, "It's good to know there's some justice in this world, at least the lightning struck a boat with insurance!" lightning flashed and the telephone beside him went up in smoke. He went off to inquire about rates for his boat the next morning! You never know when lightening might strike. Recently, the dock at The Royal Vancouver Yacht Club was hit and several boats had equipment damaged.

MEDICAL

Although there are many programmes for short-term travel, long-term medical insurance is expensive. Plans commonly used by cruisers are PPP (UK) and The Principal (US). Bluewater Insurance Inc. (US) is also offering worldwide coverage for crew on boats over 30 feet. Although costs are comparable, there are significant differences such as deductibles and amounts paid out. *(See Appendix B for addresses)*

Generally, we found fees for doctors' visits very reasonable around the world, with medications considerably cheaper in developing nations.

LIFE ON BOARD

One of the most significant differences between modern day cruising and that of twenty or more years ago is that one can be truly comfortable on a boat - well, most of the time!

Thankfully, as yacht designs have radically improved it is no longer mandatory to live in misery. I well remember my first experiences of 'big boat' cruising. In my small clinker built (lapstrake) wooden dinghy I had sailed over to the Isle of Wight to watch Cowes Week, the well known international racing event on the south coast of England. Some friends, moored on the 'trots', hailed us to join them on their 40 footer. As we clambered over other yachts to reach them I couldn't resist peering below. The berths were narrow and covered in uninviting, clammy vinyl, the stoves were tiny, everything looked damp and there was an odour - an indescribable mix of fuel, bilge and mould - which certainly didn't entice me to go to sea.

How things have changed! Modern designs have light, airy interiors with attractive upholstery and fine woodwork; large, comfortable, dry berths with regular bedding; gimballed stoves with big ovens; refrigerators, cabin heaters, walk around heads with separate shower stalls and plenty of water to use in them. In addition, one still has a boat that is strongly built, performs well and is easy to handle for two people.

Despite this reality, featured in boating magazines and by vessels being displayed to perfection at boat shows, the old-fashioned perception of roughing it persists. Even with our boat, which is very homelike below, when I suggest that our guests unpack (if they are staying more than a weekend) I frequently get resistance. "It isn't necessary," they say, "after all boating is like camping. It's easy to put our bags on the floor at night."Cruisers do not 'camp' on their boats, as this isn't acceptable for many people long-term. Successful cruisers live very comfortably in their home, which happens to be a boat.

Aboard *Bagheera* the berths are always made up. We personally like duvets (washable varieties) when it is cool, and use the cover alone when it's hot. We have a couple of Greek cotton blankets handy on the shelf in case it cools off in the night. Similar to general clothing we prefer linens with some polyester, as pure cotton ones hold moisture and crush easily. Linens are stored in what appears to be a tiny locker forward but it holds a remarkable amount - currently there are eight duvet covers, ten sheets, several pillow cases, a portable iron and a plastic table cloth from Gibraltar that has seen many a beach barbecue. Foam mattresses should be at least 10cm; we have 13cm in our cabin.

As at home we have pictures on our walls (bulkheads), although they have to be attached, not just hung. These are often souvenirs. On our main bulkhead, for example, is a handpainted Portuguese vase, a framed stitched mola from the San Blas Islands, a woven cowrie mat from Raratonga in the Cook Islands and a framed cross stitch picture I completed underway after our visit to the Galapagos Islands.

However, although our boats are very comfortable they are also serviceable. Locker space is important for liveaboards and when looking for a boat make sure this is one of your priorities. Our Beneteau, for example, has a hanging locker and cupboards in every cabin, besides a long shelf alongside the berth. We also have bookshelves on top of the lockers behind the main cabin seats. There is accessible storage under the berths, especially in the forward cabin where I only have to turn over the pillows to get at a large bin. Many boats manufacturers go for the spacious look below, and compromise on the storage room needed to live satisfactorily on board.

Also, imagine being heeled over. Are some of the lockers open so that goods will fall out? Are there enough grab rails, or could you be flung across a wide cabin? Are there fiddles, on the table and in the galley, to stop things sliding off? Could you work in the galley easily at an angle? How are the ports situated, can you get enough ventilation?

Is the lighting bright enough for you to read in the main cabin when relaxing on the seats?

The Galley

Like the kitchen at home you will spend much time in the galley, hopefully everyone on board will take their turn, just as they take their turn on watch. For convenience the galley should be close to the companionway, both for ease of passing up food, ventilation, and for the cook to be included in the conversation on deck. It is convenient if the cook can reach all the day-to-day items easily - whether cutlery, dishes, jams and sauces, tea or coffee etc. Personally I like drawers for the cutlery, one for the tableware and another for cooking items. As explained in *Provisioning*, what we have in the galley on the boat and what we have in the kitchen at home is very similar - we just seem to need more at the house! All pans and utensils should be stainless steel but even the best quality may rust if not rinsed regularly in fresh water.

Stoves are usually gimballed. Many have only two burners and we managed all around the world with this arrangement quite satisfactorily. Recently we replaced our stove with a unit that has three burners and a larger oven. Now I feel quite spoilt, especially as it is also self-igniting. Many stoves only come with one oven shelf; a second shelf comes in handy, particularly for baking flat items like cookies while baking bread. For rough weather the stove should have fiddles to retain the saucepans. A crash bar should be mounted across the front for safety and support; there should also be a safety strap to stop the cook being thrown across the boat when heeled. A fire blanket is the safest way to put out a galley fire; have one readily available. *(Also see Fuels-cooking)*

Most cruisers have plastic dishes; although many of us tried the so-called unbreakable chinawear in the past, we all found that it shattered into a million pieces of glass if it did break, so was unsuitable for boat use. Some cutlery is very sharp but can easily be ground-down to stop marring plastic plates. Buy stackable plastic glasses; twelve fit on shelves at the galley end of our main table, easily accessible for use.

Use shock cord inside the lockers to stop containers coming out as the doors are opened when heeled over and be sure to have foolproof support on the lids of the freezer; they are extremely heavy if they collapse. Non-slip mats are useful: this material can be bought by the metre in every shade imaginable. Make sure the fiddles in the galley are high enough to stop coffee cups and glasses tipping over.

A deep sink is a must, preferably two. We have a board which fits over one of ours which is not only convenient for chopping, it hides a volume of dirty dishes! We have both fresh and salt water coming to the galley, with manual and pressure pumps for both. Inevitably you get hot while cooking; a fan and opening port in the galley are a godsend.

One of the best features in *Bagheera's* galley is that the doors on the lockers above the stove and fridge stay at the horizontal when opened. This provides an extra working surface, particularly for items that are on the fridge top when you want to open it. I've seldom seen this feature but it's very practical. In addition our chart table opposite provides extra surface for entertaining.

The Head

Andy and I had to laugh. He wrote a section on heads that said they should be as small as possible to contain you in a large sea, while I wrote "the larger the head the better"; like so many aspects of boating there are different perspectives! Ideally you have two heads; most boats over 40 feet do. Preferably, one head is well aft for use while at sea while the other head forward will be more luxurious. Most heads have showers. I thoroughly recommend a separate shower stall, but you generally only find them in larger yachts.

The head itself should be mounted high enough that the rim is above sea level as anti-siphon valves can fail. Unfortunately heads get clogged and need to be dismantled quite often unless the crew is particularly careful, so good access all round and to the seacocks is needed.

Electrically operated heads are an added complication. The discharge line needs to be changed every two years; not only does scale build up but odours permeate through the hose wall. Always replace with hose designed to handle sewage. If the head gets stiff to use, pump through some cooking (not mineral) oil. Vinegar helps reduce scale.

Holding tanks are required in some countries and even where they are not should be used in populated areas, rivers and marinas. Since pump-out stations can be rare, even in countries which require holding tanks, your yacht must be self-sufficient and be able to discharge the tank at sea.

A good holding system requires a Y-valve on the head outlet to select overboard or holding tank disposal. From the holding tank the discharge can be Y-valved to allow for deck pump-out at a station or disposal overboard using a manual or electric pump, which must be of the sort which can cope with the solids and paper. The tank vent can be the source of unpleasant odours which will guarantee seasickness. This can be controlled with a vent filter and by using holding tank chemical treatments.

The tank itself is best made from fibreglass, polyethylene or linear polyurethane. Aluminum and stainless steel ones are liable to leaks from corrosion. Flexible ones can develop odours and they can also wear through due to chafe from the constant movement, which will just make your day in the middle of a boisterous passage! Very secure mounting is needed so the tank can't break adrift in a knockdown.

The head, similar to other areas in the boat, whether sleeping or the main cabin, could maybe do with some extra storage. Andy added a shelf behind the head, also one in the locker under the basin. This last gave him great satisfaction as it holds 20 rolls of toilet paper. As we get through about a roll a day on *Bagheera,* this could see us through our longest passage! You have to be careful about toilet paper clogging the head and really should only use one-ply toilet paper. We have a weakness for two-ply in our family but have to be careful. Incidentally, men too should sit down on the head when at sea!

COMFORT ON BOARD

Below

Hatches which open forward allow a through breeze to flow below when at anchor. The more the better. Cloth wind scoops which direct air down and through the hatches are effec-tive and inexpensive. Opening ports also help with ventilation. Dorades are not effective to create a cooling draught but do ventilate in cool climates.

Light-coloured decks reflect the heat and the core material makes a huge difference to the protection given from the sun's heat or extreme cold; check on this detail before buying. Thick balsa or closed cell foam is good insulation, plywood coring is not. Teak decks not only increase the insulation but give a positive cooling effect if wetted down.

Dark hulls are hot in the tropics; the lighter the colour the more it will reflect the heat of the sun. Uncored hulls need insulation material or liners with an air space between to protect against the transfer of heat from the sun or condensation when it is colder outside.

Fans make a big difference to our comfort below. We have the

German Hellas which draw a minimum of power, have two speeds and are quiet. There is one at every berth, in the galley, and two over the settees. They are frequently running 24 hours a day in the tropics and make sleep possible when no natural wind finds its way below.

We have a simple bulkhead mounted diesel heater for cabin heat which vents the combustion gases outside. Less suitable for long-term cruising are the furnace type of heaters with forced draught circulation. Although great for cool climates they do not take kindly to long periods of non-use in the tropics, where the high humidity, temperature and salinity combine to rot them out in short order.

If clothing and food etc. is to stay free from mould all storage lockers need to be well ventilated. Salty clothing should always be kept separate until the salt has been washed out. Mould has to be removed immediately otherwise it will 'run' rapidly through the boat. Spray-on bleach-based tile cleaners work well, especially on PVC deckhead liners.

Cushion covers can quickly deteriorate in a liveaboard situation, particularly in the tropics, with salt, sand, sweat and sunscreens, and the common 'tweed' style is scratchy in the heat. On *Bagheera* we use cotton slip covers fastened with velcro over the regular covers which can be easily removed and laundered. Lee-cloths are on all the berths, double berths being split down the middle. A wet/dry vacuum is useful to clean salon cushions to bilges.

On deck

Make sure that the cockpit is efficient for everyone to work in. Remember your body is your most important tool, so organize the boat so that it helps rather than hinders you. Particularly think of load, lead and leverage for handling the sails. All adults should be able to furl the genoa without help.

Most boats have dodgers with an opening portion in the centre to allow a throughbreeze (essential in the tropics). Many also have removable side curtains. Being able to see over the dodger while standing at the helm is most advantageous. Many are now seeing the benefits of fixed fibreglass dodgers with glass windscreens, as they give greater visibility and durability. Initial costs are not that much higher than for a soft dodger.

As the sun is one of the greatest hazards of cruising, a bimini over the cockpit is a must; it also protects from the rain. Ideally it should be high enough to stand under, but must clear the boom. Ours can be left up when sailing in all but the strongest winds. Side curtains on the lifelines, from forward of the companionway to the stern pulpit, help keep the cockpit dry and shield us from reflected sun's rays off the water; psychologically they also make the cockpit seem much bigger and safer at sea. An awning, stretching from behind the mast to the backstay above the boom, is rigged on *Bagheera* when at anchor. This shades much of the deck and funnels the breeze, cooling both above and below deck. Ours is also rigged to catch rain. It rolls up tightly to stow permanently across the double backstay. Although fewer boats now have these large awnings, as they are considerably more work, they are highly desirable if anchored for a long period of time in the tropics.

Gates in the lifelines are useful to facilitate boarding but should be taped against accidental opening at sea.

The further you go, the more cockpit cushions you need for night watches! They must be waterproof, such as closed cell foam, easily manageable in size and comfortable. Flotation cushions can also double for safety. Have earphones on a long cable from your radio so you can listen to world-wide news and entertainment; it's amazing how quickly your watch will pass by. During the day we really enjoyed our outside speakers that cast Wagner, the Beatles or Roald Dahl's Revolting Rhymes into the wind.

COASTAL CRUISING

Much of your time while cruising will be spent day-sailing and at anchor. The life is very pleasant, as distances are short. You wait for good weather, or, if you do decide to head out, the trip is soon over. At anchor the breeze flows through the boat so even in very hot climates you generally stay relatively cool. You meet up with a group of other cruisers and frequently get together on the boats, or go ashore to try the local fare. You might all decide to have a beach barbecue. For this a portable lamp (the 12-volt rechargeable camping lights work well) is a necessity if you eat after dark, otherwise you will crunching sand with your lobster! A metal rack or sheet is invaluable for cooking on the embers. Australian friends had a 3' x 2' x 1/2" aluminum sheet that cooked many a fine meal as we cruised from Cape York to Darwin.

Periodically most boats go into marinas to plug in to shore power

for tools, use water for laundry and washing-down the boat, also for accessibility to stock-up on food. Be warned. This is the time when the boat is often in chaos - and when you have a stream of visitors.

LIFE AT SEA

Without doubt the passages that are so appealing to some are the source of dread and fear to others. In reality, some passages are a little too exhilarating, others are boring, while most are somewhere in between - pleasant enough. At the end, die-hard sailors are generally as pleased to sight land after many days at sea as those who regard ocean voyages a necessary evil!

There is no guarantee that ships will keep to the shipping lanes or that local fisherman will observe your right-of-way. Experienced voyagers keep watch at sea 24 hours a day. There are several different strategies used and crews work out what works best for their individual preferences. Some do 2-hour watches while others do 3 or 4. Some only do watches in the daytime, while others on board cover the nights. Some only have formal watches at night; during the day, whoever is on deck keeps a look out. If someone scans the horizon every few minutes, so long as conditions are good and there is no traffic, all should be well.

On passage in *Bagheera* we always keep a 24-hour watch routine. This is hard for the first day or two but then becomes acceptable when one's body has adapted. It usually takes me three days to catch up on sleep and to get my sealegs. Andy and I do three hour watches, with the boys sharing one three hour period during the afternoon. This means we alternate watch times daily. We change watch on the half-hour because it seems to make the time pass more quickly as the first half-hour is spent getting oriented and comfortable with a cup of tea etc. and the last half-hour taken up with plotting a last fix, clean-up and waking-up the person for the next watch. Whoever is on 4:30-7:30 watch also cooks dinner. Having snacks available for watches is important and many swear by their thermos flasks of coffee. If we have a guest on a long passage they generally also stand watches which gives us more sleep; the down side is you lose your privacy and might have to wear clothes!

At sea a log is kept at hourly intervals with time, course steered, log reading, nautical miles covered in last hour, wind speed and direction, barometric pressure, position (electronic, celestial or DR). Also noted is any significant information such as ship sightings, gear problems, weather changes or radio contacts. Reminders for the next watchkeeper of weatherfax broadcasts to be printed out or light characteristics for an expected landfall are also entered. In between, we listen to the radio and talk to our cruising friends, read, listen to music, bake bread etc. or play games with boys. I also bring my journal up to date, reckon our finances, read up on our next landfall and write letters and articles.

Keeping watch during the day is generally not difficult, although it can be busy when close to a port, in an area of tricky navigation or crossing shipping lanes. Radar is useful in these situations in that it shows whether you are on any collision courses. Incidentally, know where the shipping lanes are so you can keep away from them unless absolutely necessary. We have friends who were in the shipping lane all the way from Langkawi to Sri Lanka. They averaged seeing nine ships every watch and arrived exhausted. If they had sailed a few miles north or south they would have been clear.

Being on watch at night varies dramatically. When the moon is high and clear the whole sea is lit up; when there is no moon it can be unbelievably dark and spooky. This is in dramatic contrast to your cosy ship below and it is sometimes quite a shock to come up on deck to a black, raging sea. It is easy to understand how sailors imagine sounds in the night. The most scary incident I had was when there was a loud sigh and hot breath down my neck. Even though I knew Andy and the boys were sound asleep I involuntarily called out "Who's that!" Of course no one answered, but as I turned a ripple caught my eye. It was a dolphin disappearing into the gloom - he had just been taking an inquisitive look!

Many wonder about getting along with each other in such a small space for long periods at sea. In fact, you probably won't be doing many long passages and by the time you realize you can't stand your companion you will be arriving at your destination! Without doubt, however, there are crews to be seen abandoning ship on reaching the dock, refusing even to take the lines! Others feel that coastal cruising is difficult to manage interpersonally as more decisions have to be made, in comparison to the passages with alternate watches, where they hardly ever see each other for long periods.

One of the most important aspects of long passages is not getting overtired. Because we can handle the boat alone it is very seldom that either Andy or I wake the other up mid-watch. At the change of the watch we assess the weather carefully, having listened to forecasts and looked at the weather maps and at the sky. If in doubt we will reef the mainsail at that time. If the wind comes up a substantial amount, the watchkeeper will furl the genoa. *Never be over-canvassed; it is the best way to scare yourself and it can lead to all sorts of failures on the boat.*

Those who are looking for excitement are surprised that we weren't in any really bad storms on our six-year circumnavigation - although I am able to satisfy them with our lightning strike! In fact we did suffer gale force winds regularly in the UK, several storms in the Med, numerous line squalls and regularly had passages with 25 knots or more. A front with gusts up to 60 knots hit us just before our landfall in Australia.

We also sailed across Bass Strait in a full gale. But, one tends to get used to big seas being the norm and they are no longer threatening. When sailing across Bass Strait, when we were on the wind, for example, Jamie aged five, wedged himself in the galley, filled the sink with water and played quite unconcerned with his Lego boats.

So many people ask us about privacy and our 'private life' that Andy suggested that we should have a section on *Sex in a Seaway!* As he didn't volunteer to write it, I decided to leave this up to your imagination - suffice to say it doesn't seem to be a problem!

GUESTS ON BOARD

Whether friends from home, relatives, other cruisers or locals, having guests on board is fun and part of the pleasure of the cruising life; however, these visitors can also be overwhelming. The main problem with guests from home is the structure they impose on you. As their holidays often have to be confirmed several months before the visit, one's own cruising plans can be curtailed. This may either involve hanging around because you are ahead of schedule or pushing through bad weather to meet the deadline. Guests should be aware that you may not be able to reach the appointed meeting place in time and be prepared to stay at a hotel until your arrival, or catch you up.

Once on board, and given time to relax, the financial arrangements need to be sorted out. We usually put equal amounts in the kitty, and agree to cook on alternate nights; but inevitably your cruising expenses increase. Not only will you prepare more sophisticated meals, you will drink more and will frequently find that on your friends' cooking night they decide that you should all eat ashore because they are on holiday! In the cheap places this is really fun to do but where expensive you have to feel comfortable saying "no!"

Visitors also need to be shown around the boat and instructed on how everything works, especially the head, how to conserve water, and safety aspects such as using the stove. We get used to the systems on our boats but it is easy for a newcomer to abuse these inadvertently. All of our friends know to bring soft bags but I also ask them to bring an extra, to take home for us some of the souvenirs that are weighing down our vessel. The boys and I do quite well hiding these items from Andy, but it is the higher waterline that always gives us away!

Sundowner parties are very much part of life afloat. Swimming over or taking the dinghy to another yacht in the anchorage, chatting and getting together for a drink at the end of the day is the essence of cruising camaraderie. Make sure you have a light for the cockpit. A weekend of fun with these people, as you all enjoy a new destination, creates closer friendships than you have ever had with many of your neighbours at home. Subsequently you may either cruise together or talk on the radio and inevitably meet up further down the line.

You will also get visits from the local people, particularly the children, and they all love to come on board. Trading or giving gifts is common in the more remote areas. A problem is that while the locals give products from the land and sea, you have to come up with gifts from what you carry on board. So be prepared. Our typical gifts were fishing hooks and line, soap, t-shirts, (although in some of the more frequented areas they wanted designer shirts!), coloured pens and pencils for children, also outgrown children's books and clothing, fuel to fishermen for their outboards, occasionally canned goods and specially obtained local items such as kava root in Fiji. We frequently entertained local people on board, serving large quantities of newly baked bread and cakes, with juice and coffee or tea. The boys quickly made friends and disappeared into the village to play, often returning with shells and carvings.

However, with constant visitors it is hard to get anything done - like school for example! So generally we would only spend a day or two anchored off the villages, enjoying going ashore to see people's homes, meeting the chiefs, taking books to the school and entertaining on board. Then we would head off to an outer island to dive and get some schoolwork behind us.

YOUR NEW IDENTITY

Finally, not only do you have a special life, you also have a new identity. This is derived from your boat name, so think about choosing it carefully! We became Andy and Liza Bagheera, the Bagheeras or the Bagheera's parents and still have Christmas cards addressed as such.

Bagheera was the black panther in the Rudyard Kiplings' Jungle Book. Not only were the stories our childhood favourites, but we felt the sleek, fast Bagheera was symbolically perfect for our first racing boat. It also perfectly suites our Beneteau 38, our seventh boat of the same name, which sped us across the oceans. You will be saying and hearing your boat's name a huge amount while you are cruising, so give due consideration on what to call her and any nicknames you might acquire. We have heard several in our day; the most memorable was for a charter boat in the Caribbean called *Nightwind* - which became known as *Fart in the Dark*!

LIGHTNING

BAGHEERA'S STRIKE

Of course it happened at three in the morning. Doesn't it always? We were heading south from Maputo in Mozambique, bound for Richards Bay in South Africa, when a rapid pressure drop and lightning on the horizon ahead presaged some unpleasantness. As the wind strength began to increase I woke Liza and meanwhile started the engine to make it easier to hold the head into wind when putting in a deep reef.

In no time there was lightning all around us and before Liza had time to complete donning her wet weather gear and join me in the cockpit there was a flash and a roar as if a hand-grenade had gone off in my face. I had a fairly severe jolt from the wheel and must have been confused for some seconds. When I gathered my wits and could look around I saw that a stream of sparks was trailing downwind from our masthead and realised that we had been struck.

I yelled to Liza below to check the bilges. She had heard the noise but hadn't realised that we had been hit until then, but as the VHF radio was spurting flames and ominous clouds of smoke were coming from the engine compartment she soon realised that we had a problem. Having ascertained that we were not sinking and killed the engine we swopped places and I went below to assess the damage.

The engine fire had put itself out. It had been caused by the alternator which had shorted out and literally melted, taking with it one of the battery banks. The main VHF and SSB radios, wind instruments, log and sounders, the weatherfax and radar and the satnav were all dead and emitting the unforgettable smell of fried circuitboard. Some lights still worked, as did some of the fans once the fuses were replaced. We later found that the windlass had not been damaged, nor had the portable VHF or small tiller-type autopilot which we kept for a spare. A portable electronic typewriter and the navigation calculator which were turned off and not connected to the yacht's batteries were also damaged. A colour TV set, also unconnected, was found to have the half of the screen nearest the mast only showing purple.

A considerable amount of wiring including the complete engine harness had burnt out. The top five feet of the mast had changed colour where the heat had affected the anodised finish and the masthead itself was a scorched wasteland, stripped of the VHF antenna, wind instrument transducer, windex, trilight and anchor light. The top insulator in the backstay which we use as our SSB antenna had a hole blown in its side where the strike had met an obstruction and flashed back to the mast. The magnetic compass was several degrees off.

We were in an unpleasant predicament. It was pitch dark, there was driving, heavy rain, continuous lightning and a full gale of wind. We were caught between a rocky, steep to and unlit shoreline and the infamous Aghullas current, which in a strong southwesterly builds up into some of the most violent seas in the world. Without visibility or any aids at all we tried to hold position in the mile or so between the current edge and the shore, creeping in until we could hear the roar of the surf and then edging out until the seas became untenable.

When daylight eventually came and with it an easing of the wind we were mentally and physically exhausted. It was an immense relief when later that day a yacht which we had met in Maputo and with whom we had stayed in contact with our portable VHF caught up with us and escorted us down to Richard's Bay.

ABOUT LIGHTNING

It is estimated that at any given time there are roughly two thousand thunderstorms in progress over the earth's surface. Together they may produce six thousand lightning discharges each minute, over eight million each day. Particularly in the tropics, sailors will encounter thunderstorms so frequently that it is all too easy to become blasé and to forget the very real danger that lightning represents. Lightning does strike yachts, sometimes with fatal results, and with this in mind a strategy to minimise the likelihood of a strike and to reduce the possible damage to both crew and vessel needs to be put in place.

Unfortunately there are no hard and fast rules. For such a common and well studied phenomenon, lightning continues to surprise and confound the experts. There are even differences of opinion as to whether the rig should be grounded or isolated and whether through-hull fittings should be bonded together or not. The South African Lloyd's surveyor who dealt with our damage after a strike off the Mozambique coast told us that the results of a strike were never the same and that just the week before he had inspected a yacht which had sunk because lightning had perforated dozens of holes around the hull at the waterline.

Having experienced a lighting strike twice in my life I have developed an interest in the subject and strong opinions as to protective measures. Hopefully this will help other cruisers to decide on their own strategies.

We know that in a thunderstorm a massive difference in electrical potential builds up sufficiently to cause an electrical 'short' between the cloud and the surface. This is the lightning itself and it will find the line of least resistance to the sea, which could be through your yacht and its conveniently tall rig. The incredible power involved in one of these discharges can be in the order of 200,000 amps at up to a billion volts, enough to light a small city and certainly enough to blast its way through a hull if it cannot find an easy way to the sea. Other potential dangers are from electrocution and temperatures high enough to fuse steel.

Before a discharge there is a period as the differential builds up when there is a flow of ions upwards from potential strike targets, often visible as St. Elmo's fire. It is believed that this flow forms 'streamers' which are the precursors to a possible strike.

Thunder is the noise created as this massive energy burns its way through the atmosphere and is a relatively harmless side effect, other than to increase terror in a frightening situation.

A second side effect is invisible but has the potential to cause a huge amount of damage to the vessel's gear. This is called the electromagnetic pulse (EMP). Put in simple terms it means that accompanying the lightning discharge is a massive, fluctuating magnetic field.

Just as we create electricity in a generator by the movement of a conducting wire through a magnetic field, and although the electromagnetic pulse lasts only tens of microseconds, its strength is such that a huge voltage is created in every bit of wiring, every printed circuit and all other electrical components on the vessel. The results are burnt-out wiring, dead circuit boards and possible fires. It should be noted that this will happen to electronic and electrical equipment regardless of whether they are in use or connected to the batteries or an antenna.

TO GROUND OR NOT TO GROUND?

Those who advocate not grounding the rig argue that this way the yacht does not offer the shortest route for the lightning to go between the cloud and the sea and therefore there is only a small likelihood of a strike. We cannot agree with this strategy for two reasons. Firstly, a thunderstorm is almost always accompanied by rain and a wet mast is a slightly better conductor than the air around it so becomes the likely focal point for a strike. Secondly, if you are struck the results will be devastating and life threatening because the discharge has not got an easy route through a conductor to the sea. Anyone who needs to be convinced should go out and inspect lightning-struck trees, which being wet and high were in a similar state to an ungrounded rig.

GROUNDING SYSTEMS

By providing an easy and direct route for the lightning from the masthead to the sea we prevent structural damage to the hull which could result in sinking. Remember, however, that this will not stop damage to a yacht which is out of the water and if stored ashore in a lightning prone area a heavy cable from the rig leading to a metal stake driven into the ground may be worthwhile.

There are some cruisers who advocate hanging a length of chain from a lee shroud into the water during a thunderstorm, hoping that this will provide a discharge path. This simple strategy is flawed. Not only could there be a risk to the person who is attaching the chain should there be a strike, there will inevitably be damage to the topsides due to the flailing of the chain; also, the conductivity between the links may not be sufficient to stop a damaging side flash to an easier route, which may be through the hull. For those who want an external ground, a length of rigging wire permanently clamped to an uninsulated backstay and allowed to trail is far more likely to provide protection.

Internal grounding is relatively simple and consists of heavy duty copper strapping connecting the mast and/or rigging to an external ground below the waterline. On non-metal hulls this ground can either be a keel-bolt on a yacht with an external, bolt-on ballast or a large ground plate. Connections must be kept clean and corrosion free, the strap should not pass through bilge water or close to a metal through-hull fitting and no bend in it should have a radius of less than 14 inches, since lightning will not turn sharp corners and will simply flash to a more direct route, possibly straight through he hull.

A more sophisticated ground strap can have incorporated in it a 'positive gap' connector. This is a unit which looks like a cartridge fuse with the terminals separated by a minute gap, and its purpose is to break electrical contact in the strap to deny a path for the flow of ions to the masthead and therefore reduce the likelihood of streamers forming. Because the gap is so small the discharge during a strike will easily jump across to disperse through the ground plate. These units are also available for inserting into radio antenna cables. Some manufacturers such as Beneteau incorporate this system as standard in their cruising boats.

On the question of the bonding together of all through-hull skin fittings, Lloyds and several other authorities say no. The American Boat and Yacht Council says yes. What to do? We go with Lloyds every time and believe that metal skin fittings are a weakness in the hull; these should not be exposed to potential damage by having millions of volts discharged through them. There are several records of yachts sinking because a through-hull has been blown out by lightning, so why risk this?

ION DISSIPATION

Another approach to minimising the risk of a strike is to try to make it easy for the ions to dissipate from the masthead, thereby bleeding off some of the differential and reducing the chance of streamer formation. The old-fashioned 'lightning conductors' found on church steeples do this. Ions will flow off a sharp point so any conductor should be as high above the masthead as possible and be needle-sharp at the top. There should be good electrical connection at all times to the ground plate. Several needle points are better than one and there are marine dissipaters on the market that incorporate a mass of sharp ended whiskers.

THE ELECTROMAGNETIC PULSE

There is no practical way to protect an entire yacht against the loss of electronics and electrics should it be struck. Luckily the damage is not usually life-threatening, but the cost of repairs can be huge.

I have never seen or heard of anyone doing this, but believe that a 'Faraday's Cage', an all-metal box which is grounded could be used as a storage container for the portable GPS and VHF and a spare quartz watch. This box would shield the contents from the magnetic field during a strike and they would still be useable when all other electronics have been fried. An alternate might be to stow these items in an oven, preferably grounded, during thunderstorms.

MAINTENANCE, SPARES AND TOOLS

There are some who have been cruising for several years who still rely on professional help to maintain their boats. These boaters have to stay close to civilisation. Most long distance cruisers, however, are self-reliant in fixing most of the problems that arise. This is not only more economical, it also gives them the flexibility to wander off the beaten track.

A routine of preventive maintenance will catch most problems before they become crises, enabling repairs and replacements to be done in the calm of the harbour. Inevitably, however, there will be some repairs that have to be done at sea.

The following list is based on *Bagheera's* maintenance schedule, including the spares and tools carried while we circumnavigated. Hopefully this will help in the organization of your boat.

ENGINE, GEARBOX AND SHAFT

The operator's manuals supplied with most marine diesels assume that engines will be serviced by the local dealer. We replaced it with the workshop manual for our Perkins 4-108, an indispensable service and troubleshooting guide.

Lube oil and filter changes are done every 100 hours or less, fuel filters every 200 hours. The gear box lube is checked at the same 100 hour intervals but is only changed annually. Sometimes, however, these changes are done before they are due as we know that for the next several weeks we will be away from a place where the old oil and filters can be properly disposed. Injectors are serviced professionally, if possible every 400 hours.

As fuel is of dubious quality in many places special care must be taken to filter out water and solids when filling the tank and again from the engine fuel line. Biocide should be added at every fill *(see Fuels)*. At regular intervals sample the bottom of the tank with a small suction pump to check for contamination. On passages a long syphon pump can be used from the jerry cans on deck so they can be emptied from where they are stowed.

Daily checks include oil and coolant levels, belt tensions plus an inspection for any signs of trouble such as oil leaks or water in the filter trap.

Added to the standard installation are: two extra fuel filter/water traps, in-line electric fuel pump, oil pressure and water temperature gauges, exhaust overheat alarm, high capacity alternator with 'smart' regulator.

Supplies carried. Lube and gear oils, lube and diesel filters, 'V' belts, coolant corrosion inhibitor, diesel biocide, engine touch-up paint, gasket compound, Locktite, fuel hose and clamps, assorted metric fasteners.

Spares. Injectors, fuel pump, raw water pump impellers, seals and gaskets, alternator and regulator, complete engine gasket set, hoses and clamps, heat exchanger end caps and zincs, starter switch and relays, raw water intake filter, dripless stern gland bellows and face-plate.

Tools. Lube-oil sump pump (permanently hooked-up), imperial and metric socket and open end wrenches, Allen keys and feeler gauges, 'Baja' fuel funnel/filter, small brass hand pump and nine foot siphon pump.

ELECTRICS

The care and feeding of the batteries is the key to ensuring reliable electrics. We built up two banks each consisting of three 115 amp-hour deep cycle batteries which are charged from the engine high output alternator, solar panels, wind generator or by a fully automatic battery charger. Ammeters to show charge rate and consumption, a voltmeter to show charge state, plus a low voltage alarm allow us to monitor and control battery condition.

Batteries get warm and give off hydrogen so the battery boxes are ventilated by a silent, brushless computer fan.

Maintenance includes weekly checks of the electrolyte levels and the cleanliness of the terminals.

The boat's electrical system has become complex due to the variety of equipment and electronics which are installed; servicing is made easier by using identifying labels on all new wiring. Corrosion is inhibited at terminals, bulb sockets etc. using Corrosion Block or WD-40.

Supplies. Distilled water (occasionally, clean rain water was used to restock), tinned copper insulated cable in various sizes and colours, shielded co-axial cable and fittings, assorted terminals and cable clamps, circuit breakers and fuses, fluorescent tubes and bulbs for all equipment, electrical solder, insulating tape and shrink tubing, switches, terminal bars, fuse holders, watertight connectors, diodes and LEDs, dry cell, nicad, lithium and mercury batteries, Corrosion Block and WD-40.

Spares. Electric motor for bilge or pressure water pump, cabin fans, navigation and cabin lights, float switch, alarm buzzers.

Tools. 12 and 110-volt soldering irons, digital multi-meter, crimping and insulation stripping tools, jumper cables, electrical screwdrivers and long nosed pliers, modeller's vice, 12-volt nicad battery charger and 12-volt to 110-volt 800 watt inverter.

The 110-volt AC system was modified from new to accept from shore power either 110-volts directly, or 220-volts AC which went to a built-in transformer.

SYSTEMS

The heads, water system, bilge pumps, refrigeration, cabin heater, fans and much more are regularly checked over, cleaned and where needed, lubricated. Seacocks are serviced at each haul-out; hoses and hose clamps are replaced at the first sign of deterioration.

Supplies. Water filters, refrigerant and filter/dryers, tubing, pipe fittings and stainless steel clamps in various diameters and sealants.

Spares. Complete rebuild kits for all units supplemented by extras of items which need replacing regularly, submersible bilge pump, manual bilge pump, strum box filters, 'Y' valves, through-hulls and sea cocks.

Tools. Meters for refrigeration system, tube cutter, flaring tool and small plumber's mate.

SAILS, CANVAS AND LINES

Constant checking of the sails when in use and a thorough inspection before a long passage becomes routine. Self-adhesive anti-chafe patches need to be re-applied as soon as they show any signs of deterioration. Frayed stitching should be reinforced.

Supplies. Polyester sailcloth, nylon spinnaker cloth, dodger and sailcover cloth; self-adhesive polyester patching cloth and nylon rip-stop tape; polyester sewing and whipping twine in various sizes; beeswax and liquid whipping compound, polyester webbing, cringles, batten stock, shock cord and crimps, plastic tubing and fire hose for line chafe protection. Polyester and nylon lines in varying diameters and lengths, monel seizing wire and heat-shrink tube.

We also had a large selection of different colours of spinnaker cloth, coloured thread, waterproof coloured marker pens and coloured adhesive cloth tapes which enabled us to make up courtesy flags as accurately as possible (some are too complicated and have to be bought).

Spares. Sail slides; jib hanks; mast sheaves, a variety of types and sizes of blocks, cleats, shackles and snaphooks.

Tools. Sailmaker's needles, gimlet and palm; splicing fids; fisherman's netting tool; miniature propane torch; large scissors and razor knife; cringle punches.

RIG

Inspection of the rig is considerably eased if there is an electric anchor windlass on board, with a masthead halyard led to the capstan drum. Don't buy a windlass that has only a gypsy fitted for line and chain; a capstan is invaluable. Hoisting the dinghy on board, lifting someone to the masthead, taking up the slack on warps or the storm anchor rode or even recovering someone from the water are all tasks made easy with power assisted winching.

The furling gear and every wire terminal, toggle, tang and exit box, plus sheaves and their pins and the wire itself are carefully inspected visually and tactilely for cracks, wear or corrosion before any significant passage. At the same time masthead lights and antennae are checked and offshore chafe gear is put on, consisting of carpeting (poor man's baggywrinkle) taped to the spreader backs and at intervals on the shrouds. Shroud tension is monitored and any adjustments needed are made immediately; turnbuckle split pins are not reused and are replaced with new.

Annually, a chemical crack detection kit is used to test all metal fittings.

Any non-aluminum gear which is fastened to the mast is isolated with a plastic spacer and all fastenings are put in with anti-seize compound to prevent galvanic corrosion.

The lightning grounding cables between the mast, the chainplates and the keel-bolts is inspected and if needed the terminals cleaned to ensure good conductivity.

Supplies. Crack detection kit, anti-seize compound, lanolin and teflon lubricants, wire clamps, assorted toggles, shackles, cotter and split pins and rings, Locktite, monel seizing wire, rigger's tape, carpeting, silicon sealant and mast boot material.

Spares. Turnbuckles, sheaves and pins, rigging wire and mechanical terminals, masthead trilight and anchor light, VHF antenna and Windex unit.

DECK AND TOPSIDES

As any weakness will show up when you have your hands full coping with extreme weather, routine inspection of all mechanical systems, with replacement of any parts that show the slightest wear, is important.

The steering gear warrants particularly attentive care. The windlass, winches, turning blocks, hatch and locker hinges and catches, and wind vane gear, all should be cleaned and lubricated every few weeks. When we stayed in eastern Australia for a year, so that our three boys could attend normal schools, Andy set himself up as the 'Winch Doctor' and was kept busy overhauling or replacing some sadly neglected deck gear.

Regular washing down with fresh water can be a problem away from reliable supplies but every chance should be taken to remove salt from metal surfaces. Aluminum will start to 'pit' if salt crystals remain for long and even stainless steel will show brown oxidation marks if not washed and polished frequently.

Exterior wood is left by many to bleach out to save maintenance but a slow deterioration does occur as the surface wears and becomes grainy. Oil finishes oxidize quickly in the tropics, going black and blotchy. We favour varnishing but it does entail a great deal of work. In

171

temperate climes re-coating is needed every spring and fall and in the tropics every two months. If varnish is not kept up to scratch then the entire lot must be removed and the process started again, a major chore!

Fibreglass surfaces need any nicks or scratches repaired with gel coat, while major damage must be reglassed and finished. Staining, such as the rust specks which are so common when near an industrial area or railway bridge, and the brown streaks at the waterline, are removed with phosphoric acid. Topsides must be regularly waxed.

Fittings need periodic re-bedding in sealant which is done at the first sign of any movement or leaking.

UNDERWATER

Travel lifts or marine railways and regular haul-outs are left behind once you are away from the affluent areas of the world and bottom cleaning may have to be done by diving.

Some repairs might have to be done without hauling. For us the most nerve-wracking job was in Thailand, where we had to have our propellershaft straightened. This entailed dropping out the rudder, then pulling the shaft and stuffing cloth into the shaft tube before we filled, so that soft bung could be tapped home inside - all while anchored in forty feet of water. The process had to be reversed after repairs. Trying to get a heavy 2m of 30-mm shaft aligned and back into place under water with no visibility was an interesting experience to say the least; especially as a rag held over the inner end of the stern tube was the only thing stopping the ocean rushing in!

Where there is sufficient tide it may be possible to dry out against a wall or pilings. At Kilfi, in Kenya, we just managed this with a draft of seven feet and a spring tide of seven feet. We dug a trench on the previous low and then wriggled in at the top of the tide, then took lines to nearby palm trees to hold us firmly against the wall. A new rudder bearing was needed and had to be machined from a block of teflon in Mombasa and then rushed back to get us away that evening as the next day's tides were considerably less. It all worked out, thank goodness. We didn't relish being stuck there for a month waiting for the next spring tides.

Fibreglass requires protection from osmotic blistering, which can occur even in hulls that have been in use for years. We recommend that new hulls be treated before the first antifouling and that used boats when purchased have their bottoms stripped of paint and treated after a period of drying out. It is far cheaper to prevent blistering than to cure and repair it. Treatment consists of building up a layer of epoxy over the prepared fibreglass to at least the product manufacturer's recommended thickness. There are epoxy products incorporating metallic copper which both increases their impermeability to moisture and also deters marine growth. We have not used these but will do so before our next cruise.

Wood hulls will be attacked by teredo or 'shipworm' and possibly by gribble, both of which burrow into and weaken the structure if an antifouling barrier is not maintained in good condition. Any exposure of bare wood due to a scrape or grounding will allow these creatures access and must be re-painted at the earliest opportunity.

Unprotected steel corrodes rapidly in salt water, as does aluminum when in the presence of dissimilar metals, including copper based antifouling paints, which are all that may be used on yachts in many countries. A galvanic barrier-coat such as coal-tar epoxy is effective on steel hulls and cast iron keels, while aluminum usually has a complex priming and barrier system applied before antifouling is put on. Any breach in this protection will result in corrosion and should be corrected early. Many owners of metal hulled yachts will plan their haul-out in countries where tin based antifouling is still obtainable. If we get any sign of rust on our keel we wire-brush the area down to bare metal, apply coal-tar epoxy followed by copper antifouling paint.

Antifouling paints are less effective and have to be more frequently applied now that many countries have banned tin based toxicants for yacht use. Some marine organisms seem to positively thrive on the copper oxide based ones. For this reason we use co-polymer paints which slowly erode, these being easier to clean off underwater and also preventing a huge build-up of paint.

Propellers and shafts which are left bare will accumulate growth and become less and less efficient. In warm waters these can be kept clean by diving but we prefer to use antifouling paint which is applied over an epoxy metal primer, leaving just a small area of the shaft for the zinc anode. We use a hard racing paint which will not erode from the blades during rotation when motoring.

Supplies. Antifouling paints, coal-tar epoxy paint, metal primer and rollers, brushes, wet and dry sandpaper, masking tape and solvent, underwater hardening epoxy paste; zinc anodes.

Spares. Propeller, cutlass bearings and rudder bearings.

Tools. Propeller puller and stainless steel wire brush.

MEDICAL

Although it is important to have a well-stocked medical chest on board (several plastic containers in our case), in reality cruisers seldom get sick with the constant fresh air, lack of stress, frequent exercise from swimming and walking ashore, little exposure to germ-ridden recycled air of office buildings and brief contact with potential disease.

"You are all SO disgustingly fit and healthy," was a comment frequently heard from our many visitors. Conversely on our return to Vancouver we all seemed to get every bug that was going around, including the chicken pox!

FACILITIES

It is rare when I give seminars on cruising that I am not questioned about medical concerns related to hygiene, disease, nasties in the ocean, and the availability and standard of medical facilities.

As we initially planned to cruise the Mediterranean I hadn't been worried about medical issues. With a basic understanding of French and Spanish, and English being the world-wide language, we were unlikely to have any communication problems and I knew European countries practise first rate medicine. The Caribbean is less sophisticated, but having lived in the area for many years we knew that it was satisfactory and improving yearly. As we continued our travels west, most areas of the world had more than adequate medical facilities. Certainly, the buildings may not be in good state of repair, with paint peeling off the walls, but the medical care was generally good. Many third world countries have good medical schools, send students for training elsewhere and receive supplies and personnel from Europe and North America.

Recently we led a group charter with The Moorings in Tonga. The day after arrival there was an outbreak of typhoid. All visitors were offered the opportunity of immunization. There was great discussion amongst the group which had a heavy medical component. Finally they all decided to troop up the hill as it was an excuse to see the hospital! In the end, half had the vaccine; the others decided it was not necessary as the outbreak was small and contained. On their return they all, whether GP, ophthalmologist, psychiatrist or nurse expressed their approval of the good care and facility.

MEDICAL SUPPLIES

We, like most cruisers, carried supplies for the spectrum of health hazards with dressings, ointments, lotions, powders and medications for every aspect and function of the body, including antibiotics and even morphine. Consult with your local travel clinic and physician before leaving but don't go overboard in stocking up for every eventuality. Medications are very expensive and generally have an expiry date. Although it is wise to carry antibiotics (appendicitis and prostatitis are particular concerns, besides skin infections) and antihistamines in case of allergic reactions, specific medications can be purchased when needed and often cost considerably less in third world countries. *Make sure prescription drugs are officially labelled.* We never had any problems with our medical supplies on board; however, countries vary in their regulations; while we were in Greece, for example, an Australian girl was arrested because she had codeine in her bag without a prescription.

Carry medical books oriented both for general family health and travel; it is in the tropics that you will most likely have problems. There are many of these volumes on the market *(see appendix C)*. It's worth taking time when choosing one. I found some difficult to read, others hard to access relevant information, while others just weren't geared to practical treatment.

Many people who have recurrent health problems cruise successfully. It is important to carry more than adequate supplies of special medications, remembering cruisers' plans often change, also to obtain a duplicate prescription that lists both the generic and trade names. They should also plan their route with their condition in mind to avoid their own distress and the inconvenience of others. We were surprised, for example, to hear how many had been taken from Chagos (an idyllic atoll isolated in the middle of the Indian ocean with no resident population) to Diego Garcia (an American military base some 250 kilometres away) to be flown out for specialised treatment of previously existing conditions. As they could not be flown back to the military base, their partners were left behind to complete the long passages to the Maldives or the Seychelles alone. Some find that their previous condition had all but disappeared. Colin, for example, has suffered severe eczema both before and since our travels. While he lived on the boat and in salt water almost daily, contrary to all predictions, his skin was almost totally clear.

It is common for men over 50 to suffer from difficulties in urinating due to the enlarging of the prostate gland. This can become critical and a catheter should be included in the medical kit.

COMMON MEDICAL COMPLAINTS

Common medical complaints suffered by cruisers:
> swimmer's ear
> sore eyes
> cuts and sores
> dehydration
> insect bites
> diarrhea
> stings from marine organisms and coral burn
> bruises and stiff muscles
> urinary tract infections (cystitis)
> seasickness
> sunburn

Swimmer's Ear
For this common divers' problem there are many remedies on the market but Andy swears that a mix of alcohol, vinegar and oil works best.

Alcohol dries the ear and is antibacterial, vinegar is a fungicide (swimmer's ear is generally caused by a fungus), and oil softens wax and allows removal. Either use 50% distilled vinegar and 50% rubbing alcohol or if wax in the ears is a problem 40% vinegar, 40% alcohol and 20% good salad oil (Andy prefers olive!). After diving apply 2 - 3 drops in each ear or if an ear is already infected, 4 times each day. For a mild condition use diluted 10% Vol. hydrogen peroxide.

Sore Eyes

Due to the sun, salt and wind, and dust ashore in tropical countries, sore eyes are common, particularly with contact lens wearers. Bathe eyes frequently with saline solution. Many of us decided that is was easier, especially for watches, to wear prescription dark glasses instead of contact lenses. I have found the 'photo grey' system, where lens colour changes with light, very successful. Ultra violet rays can also cause eye damage, particularly to the cornea. Pterygium can result from continuous exposure to the sun, along with the wind, dust and salt. Wear dark glasses to reduce glare. Polarized ones are preferred as they give better vision for navigating through reefs.

Cuts and sores

For those of us reared with the maxim 'saltwater heals', it is a shock to find that in tropical waters it does quite the reverse. Within days, the tiniest of cuts can fester and grow to a sore, ugly wound. The most effective remedy is to keep the wound dry (a great 'out' for washing-up, the boys learnt!), and particularly away from the bacteria found in tropical sea water (a group of comma-shaped bacteria, the most well known species of which causes cholera and which can live 285 days in sea water!). Band-aids must be used sparingly, those that breathe (such as Elastoplast) being much healthier than the waterproof variety; they also stay on better. Once the bleeding has stopped the wound must be exposed to air (except in dusty areas cover with a light gauze to prevent infection); enclosed in the heat it will soon fester. Antibiotic ointments such as Bactroban and Neosporin may speed healing.

Dehydration, heat exhaustion and heat stroke

It is important to drink plenty of fluids in the tropics, to replace that lost through perspiration. Ten glasses of non-alcoholic liquids per day are recommended. In the past salt tablets were also prescribed but are

today not recommended. Now we have the knowledge that it is best not to work, and sweat, in the heat of the sun and we can drink Gatorade or Gastrolyte for electrolyte replacement. If this is not available one should drink anything soft, even tea with lemon (potassium) and sugar. Incidentally 'drowning your sorrows' in Caribbean rum will only create more sorrows; alcohol is very dehydrating. Tea and coffee are also diuretics. If you feel lethargic and irritable, and especially if your urine is dark yellow, small in volume and infrequent, you are most likely dehydrated.

You can easily make Gastrolyte, a glucose-electrolyte recipe, yourself.

        glass #1 . . . . 250ml fruit juice
                        1/2tsp. corn syrup, sugar or honey
                        pinch of salt
        glass #2 . . . . 250ml boiled or carbonated water
                        1/4 tsp. baking soda

Drink from the glasses alternatively and repeat until no longer thirsty.

Sip one 250ml glass for every bowel movement. Drink more if urine is low or still thirsty.

Green coconut water also makes a good rehydration liquid as it contains both glucose and potassium. Dilute with an equal part of water.

179

Heat exhaustion can happen on board when it is very hot and especially when ashore if one is walking long distances in the sun. The symptoms are lethargy and dizziness. More serious is heat stroke when all sweating ceases and the person may become delirious, even comatose.

You've heard the saying 'only mad dogs and Englishmen go out in the mid-day sun' and it's quite true; we tend to have set ideas of what we will accomplish in a day regardless of the climate. Many of the towns in the tropics are stifling, as they are built in sheltered areas in case of storms. St. Johns in Antigua is one; we all used to gather in the banks as they were air-conditioned, and few places were at that time.

My family only suffered from heat exhaustion once. Andy, Colin and Jamie went shopping in Galle, Sri Lanka, for my birthday. I was in England, for my sister's funeral, so they wanted it to be a special occasion. It was during the pre-monsoon, unbelievably hot and humid, but they persevered. Colin was very sick the whole of my birthday, and the other two not feeling well . With plenty of liquids the boys recovered quickly but Andy, although he didn't recognize he was ill at the time, was lethargic for several days on our trip to India and his reasoning was definitely affected.

Insect Bites

The itching and irritation of insect bites is reason enough to avoid them but several tropical diseases such as malaria, Japanese B encephalitis, yellow fever and dengue fever are transmitted by insects. Particularly avoid mosquitoes by applying insect repellent that contains at least 20% DEET, wear light-coloured clothes after dusk (this is when mosquitoes are most active) that cover your legs and arms, and use unscented make-up, deodorant, soap and shampoo, as mosquitoes are attracted to perfume. Have mosquito screens on the boat, use pyrethroid coils, or spray aerosols such as Raid around the room *(see Pests - Mosquitoes)*. Also take the necessary prophylactic treatments listed under 'other preventative measures' below.

Flying insects, such as no-see-ums and gnats, can come in swarms and be vicious. An Avon product, Skin-So-Soft, put on the skin (it is made for the bath) is effective in keeping them away (now sold by Off as Skintastic).

Be especially careful if bugs tend to like you. Andy suffers the most in our family. If he is around, I can relax, no mosquito will come near me, although a few will attack Duncan. Andy's worst bite was from a spider in Indonesia. It took several treatments of antibiotics to clear the complicating infection.

Diarrhea

This is usually caused by bacteria that contaminate food and water. Contamination can be by unwashed hands, human sewage in fertiliser or unsafe water used on vegetables in market stalls. Diarrhea is the most frequent illness amongst travellers, but not so prevalent amongst cruisers as they have the advantage of being able to go 'home' if the food or water appear suspect.

Generally diarrhea is a self-limiting illness that lasts two or three days and may be associated with vomiting and fever. *By far the most important treatment is re-hydration,* especially critical for children - a small child can be limp in half an hour. Imodium works well in reducing the effect (but can't be given to children under 12), or take the local remedy. To treat, avoid milk and milk products, drink plenty of fluids, especially those containing glucose for increased absorption and begin eating solid foods as the diarrhea diminishes. Antibiotics can also be taken if severe. Quinolones are presently the drugs of choice (i.e. Ciprofloxacin, Ofloxacin).

Some find Pepto-Bismol (chew two tablets four times a day) helps in its prevention but products such as Enterovioform are not recommended by any authority. Others such as doxycycline may have side effects such as extra sensitivity to sun, diarrhea and vaginal infection.

Ashore, in suspect areas, only drink water or beverages that have been boiled (at least one minute at a rolling boil at sea level), or passed through a purifier, or treated with either iodine (5 drops of 2.5% for every litre of clear water, 10 drops for every litre of cold or cloudy water and let sit for 30 minutes) or chlorine (2 drops bleach (4-6%) per litre) - *see Water* for on board supplies. Eat food that is hot and well cooked (particularly shellfish). Never eat leftover food that has been sitting for a long time, be careful of street vendors. Milk should be boiled or powdered milk used with boiled water as many countries do not pasteurise their milk. Also, be careful of cheese, home made ice cream, yoghurt and mayonnaise. Avoid salads and wash fruit and vegetables thoroughly, whether on the boat or ashore in case of poor hygiene of handlers, also because of the world-wide use of insecticides and the use of human manure as fertilizer. It is usually safe to drink coffee, tea, any carbonated soft drinks (if it doesn't fizz don't drink it - it has probably been concocted locally and put into Coke bottles), beer, coconut milk and bottled water (be sure to break the seal yourself).

Far more serious than diarrhea is dysentery. It is not common amongst cruisers and I was the only one who suffered from it on our boat. It was just after we had left Madagascar. Dysentery is diarrhea containing blood and mucous; it can be caused by viruses, bacteria or parasites. The treatment of choice for bacterial dysentery is Cipro, for amoebic dysentery take Flagyl. Bactrim was also suggested in our backpackers' handbook. This is a recognised,general purpose antibiotic that we had been recommended in Singapore and we had it on board.

Besides diarrhea, food and water that is contaminated can also give you such diseases as typhoid, giardiasis and worms. There may also be worms or worm cysts in under-cooked pork, wild game, fish and water-plants such as seaweed.

Stings from marine organisms and coral burn
(See Dangers) Always have a good supply of white vinegar to treat jellyfish stings.

Bruises and stiff muscles
Having sufficient handholds and using them automatically drastically reduces falls and bumps when the boat lurches; also develop foolproof techniques for climbing in and out of the dinghy. We particularly notice the extent of bruising that can happen when guests are first on board.

Stiff muscles occur with stress and strain. Avoid the stress by being comfortable with the situation - not always immediately possible! Strain can come from using equipment that is awkwardly positioned such as a winch. Organising equipment for manoeuvres to be convenient for all the crew is discussed in *Life on Board and Safety at Sea*. This is an important aspect of not only successfully, but also safely, living on board. If a job is too much work it will be put off, including reefing the sails when the wind is building.

There are some areas on the boat, where one spends considerable time, that can be made more comfortable. The cockpit is an obvious example. If night watches are uncomfortable you will end up aching. Make sure you have a selection of cockpit cushions so you can be surrounded by padding. If the foam on your berth is too hard or too soft, too thick or too thin and you have a back ache in the morning, change it. We always put a layer of softer foam on the top of ours; now one can obtain the ridged posturepaedic varieties (always have a pad on top as foam can be hot).

Keep a muscle relaxant in your medical kit (my family likes Tiger Balm) and exchange frequent backrubs with your partner!

Urinary tract infections

Yeast infections and cystitis can be very uncomfortable and debilitating on a boat. If you are prone to these infections make sure that you have good supplies of medication on board. I use Wintomylon for cystitis; it works rapidly. Also important is drinking several tumblers of water. Avoid wearing wet bathing suits or sitting on wet salty cushions. (Hemorrhoids are also a common complaint - carry Preparation H.)

Seasickness

(See Seasickness) You CAN overcome it!

Sunburn

It is hard to emphasize enough the dangers from the sun. When we first lived in the tropics in the sixties no one realised the long-term effects of sunburn. Both Andy and I are fair-skinned and freckled, so are high risk for burning although both ultimately tan, and we did immeasurable harm to our skin. In Australia Andy had 56 liquid nitrogen treatments to his face and hands for pre-cancerous tissue and has had several more treatments since. I had a small mole that bled and distorted on my arm. A biopsy showed it to be malignant, only a pinprick of a melanoma but a centimetre all round had to be removed. I had the surgery completed in Panama. It was our only expensive medical bill, $500, of which I recouped only $90 on a medical plan.

Use a sunscreen with a sun protection factor of at least 15, and one as high as is available on one's face. Wind, salt and sun together are dynamite for damage as well as horrendous for wrinkles. Limit time spent in the sun between 11 am and 2 pm and wear a hat, particularly if bald! Remember you can still get burnt when there is a cloud cover. All experienced cruisers now have bimini sun covers over the cockpit and many have side curtains on the life lines to stop the burning from the glare off the water. Be especially careful with children as this is when the main long-term damage is done.

RESOURCES

When you travel outside Western and Central Europe, U.S.A., Canada, Australia, New Zealand and Japan, certain immunizations may be needed. As several diseases are on the rise it is important to have up-to-date information. Obtaining this and the necessary vaccinations requires careful planning as there are only certain places that offer them, although due to the dramatic increase in travel, especially adventure holidays, travel clinics are now common in the major cities of first world countries. It is important to visit a clinic at least six weeks before you leave for infected areas. Constant updates and advice on immunisations and high risk areas for malaria are provided by world wide organizations such as the World Health Organization and IAMAT (International Association for Medical Assistance to Travelers). In addition, IAMAT has listings of English-speaking doctors and health institutions worldwide. Several national departments also provide information. On my recent visit to a travel clinic at the Vancouver Health Board, I was given not only considerable informative literature on specific diseases but also a general travel booklet put out by the government. This included a number to call in the Quarantine Health Services of Health Canada in Ottawa for medical update as well as a list of names, addresses and phone numbers of all the Canadian Missions around the world. Other sources of medical information are Centres for Disease Control, Atlanta USA. *(See Appendix B for agencies and Appendix C for recommended reading)*

IMMUNIZATIONS

Check you are up to date on all childhood vaccinations such as **polio**, **tetanus** and **diphtheria**.

Typical additional vaccinations cruisers might need:
Hepatitis A (also called infectious Hepatitis) - a viral infection of the liver, found world-wide, which is transmitted in food and drink or by ingesting contaminated water during swimming. Two boosters of Havrix, with another 12 months later, will give you 10 years of protection.

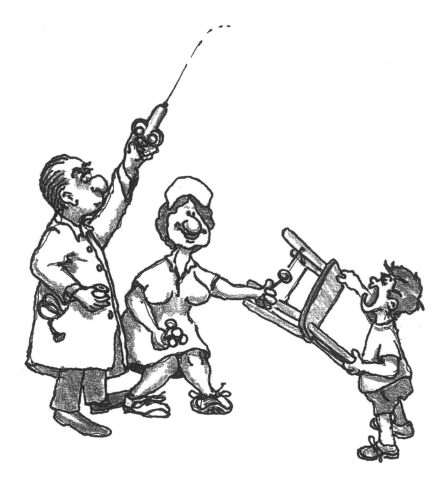

Yellow fever - a viral infection of the liver and other tissues transmitted by mosquitoes in the tropical areas of Africa and South America. Urine becomes dark, stools clay coloured and skin turns yellow (jaundiced). One injection protects you almost 100% for 10 years.

Typhoid fever -a bacterial infection of the bowel and blood, found world-wide and again spread through contaminated food and water. Symptoms include fever, headache, diarrhea or constipation, vomiting and a rash. Avoid by making sure food is safe; the typhoid vaccine does not protect you completely. One injection provides 3 years of protection. Four oral typhoid vaccine capsules last 7 years.

Additional immunizations might include **Meningococcal Meningitis, Japanese B Encephalitis** and **Hepatitis B** depending on your travels.

Don't be in too much of a rush to leave after you have immunizations, in case you have an allergic reaction. Common ones, other than redness and soreness at the injection site, are fever and headache, difficulties with breathing or swallowing, swelling around the mouth or tongue, hoarseness or problems talking, feeling itchy all over and wheezing in the chest when breathing.

OTHER PREVENTATIVE MEASURES

Malaria

No vaccine is available to prevent malaria; avoid the disease by protecting against mosquito bites and taking anti-malarial drugs.

Malaria is found in virtually all tropical countries. In much of the world, transmission only occurs in rural areas; Africa, Asia and Oceania have exceptions. The disease is carried by the Anopheles mosquito, which bites between dusk and dawn. The symptoms are similar to flu, including fever, chills, sore muscles and headaches. Symptoms generally occur less than 10 days after exposure but can begin over a year later.

In additional to the precautions for not being bitten (*see Insect Bites)*, you should start prophylactic drugs one week before travelling to a malarious area and continue for four weeks after. Chloroquine is generally the drug of choice for Central America, mefloquine (Larium) used in Chloroquine resistant areas. Recently, however, some areas in the north of Thailand became Mefloquine resistant. It is thus important to be on top of the current situation. If possible consult a physician trained in travel medicine or ask your 'business manager' to find out at home. Have Fansidar on hand for emergency self-treatment.

Cholera

A serious infection of the intestine found in Asia, the Middle East, S. America, Africa and some parts of Europe. Symptoms are the sudden onset of profuse, watery diarrhea as well as vomiting. Although it used to be popular to immunize for cholera it is now NOT recommended as the vaccine does not prevent the disease. As the bacteria are spread mainly through food and water, carefully monitor all intake if prevalent.

AIDS/HIV

A global disease that attacks the body's immune system. As it is usually sexually transmitted, if needed, always carry latex condoms; local varieties may not meet the safety standards set by the World Health Organization. Be aware that some countries have introduced AIDS testing for foreigners.

Rabies

Rabies is more common in tropical countries. Avoid contact with animals and do not feed or pet cats, dogs or monkeys. If bitten go immediately to a medical centre for a vaccination.

Other risk activities to avoid

— receiving injections (if diabetic etc: carry your own needles)
— having skin-piercing procedures such as tattooing and acupuncture
— accepting blood products for non-life-threatening situations
— swimming in fresh water. In most tropical regions, except Asia and Central America, there is a risk of schistosomiasis (bilharziasis). This infection is acquired through a parasite that may enter the skin during contact in slow-moving fresh water.

It wasn't until the Indian Ocean that we had to have shots for yellow fever, Hepatitis A, typhoid and, at that time, cholera was advised. Those of you who have read *Still Cruising* may remember how traumatised Colin was after having watched 30 boat loads of adults coming from a clinic in Darwin complaining about the pain!

We first took malaria pills in Venezuela. I gave them to the children in strawberry jam and they have never eaten strawberry jam again! In the Indian Ocean we took malaria pills for one and a half years. During our travels many doctors advised us not to take them for an extended period because of side effects; Andy for example, developed eye troubles. They recommended that a three-day treatment of Fansidar (sulfadoxine and pyrimethamine) should be taken as a treatment, and contact made with a doctor as soon as possible. The problem, of course, was confidence in oneself in being able to diagnose the symptoms, especially worrying when one was in the middle of the ocean. It is something to think about, however, as often only certain areas of a country are affected, such as Kruger Park in South Africa.

DENTAL

A small cotton ball soaked in oil of cloves will help relieve tooth ache. When the pain has subsided a mixture of oil of cloves and zinc oxide, inserted with a flat ended toothpick, will set up and seal the cavity.

INSURANCE

(See Insurance - Medical) for companies that will insure for cruising long-term.

Be sure to ask certain questions about the policy. Does it:
* pay foreign hospital and related medical costs and if so does it pay up front or do you pay and get reimbursed later?
* allow for cash advances for medical costs;
* provide for your medical evacuation to your home and someone to accompany you;
* exclude a pre-existing medical condition;
* pay for the preparation and return to home of your remains should you die while away;
* have a high deductible and annual maximum?

Besides having details of your insurance on the boat, give copies to your business manager back home. Always get a detailed invoice from the doctor or hospital. Trying to get copies of the paperwork after you have left, particularly if in a different language, can be very frustrating.

VISITORS AND JET LAG

This may not be relevant to you, except maybe when you make a visit back home, but it will be to your guests. We have all experienced tiredness after crossing time zones, had an upset stomach and disturbed sleep. It will, in particular, take your guests time to adjust to the heat and humidity of the tropics if that is their destination, as well as being on the boat. Encourage them to cover up, stay out of the sun, eat light meals, drink a lot of water and juice (stay off alcohol!), and give them a day of rest before heading out. It might be beneficial for some to spend their first day in a hotel.

NAVIGATION

When venturing away from familiar waters it quickly becomes apparent that what we are used to at home isn't necessarily applicable elsewhere. Buoys and channel markers, chart symbols and datums, measurement units etc. differ from one country to the next. US sailors are particularly surprised to find that the rest of the world marches to a different tune (see Differences).

Furthermore, when cruising in the more remote areas, surveys are found to date back decades or even centuries. In northern Australia, for example, soundings are still used that were made by Flinders in the early 1800s. Whole areas of the oceans have yet to be surveyed. Wording such as "breakers reported 1907" or "Flatulence Island is reported to lie 1 mile southwest of the charted position" will prompt a cautious mariner to navigate with special care. Old French charts even have the prime meridian through Paris!

American cruisers using charts produced by most other English speaking nations will find some important differences (and, of course, vice versa). US charts are less graphic, British Admiralty use more pictorial symbols such as for buoys, where the shape is shown on the chart, kelp beds and tide rips. It is important when buying foreign charts that the list of symbols is also purchased. Although older US and Admiralty charts are in fathoms and feet, more recent use metres and tenths. Always check the chart so that you are not caught out. Most depth sounders can be switched from feet to metres. On the US charts depths are measured from Mean Lower Low Water, which means that there will often be minus tides. Admiralty charts use the approximate Lowest Astronomical Tide, which means that virtually always there will be at least as much depth as shown on the chart, which is far easier to work with. Similarly, height clearances are overstated on the US charts as they are measured from mean high water and half of all high tides will be higher than this. Admiralty charts show a safe clearance from the highest likely astronomical tide.

Get as much practise in navigating and piloting in new areas as you can, so that you take these differences in your stride. Gathering together the necessary charts and publications before you leave, or when you are assembling a new portfolio of charts during your voyage, requires considerable time and planning.

NAVIGATING BY ELECTRONICS

Few of us use traditional methods of navigation any more except to keep in practise. Modern electronics give continuous, usually accurate information and have made ocean voyaging safer for everyone, and therefore more enjoyable. Areas such as the Tuomotus, which are low, reef encumbered and subject to strong and unpredictable currents, in the past were given a wide berth by most yachts but are now regularly explored. Furthermore, all crew members can now easily learn to use these aids; in the past there was often only one competent navigator on board, a dangerous situation should this person be incapacitated.

GPS is now the primary position finding tool, giving not only a continuous and usually accurate position, but also course and speed over the bottom and time and distance to go. Depth sounders have replaced the lead line. Radar helps us see in the dark and fog. It is all too easy to rely completely on what those dials are telling you. However, common sense should make you skeptical;positions at sea should be logged regularly so that in the event of total failure a DR plot can be started from a known position. Never lose a chance to confirm a GPS position visually, by radar or depth sounder when close to land. Remember the charts are often not as accurate as the GPS. For more information see *Electronics*.

ASTRO NAVIGATION

Commonly known as 'celestial', navigation by sextant and chronometer was the only way a yachtsman could find his way across the oceans with reasonable accuracy until the advent of electronic aids. At times cloud cover or the lack of a horizon would mean that days could elapse without being able to take a sight and prudent sailors were very conservative in their chosen routes.

Today navigation skills are almost obsolete, which is a pity because it makes ocean voyaging seem too easy and encourages some who are unfit to go to sea. Many sailors do not bother to carry a sextant, almanac and reduction tables. Of those that do, only the most disciplined use them regularly to stay in practice because the truth is that electronic aids, particularly GPS, are both more accurate and reliable. We continue to carry a sextant because we experienced total loss of all electronics from our lightning strike.

Celestial is fun and easily self-taught with the help of a good instruction book. Concentrate on the practice and don't worry about the theory at first. Simple noon and Pole star sights for latitude soon progress to position lines derived from morning and afternoon sun sights; planet, star and moon sights quickly follow. Distance off measured by vertical sextant angle, and position using horizontal sextant angle and compass, are equally easy and useful.

CHARTS

Charts are a major but necessary expense. They are needed not only for the planned route but also for any possible diversions due to weather or emergency. Because aids to navigation such as buoys and channel markers are unreliable or non-existent in many third world countries, detailed charts for approaches and anchorages must be carried. Chart plotters are becoming popular but may give insufficient information and, being electronic, cannot be relied upon so should be used in addition to rather than a substitute for paper charts.

Some economy can be achieved by using good cruising guides which have detailed sketch charts of anchorages, that now cover the more popular areas. Many chart books are also available. There are also some excellent commercial reproductions of US charts that can be obtained to cover most of the world and which are inexpensive. A brisk trade is carried on between the cruising fraternity and it is often possible to obtain complete folios from a yacht which has already cruised the area.

Outside US waters most cruisers prefer the charts published by the British Admiralty, which cover the whole world, or those produced for their own waters by many British Commonwealth countries such as Canada, Australia or South Africa and which are similar to the British ones. Compared to the US charts they use better paper, are more uniform in size and, most important, are up to date with the latest amendments when purchased. Be prepared for the differences in symbols and chart datums. If US charts are purchased, ensure that you send to the Hydrographic Office in Washington DC for all amendments to update them.

Cataloguing charts

When there are several hundred charts on board it is important to be able to find the sequence of charts quickly as they are needed, also to be certain before heading out that the folio for the route is complete.

Our simple method uses the chart catalogue. As charts are acquired we highlight the outline directly on the pictorial catalogue so that a series of rectangles overlapping each other from the start of the passage to the end will confirm that we have all the charts we will need. Charts are then stowed in folios covering each segment of the voyage in numerical order. At sea, as the limits of one chart are reached it is easy to identify by number from the catalogue which is to be needed next.

Stowing charts

To roll or to fold? Both methods have disadvantages.

Rolled charts take up a considerable amount of space and a couple of hundred charts would occupy a whole cabin; they also like to remain rolled up and have to be nailed down to the chart table! Folded charts can quickly lose printing definition at the creases, which of course always coincide with a tricky passage into your destination anchorage!

We fold ours once. The folio in use is kept in the chart table. Others are stored flat under berth cushions in the type of oversize, tough plastic garbage bags used by gardeners.

Routing or Pilot charts

Luckily we can use the experience of generations of seamen by acquiring a set of the Routing charts put out by the British or the similar US Pilot charts. Any yacht venturing away from home waters should have these on board.

The amount of information of these charts is astounding. They present in graphic form the averages of many years of meteorological and oceanographic data and are indispensable to the navigator selecting the quickest and safest route. Charts are printed for each month of the year and the navigable seas of the world are covered by five sets: North and South Pacific, North and South Atlantic and Indian Ocean. From them we get percentages of frequency and strengths of wind from various directions, frequency and force of gales, frequency and historic tracks of hurricanes, direction and strength of currents, information on atmospheric pressure, visibility, wave heights, pack ice and iceberg limits, sea and air temperatures and much more.

PUBLICATIONS

Cruising guides where available are particularly useful because they are oriented to the small boat sailor. They do vary in quality of content and accuracy, so when a choice is available such as in the Caribbean some research will pay off.

The *US Sailing Directions* or the UK *Admiralty Pilot* Books provide information on weather, the coastlines, harbours and facilities. Lists of lights and aids to navigation, tide and current tables, radio stations and weather services, current almanac, and sight reduction tables and plotting sheets will also be needed. A publication which we find invaluable is the British *Ocean Passages for the World*, also see Jimmy Cornell's *World Cruising Routes*.

COMPASSES

The principle aid to navigation on board is the steering compass. This shows the direction being steered relative to magnetic north. It does not show the actual course over the bottom which is affected by variation, compass errors, steering inaccuracy, leeway and currents.

It is usual to find several compasses on board a cruising yacht. *Bagheera* has a binnacle mounted main compass, with a smaller spare mounted at the chart table. There are also two hand bearing compasses and the electronic compass with a digital readout for the autopilot.

Many production yachts have compasses that should be upgraded for ocean passages. Requirements include a large card which is easily read, good damping which gives the card stability in rough conditions, corrector magnets so that deviation errors can be minimised and good night lighting. Compasses which are looked down upon, normally have flat cards with the lubber line at the forward part. Headings are read off the bow side of the card. Direct reading cards are more usual on bulkhead units. These are read from the side nearest the person. Sunlight will damage a compass and a cover should be in place whenever the compass is not needed.

Most vessels have the steering compass mounted on the binnacle immediately in front of the helm position. Tiller steered boats may have them bulkhead mounted. Always check that the 'lubberline', or direction indicator, is true to the centreline of the hull, otherwise a permanent error will be present. Any electrical wiring near the compass must be 'twisted' cable so that it does not interfere with the compass reading.

Magnetic compasses are still the most popular steering compasses although electronic units using fluxgate sensors are now available. The latter are more expensive and like all electronics prone to failure, but have the big advantage of being self-calibrating for deviation and being unaffected by dip. A magnetic steering compass must be 'swung' and corrected to minimise deviation errors, any residual ones being recorded on a deviation card. The accuracy of the compass should then be checked at every opportunity when steering on a known heading as errors will occur with changes in nearby equipment or machinery, or a close lightning strike *(see Lightning)*.

Dip is the downward component of the earth's magnetic field. Only at the magnetic equator are is there no dip problem; at the magnetic poles the needle will want to point straight down. To compensate the manufacturer adds a small weight to the compass card which counterbalances the downward pull; however, this only works within a limited zone. Take a compass which is balanced for Europe or North America to the southern latitudes and the weight actually works with the dip to increase the downward angle causing it to eventually bottom out. When this happens the compass ceases to work. This happened to us in Sydney, Australia. When we were heading due south, we were most surprised to find the compass indicated we were going north! When planning to cruise between 30 degrees north and south a unit without dip compensation will work well. For higher latitudes compensation will be needed. It is usual that the compass will have been corrected for your home waters. A second compass should be carried if your cruise takes you to the other side of the equator, so when ordering a compass, specify the cruising area.

Small, portable 'handbearing' compasses come in all shapes and prices. They are an indispensable aid to coastal piloting. We carry an

Autohelm electronic unit which memorises several bearings at the press of a button, also a magnetic 'hockey puck' compass. Accurate bearings in rough weather requires practice and wearers of glasses should check that steel frames do not build in errors.

Radio compasses are in fact radio direction finders and use a source of radio signals for direction, rather than the earth's magnetic field. Developed for aircraft, they can also be useful on a boat.

BINOCULARS

You get what you pay for with binoculars and cheap units are not appropriate for a yacht. As binoculars are essential for safety and piloting as well as for fun, invest in a pair which has good optical quality and light gathering ability. They should be sealed against moisture and armoured against minor shocks.

Binoculars are sized by two numbers such as 8 x 21. The first number is the magnification. Although it would seem advantageous to magnify an object as much as possible a problem arises in that the more an object is magnified the harder it is to keep the object steady, especially on a moving boat. Increased magnification also reduces the transference of light. The second number relates to the diameter of the large front 'objective' lens of the binoculars. This determines how much light the binoculars can gather; it is especially important in low light.

Focussing can be by a central focus knob, or each side may be adjusted independently. Most waterproof units have the latter. The best marine binoculars are sealed and filled with nitrogen. Also available are ones with a built-in bearing compass.

For the average cruising yacht a pair of 7 x 50 will be ideal, while on smaller vessels 6 x 30 will give a steadier image.

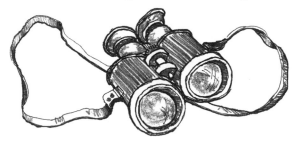

To enhance **night vision** night scopes are becoming popular.

OFFICIALDOM, VISAS AND PAPERWORK

It is always a thrill to see land take form after many days of scanning an empty ocean horizon and there is a never-failing sense of anticipation as one approaches a new country. The last few hours are used to clean below but there are always diversions on deck. Birds are sighted and have to be identified; then the fishing line is spinning astern with the increased abundance of fish close to shore. Smells and sounds waft over the water; the fragrance of flowers, cooking aromas, or the unfamiliar noise and bustle of a city. Particularly appealing are the spice islands with their pungent drifts of cinnamon, cloves, nutmeg and allspice. "A banana bread island," declared Jamie on his first visit to Grenada in the lower Caribbean.

Landfall in a new country has to be at an official port of entry, with heavy penalties in some countries if one stops ashore en route. You need to be prepared for arrival well in advance, as the last hours of approach can be busy. Navigation has to be stepped up, with pertinent charts, cruising guides, pilot books or sailing directions, lists of lights and tide tables at hand. Sails and sheets must be stowed, covers put on and the anchor, or fenders and lines organised. You might have to anchor, or tie to a dock or mooring buoy. One crew member usually spends some time on the radio (usually VHF Channel 16) raising the port officials for instructions. If there is a period in sheltered waters you can start unlashing the dinghy, assembling and inflating it. It is thus safest to plan your arrival in daylight, when you are fresh. Slow down or heave-to until dawn rather than try a risky night entry, particularly if detailed charts and aids to navigation are limited.

ARRIVAL AND DEPARTURE PROCEDURES

Clearing procedures and officials vary greatly around the world. Some require you to stay on board, others that you go ashore; this may be just the captain or both captain and crew. For a smooth entry it is important to know the ports of entry, and correct procedures and to have acquired any necessary documents and visas in advance. Jimmy Cornell's *World Cruising Handbook* is very useful in this respect, besides giving much other information. We are fortunate that English is the

international language for port authorities, as well as the language most commonly used for communications at sea.

A clean, tidy boat and a spruced-up crew does wonders in speeding up the clearing-in procedure, as does patience, politeness and deference! Not being naturally patient, Andy takes along his latest novel or magazine if he has to go ashore. If you get aggressive the process will take double the time.

Most officials work from Monday to Friday, regular working hours, sometimes Saturday mornings, otherwise there is a overtime charge. The problem is that in paradise one never keeps track of days of the week. You wouldn't believe how many times we managed to make our arrivals on a Sunday! Generally we would wait at anchor until Monday morning and feel we had gained one bonus day of relaxation.

Organize **boat documents** (*see The Boat* - for boat registration and documentation details), **personal documents** (passports, visas, etc:) and **copies of crew lists**, at least four, with boat name, nationality, registration number, gross registered tonnage and crew names, nationality, date of birth, passport number, place and date of issue.

On page 198 is a typical crew list. It is customary to have categories for crew and passengers, although you list your guests as crew, otherwise they may be considered charter guests.

A ship's stamp makes these look far more official, and is often demanded. Most stamps have some representation of the boat, or something nautical, the vessel's name, number and home port (they are also fun for visitors' books!).

YACHT _____

NATIONALITY _____ PORT OF REGISTRY _____

OFFICIAL NUMBER_____ G.R.T._____
(registration or documented)   (Gross registered tonnage)

CREW LIST

NAME	NATIONALITY	DATE AND PLACE OF BIRTH	PASSPORT #	DATE AND PLACE OF ISSUE
Captain				
Crew				
Crew				
Crew				
(include friends on board)				
Passengers *none*				

NUMBER OF CREW _____ SIGNED _____ (Captain)

NUMBER OF PASSENGERS___*none*_____ DATE _____

Most countries require a **clearance document** from the last place visited before they will process your arrival. Keep this with your ship's papers. For example, we knew a couple who left the harbour in Raratonga (Cook Islands) when the wind made the harbour untenable. Once at sea they decided to head west then found they weren't able to clear into Tonga or Fiji.

Some countries will issue you a cruising permit; this might be open or restricted. If restricted, and you have a choice of cruising areas, make sure you list absolutely everywhere you might want to go. Sometimes there is a **cruising fee**. Usually this is only a few dollars, although the steepest we paid was $200 for Indonesia (down from a previous $500!). Be warned that in several countries you have to check with officials at every stop, and they love paperwork world-over. After our two week visit to Fiji, for example, they had 32 pieces of paper on us!

One of our memorable experiences was the initial clearance in Fiji's capital, Suva, that had taken more than one and a half days with security at a maximum after a military coup. Every possible government agency came on board, including the army in full battle regalia. They were very stern as they asked us if we had any guns on board. "Absolutely not," replied Andy, but Jamie, aged four, contradicted him. "Oh, yes we have." The officials leapt to attention, their guns ready. Two seconds later Jamie rushed from his cabin and triumphantly held up his water pistol for their inspection! There was a look of disbelief, then a big smile and soon tears of laughter were rolling down the soldiers' faces. All further questions were dispensed with.

Having children on board was a real asset; it was a rare bureaucrat that didn't have a smile for them and Andy took full advantage of it! We, like most cruisers, never had problems with officialdom. Interestingly it was always the same people who did. Again like most other cruisers we never bribe..

Tea or coffee is offered when officials arrive; they are curious and always like to sit below. After the basic information is collected questions related to drugs and alcohol are frequently asked, although in Cuba they wanted to look at our photo albums. We have a substantial supply of medications on board, including morphine. There was never a problem but we always made sure they were officially labelled with prescriptions. When asked about alcohol we tell them that there is beer in the fridge and offer it around. Usually it is rejected, but when the paperwork is over many officials will happily imbibe. Most enjoy talking about their countries and we find them extremely informative both with practical and sightseeing suggestions, as well as giving insight into the local political, cultural and economic situation.

A few countries will hold your passports for a day or two, others until you leave. This can be a nuisance if you have to collect them to change money or pick up a parcel, so it is best to arrange to do everything at once.

Note: It is a good idea to have copies of all documents. Keep one set of copies on the boat, one back home.

VISAS

Visa requirements are the same whether arriving by plane or by boat; a poor reception will be given by the officials if you do not have them. Usually countries demand these be acquired in advance, a few allow them to be purchased on arrival, but they are generally more expensive that way. Yachts who try to circumvent visa requirements make it difficult for others by hardening the attitude of the authorities.

Jimmy Cornell's book and other travel books give details of the requirements; however, be aware that regulations are constantly changing. They vary widely for different nationalities, so find out from an informed source. They also can differ greatly in price, as we found out when using a mix of both British and Canadian passports. A European Community passport allows easy access to all the French and British overseas departments and colonies.

Most visas are limited in time which can be an operational problem when crossing an ocean. For example, I obtained Jamie's Brazilian visa in South Africa but we were delayed in Cape Town waiting for autopilot spares; then the winds were light in the South Atlantic so the trip was slow. The officials were not impressed that when we arrived in Fortaleza the visa had expired by two days - we had been quite oblivious of the fact!

COURTESY FLAGS

It is traditional and good manners when you enter to fly the flag of the country you are visiting from the starboard spreader. It is technically correct to carry your yellow Q (quarantine) flag from your port spreader, as you should not fly a courtesy flag and signal flag together. Many, however, fly both on the starboard side. Unfortunately buying a flag in advance is often considerably more expensive than purchasing it in the country itself. Although it may offend, it is rare that officials take action. In Turkey, however, they did make yachts that were flying a frayed or faded flag put up a new one that day. In Indonesia it was obligatory to fly a courtesy flag at least as large as the ensign (there were a lot of very large courtesy flags and some very small ensigns) and in the Dominican Republic, officials tried to insist that new arrivals buy a flag from them at an exorbitant price.

Many cruisers make their own flags and they have a supply of colour-fast fabric, particularly red, white and blue, on board. Self-adhesive spinnaker and sail repair material can come in handy for stars etc., as can permanent markers, but accurate reproduction is necessary to avoid offence. If staying a long period in a country, flags need to be sturdily made, preferably with a sewing machine, or they will fray quickly, particularly in the tradewinds.

CREW

The owners of a vessel are responsible for any crew that is taken on board. Either a return ticket to their country of origin or cash in lieu of the ticket and their passports should be held by the skipper from the onset of the voyage. Although you might feel awkward about demanding this, you must insist. We have seen many distraught owners having to pay for airfares of pick-up crew on their arrival in a new country .

PETS

A *ship's cat fits the cruising dream, a dog provides good security, but the reality is not so easy. Those who want to sail with a cat or dog need to plan their route to avoid countries where the authorities impose a quarantine period of several months (because rabies has been eliminated) before the pet can go ashore. This includes much of the former British Empire.*

Penalties for infractions can involve the pet being destroyed and huge fines for the owners. Rabies shots are not acceptable as the animal can still be a carrier.

In many places you may not even lock the pet below and take your boat to a marina or fuel dock but must carry everything out in your dinghy. Some countries like New Zealand have quarantine officials who make regular unscheduled visits to the yacht to check on the pet and the boat is charged a hefty service fee each time.

Our boys all wanted pets. After suggestions such as a large terrapin and a piranha we settled on a budgerigar, a tiny and very endearing parakeet. This did not worry most officials, although it was sealed in its cage in Australia to ensure that it could not fly off to join its wild cousins.

We have many a fond memory of our budgies and a few traumatic ones. The birds were a great source of company and amusement for the boys. They would sit on their shoulders while they did schoolwork and chew on their books in sympathy. We always let them fly around the cabin although their cage was obviously home. This was a round filigree metal and olive wood decorative affair that hung on the teak arch between the galley and the main cabin. It was fastened with shock cord when underway, and the birds never seemed to suffer from seasickness. We bought the cage in the Souk in Tunis and, as our first bird came from Sidi Bou Said, it was named Sidi Bou.

We had a few antics with Sidi Bou mainly because we forget to trim his wings. When clipped, although he could fly around the cabin, he couldn't fly up and out. Just a few extra millimetres of growth on those feathers, however, and in a flash Sidi Bou could be out of the companionway. This is what happened just as we were about to leave Gibraltar! Resting only momentarily on *Bagheera*, Sidi Bou took off from boom to boom in the crowded marina with Andy following in hot pursuit. As boats are locked up and left in Gibraltar, many of the decks were cluttered with dinghies and jerry cans; to the boys' distress Sidi Bou definitely had the advantage. Raised by our cries, other crews came running to the dock. "Come on Andy," they urged, "faster, faster! Oh! you were so close!" Finally Sidi Bou came to the end of the row and ahead was a large expanse of water. Whether realizing the problem or just plain exhausted, at this point, Sidi Bou graciously condescended to hop into his cage. What a relief; we could now leave for Madeira. It hadn't been much of a delay. Friends of ours held up the entire Panama Canal when their bird chose that moment to go for a swim!

Now that we are living ashore we are back to cats, turtles and fish galore! In fact, Jamie's black cat Frisket (she's a perfect miniature Bagheera) has just had four kittens. She waited until the Easter weekend when we were cruising to have them and happily gave birth above the hanging locker in our forward cabin!

PESTS ON BOARD

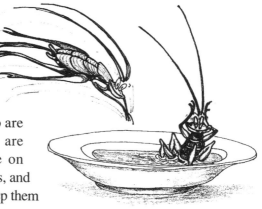

COCKROACHES

I hate to tell those of you who are squeamish, but cockroaches are a fact of life when you live on board, particularly in the tropics, and a constant battle is waged to keep them off the boat.

Cockroaches come in a variety of sizes. Some large tropical species fly on board but are usually easy to find because of their size. The real pests are the small cockroaches found throughout temperate and tropical climes. These get aboard along warps and gangplanks, in containers and on produce. Common practice is to discard all boxes and packaging ashore, then to inspect all containers that have to come aboard, particularly in the folded ends of cartons, for eggs or young 'crawlers'. All produce should be cleaned immediately, especially stalks of bananas which can house an entire colony. You can be assured that this colony will become a nation state in a few days. Leaving the banana stalk in salt water for a short period works well for also getting rid of the spiders and centipedes! Where you use a plank to get ashore, as is common in the Mediterranean, it is wise to suspend it a few inches above the ground to foil would-be insect boarding parties.

When you find a cockroach on board assume that there are more. There are many different commercial baits. Roach hotels that contain the poison in sealed units are popular, particularly when there are pets and children on board; 'pellets' of boric acid mixed with icing sugar is a good home remedy.

WEEVILS AND FLOUR MOTHS

These pests lay eggs in anything that is made of grains, seeds or nuts. They can penetrate plastic bags and cardboard packs so all cookies, rice, cereals, pasta etc. have to be in robust sealed containers. Bay leaves seem to discourage them. The traditional sailor may prefer to ignore them since the Royal Navy of Nelson's day appears to have flourished on the extra protein in the weevily ship's biscuits!

RATS

Only a rat you are trying to catch will show you how many inaccessible nooks and crannies you have on your boat. Catch it you must, however.

A dead rat festering on board is not only an unpleasant experience, it is a health hazard. Alive, rats are extremely destructive and can eat through wiring, strong plastic containers, even lead. They are uncommonly dextrous and can traverse along long mooring lines. We had one such visitor in Turkey. It gave me quite a start when I opened a cockpit locker in a remote anchorage to find two beady eyes staring up at me quite unabashed. Slamming the locker shut, I rushed below for a tennis racket, closed all the ports and the companionway, and gingerly opened up the locker again. Quickly scooping the little animal up I batted it overboard, feeling, I must admit, a little guilty - until I found out it could swim!

Rats will try to scramble aboard if they can from the dock or wharf. Raising boarding ladders and putting large funnels on the mooring lines facing shoreward will help deter them. Be particularly diligent in rat-infested areas such as commercial harbours.

Use baited rat traps but if they don't work hunt the beast down and stun or kill it when it appears - it will, eventually!

MICE

Mice are almost as destructive as rats but fortunately they have smaller teeth. Set mouse traps to eliminate mice before they have time to multiply.

TERMITES

If allowed to get established on board, termites might weaken bulkheads etc. Professional fumigation seems to be the best method to get rid of them. It is preferable to use a gas which disperses rather than one of the highly toxic chemical sprays which can linger and affect health.

MOSQUITOES

If mosquitoes like you, be prepared. Duncan, Colin and Jamie and I never have to worry if Andy is around. Mosquitoes love him and he has many a scar from ulcerated mosquito bites received during his early days in the Caribbean.

As several tropical diseases can be carried by mosquitoes, they must be kept out of the boat. Cruisers that have been out for a while have mesh screens. These have different modes of attachment; we use Velcro for all ports and hatches, including the companionway.

An awareness of malaria, dengue and yellow fever danger areas is important. Contact your local health department or look in travel books. Appropriate medications and immunizations must be arranged ahead of time *(see Medical Issues)*.

Wear long pants and long shirts, particularly at dusk, and use a mosquito repellent. I prefer creams as aerosol sprays are unpleasant to breathe, the metal canisters can rust on the boat and they don't fit easily into a pocket. Many brands are on the market; often the local ones are the most effective. If you find one that works for you buy it in bulk. Repellents that contain 20% DEET (N,N-diethylm-toluamide) are widely recommended for most bugs, particularly mosquitoes. Many people burn the green pyrethrum coils but we became allergic to the smell which pervaded the upholstery. Then we found a 12-volt unit in Australia that uses pyrethrum tablets and works effectively with no odour. Avon's Skin-so-soft bath oil works well for repelling both mosquitoes and no-see-ums (now Off-Skintastic). If cruising in the Mediterranean look for the restaurants that are surrounded by Citrosa plants; they kept even Andy protected from mosquitoes.

BIRDS

Frigate birds and boobies at sea, as well as gulls, crows and a variety of other species in harbour, will persist in trying to use the masthead as a perch. We have even seen pelicans do it. The 'visiting cards' which splatter over the sails and deck are minor irritants compared with the cost of replacing wind speed transducers, windexes etc. Vertical obstructions such as VHF antennae and lightning rods help deter them, as does a burgee flying from the masthead.

PROVISIONING

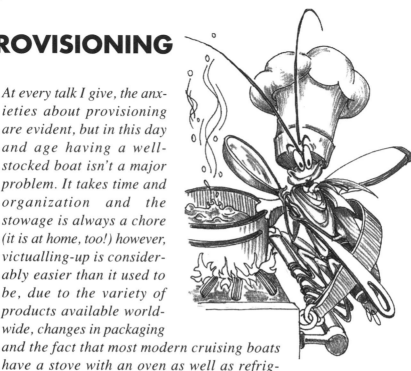

At every talk I give, the anxieties about provisioning are evident, but in this day and age having a well-stocked boat isn't a major problem. It takes time and organization and the stowage is always a chore (it is at home, too!) however, victualling-up is considerably easier than it used to be, due to the variety of products available worldwide, changes in packaging and the fact that most modern cruising boats have a stove with an oven as well as refrigeration. Also, as bulk buying has become common in regular life, filling several carts at one time is no longer so overwhelming.

Cruisers are commonly advised to make recipe lists with corresponding shopping lists and to keep inventories of goods on board. In reality, very few cruisers do this long term. A list for a first long passage is beneficial both practically for purchasing supplies and for one's peace of mind (especially if you are a 'list' person), but for subsequent trips most cruisers just check through the lockers and make a note t of the items required. Again, just like at home, there are staples that they automatically include in every shopping. In fact, most cruisers find that making a comprehensive list is far more frustrating than overlooking the odd item. (Just don't forget the toilet paper!)

Although in the past, famous sailors have written about their incredibly long voyages at sea (I seem to remember that the Smeetons took 70 days from Panama to the Gulf Islands in the Pacific Northwest), your long trips will be a fraction of this time and you won't be making that many. Not only are most modern boats considerably faster than they used to be, modern cruisers also power through the doldrums, and with countries, such as

Indonesia, facilitating easier entry for yachts, island hopping is becoming the norm. We had only four long passages during our circumnavigation. The first was a 17-day crossing of the Atlantic (2700nm); the second, from Galapagos to the Marquesas in French Polynesia, took 19 days (3000nm). There were two passages of 12 days in the South Atlantic; other trips were seldom more than a week. It was rare for *Bagheera* to average less than 150nm a day, whereas 100nm a day used to be considered exceptional.

To last us from Panama to Tahiti, I stocked up for four months. This was the longest period I catered for and, in fact, I found you could buy most items in the Galapagos Islands and everything in French Polynesia, but it was very expensive. Also because of the risk of ciguatera *(see Fishing)* I had known that we couldn't supplement our diet with reef fish. We eat very well on trips; the constant fresh air stimulates appetites and there is all the time in the world to be creative with menus. Conversely if it is rough and uncomfortable to cook, you won't want to eat much either.

It isn't necessary to load the boat down to the gunwhales. After all, there is only so much you can eat, and it will probably be the same as your normal diet. I well remember the owners of a 30' boat who took part in the Atlantic Rally for Cruisers; they had ten crates of fruit piled high on the coach roof, only part of the array of food that entirely covered their decks plus the dock beside them. This was their fourth day of shopping and stowing, and there was just one couple on board.

Although there must be enough food on board to allow for an emergency situation, the weight of overstocking stresses the vessel and slows your sailing performance - safety considerations in themselves. Also, certain countries have food restrictions, such as taking meat, fruit and vegetables into Australia and New Zealand (even Australian canned meat bought in Fiji wasn't acceptable). We benefitted from many a leg of lamb and pork in Tonga and Fiji given to us by cruisers who still had freezers half filled from the United States and Canada. Even if they had eaten frozen food morning, noon and night they would still have arrived with food that would have been confiscated.

AVAILABILITY OF SUPPLIES

People the world over eat! As most of your cruising will be coastal or island hopping, supplies will always be readily available. We found we could get virtually all staples in every major centre around the world (and most minor ones) even down to maple syrup and peanut butter for the boys. However, brand names vary and it is sometimes necessary to search through several stores.

Rather than availability, adaptability is the key to successful provisioning. If you can't find an ingredient for a particular recipe then substitute; the new dish might be better than the original! Accepting that products are going to be different from home is important, to avoid frustration when shopping. Trying the local fare is a significant and enjoyable part of visiting a country and getting to know the culture. Wandering through the colourful local markets, being enticed by lively market ladies to taste an unknown fruit, and trying dishes in restaurants that had been ordered by local people were highlights in our travels.

STOCKING-UP

I mentally divide stocking-up into three types - **general, emergency** and **luxury**.

General. We found supermarkets in every port around the world. Shopping for a passage is like any regular visit to the grocery store, only you will fill several carts instead of one, and buy more canned and packaged goods. I shop, when possible, at least two days before we leave. This allows time to stow and to purchase any goods that have been forgotten or unavailable in the main shop. We always eat out on the evening of a large provisioning expedition - I've earned it! Along the way as we coastal cruise I top up with products when I see them, especially when they are reasonably priced and we have heard prices are higher 'down the line'.

When completing a major shopping it is prudent to try new brand names in advance to see if they are approved by the crew. As storage is limited, you don't want to buy an item in bulk that no one likes, besides it being uneconomical. For example, on our boat, only Heinz baked beans are acceptable. Even pasta and rice vary in quality; some are very glutinous and require extra water.

Make sure cans are neither dented, nor bulging at the ends. The contents of those bulging are probably 'off', in particular they might have botulism which can be fatal. We saw a boat that had been towed half the way across the Indian Ocean as the crew had died from eating a can of botulism-infected mushrooms. Write the date and contents on the can in permanent marker. Although modern boats tend to have shallow bilges and are not so commonly used for storage, goods in lockers may also get wet with labels subsequently coming off. The date is important to make sure cans are rotated.

The proportion of canned goods will depend on your refrigeration. Until Australia we only had a 12-volt fridge and however creative the cooking, all food in the end was mushy. In Australia we installed a holding plate freezer system and it made a great difference to the menu on board. Even though we only had room to make the back part of our refrigerator into a freezer, it carried at least a month's worth of meals. Where possible, get the butcher to freeze meat to a very low temperature before bringing it on board and have them package it in meal-sized portions. Vacuum-packed meat, which only needs refrigeration also boosted our supplies.

Besides cans, freeze-dried goods are readily available; on board *Bagheera* we particularly enjoy 'Surprise' peas.

Put dry goods in airtight plastic containers to keep them fresh and weevil free. It also gets rid of excess garbage *(see Garbage)*. Bay leaves in flour help keep out the weevils. In many places, special bread flour, called strong flour, is sold (check the date on the package as it has a shelf life); with instant yeast it makes excellent bread. In other places we bought bread flour from bakeries. I always made three loaves at a time, although I was lucky if they lasted two days! If you have

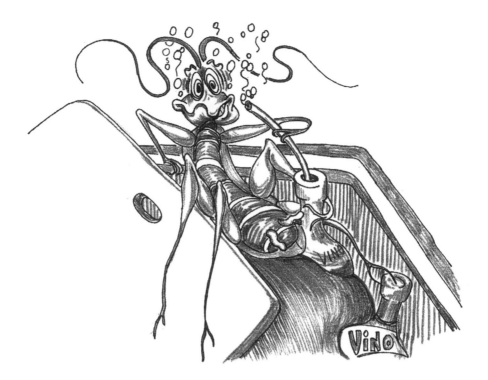

a second shelf in your oven (many only come with one) cook a pie or cookies at the same time.

Everyone needs fluids in the tropics. We all had one special drink a day on a trip, with water the rest of the time to quench our thirst; if space permits have a bottle in the fridge. Because filtered water tastes flat, crystals, concentrate and iced tea are popular. *(See Medical - dehydration and Water-purification).*

As with all goods, we stock up on beer, wine and the odd bottle of gin where inexpensive. Those of you who have read *Just Cruising* may remember Andy's purchase of 83 bottles of wine in Portugal that he stowed around the inflatable water tanks. When we could hear the bottles clinking we knew we were getting low on water! Both bottles and aluminum cans have to be stored carefully. Consumption depends on our social life and refrigeration. We were amazed how much South African white wine we still had left when we reached the Caribbean, after our refrigeration had broken down just after leaving Cape Town. Incidentally, don't forget a supply of alcohol for fish *(see Fishing).*

Ideally, produce should be purchased the day of departure. Produce should not only be as fresh as possible, it should not be washed;

machine scrubbed supermarket vegetables rot quickly. Dry vegetables in the sun before storing. Some items such as potatoes (not new), cabbage, onions, yams and squash last a long time (a squash received in South Africa was still good to eat in the Bahamas 5 months later). We never finished a trip without having produce left over. Baskets and nets work well for storage, as produce needs to be exposed to circulating air (never keep produce in plastic bags). We keep ours in cockpit lockers which are frequently opened up. Check items daily; if one item goes mouldy it will spread quickly through the rest. Apples (particularly Granny Smith) and citrus wrapped in sheets of paper towel, placed where they can't bruise, keep well. Unwashed lettuce in newspaper, sealed in a plastic bag in the fridge, keeps for weeks, particularly iceberg. Change the newspaper and wilted outer leaves regularly. The Evert Fresh plastic bags are very useful to have on board if you can find them; they are also reusable. By absorbing the ethylene gas they extend the life of produce from 50-100%, or use regular Ziplock bags.

A stalk of bananas is great for keeping hunger at bay, particularly with children on board, but don't get one too large as bananas all tend to ripen at once (we tried many different ways of storing them). Remember to give the stalk a quick dip in the ocean to get rid of cockroaches and spiders.

*To be safe destroy bacteria by washing all salads and fruit in either potassium permanganate, which doesn't taste but can dye your hands, or add drops of chlorine or iodine (**see Medical**).*

Many long distance cruisers sprout beans; these were used by Captain Cook and are highly nutritious. We liked the Chinese mung beans best; they can be eaten raw in a salad or cooked in stir fries, casseroles etc. Soak the beans in salt water before using, throw out any that float along with pieces of twig, also look for stones, then rinse and put in a glass jar and cover with fresh water. It takes about a day for the beans to sprout depending on the climate, then strain and rinse every day until ready. At this stage there should be no liquid in the jar. Placing the beans in the light will increase their vitamin C content, while the dark increases vitamin B. It will take 3-5 days before they are ready for harvesting, depending on the temperature. Many cruisers also make yoghurt on board. Whether used on cereals, in sauces or dips or as a snack it makes a delicious and nutritious addition to your diet on a passage. Having said that, you ideally need a calm anchorage and steady temperature of 105-115°F. for it to set. Powdered milk works well for yoghurt. Bring the water to a temperature of at least 105°F. to activate the culture, but not too hot or it will kill it. Some make yoghurt in a thermos to maintain the temperature, others use the engine compartment or put it in the sun. Cultures can be obtained either from a spoonful of the last batch or dried supplies can be bought at home from a health food store. I recommend buying dried culture; we found yoghurt became sour after a few repeat batches. It also allows you to have a break in production. Dried yoghurt also now comes in foil packages to which you only have to add water. I gather it is delicious.

Fresh eggs (that have never been refrigerated) can be kept for several weeks by sealing with a thin layer of Vaseline, or dipped in boiled water for 5 seconds or being turned every day to keep the yolks suspended. However, always crack them separately, the smell will leave no doubt as to whether they are off! Having your own plastic egg cartons can be useful when purchasing eggs. Margarine in the plastic tubs stores well if kept cool and in most countries canned butter is available; for long term storage cheese can be vacuum packed or immersed in salad oil in a jar. Home vacuum packers are inexpensive and can be used on a regular basis to keep food fresh.

Many of the items that we commonly refrigerate, such as mustards, sauces, jams etc. usually don't need cooling. If you are keen on fishing, stock up on ingredients for marinades, such as Worcestershire sauce, certain vinegars, dill, Tabasco, Japanese Soya Sauce, Wasabi mustard, etc.

Also get plenty of nibbles for sundowner sessions, kids and night-watches.

The **emergency** shop is purchased simultaneously but includes a variety of provisions that are kept separate in case a situation arises that causes the boat to be much longer at sea than planned. These supplies are continuously rotated so they do not get stale or out of date. I like to have at least one month's extra provisions, and generally have considerably more, beyond our estimated day of arrival at known shopping facilities. We also have a container full of items for the liferaft such as dried fruit and nuts, granola bars, chocolate and condensed milk.

'**Luxury**' items are personal favourites, such as particular brand name products, goods that are easy to prepare like muffin mix and items you can't live without, such as peanut butter for North Americans and Vegemite for Australians. Not liking powdered milk, we stocked up heavily with cartons of UHT (Longlife) milk, also on Hellman's mayonnaise. Special shampoos and sunblock were also items I would buy in bulk. When we find a favourite product that we've not had for a while, it's a cause for a celebration!

EQUIPMENT

Most cruising boats have a two- or three-burner stove with an oven and cruisers usually cook and eat as they do at home. Stackable stainless steel pans work well; also a non-stick frying pan. Our oven takes three bread pans across but as pans vary in size it is worth measuring the oven so you can fit in the maximum, likewise for roasting and muffin pans. Few cruisers use pressure cookers much these days, particularly because of sophisticated stoves and the trend towards lightly

215

cooked food, although for those who like dried beans and legumes or stews, they do save gas. They are also good for conch and octopus; we either beat these to tenderize them (a hundred throws on a rock by Duncan and an octopus was tenderized to perfection!) or cut them up finely. A pressure cooker is needed if you plan to do canning/bottling (the water bath method generally not being safe on a boat). When buying a pressure cooker, ensure it is big enough to take preserving jars and that there is a reliable control to maintain a steady 10-lb. pressure. Special canning cookers are also popular. If using the pressure cooker for food, most favour stainless steel not aluminum. For us, a large pan to cook crab and lobster was indispensable; incidentally, always cook these in salt water.

Have tables for recipe conversions, measuring cups, etc. A general purpose cookery book is always useful. Local cookery books can help with cooking and for identifying produce in the markets; even meat cuts are different, for example between North America and Europe.

PRE-COOKED MEALS

It is a good idea to pre-cook some meals for the beginning of the trip as you might not yet have your sea legs, or be busy navigating. It has become popular to can food either as a pre-prepared meal, such as a pasta sauce, or to preserve raw products. Cruisers like canning meat as they can take advantage of favourable prices. We well remember the beef filets in both Fiji and Kenya, if I had been a canner I would have filled the boat with it!

STORAGE

Storage is the key to an efficiently run boat, in particular a well-run galley. Frequently used items such as coffee, tea, sugar, jams, ketchup, mustards, condiments, etc. need to be ready at hand, in lockers that are easy to use whatever the heel. Shockcord across the front works well. Spice racks are useful as the typical small jars easily topple and roll around.

Assess a boat carefully for its accessible storage before buying. How much there is will greatly influence your enjoyment of living on board. Rather than lists, my way of keeping inventory control is by glancing in the locker. If it is getting low, I had better get shopping! In reality this is an ongoing mental process. To be able to do this I have a definite place for every type of item - although admittedly new products catch my eye that don't seem to 'belong' anywhere!

Often the largest storage areas on a boat are the least accessible, such as under the berths. Try to divide these up so that you don't have to dismantle the entire bed. For example, we have a deep bin at the aft end of the v-berth. As it has a separate wooden cover I only have to move the pillows to access it. These less accessible areas become my larders. I visit them about once a week to replenish the lockers that are readily accessible.

When provisioning for a long period of time, such as my stock to last the four months between Panama and Tahiti, you may have to become creative with stowage. Knowing that we had a crowd on board and that children's appetites are always increasing, we had the mattress in the port aft cabin divided in half longitudinally, and Andy installed a removable wooden lee-cloth down the centre of the berth. On the two long trips I doubled up the two mattress sections and had the outer half of the berth free for storage bins. I used cardboard boxes, inspected carefully for cockroaches. Each box was allocated for certain types of cans and dried goods, and the bulky cereals, paper towels, etc. tucked behind. With a few colourful cushions as a disguise no one was any the wiser, although I did have to anticipate little fingers stretching across to the granola bars in the night, as this was in Duncan's and Colin's cabin!

We also decided to allocate our second, small, aft head for storage. This became the place for the long-life milk, often several crates of it. In the Canary Islands we bought wine in similar one-litre cartons. Somehow they had ended up under the milk and the weight was too great. Half way across the Atlantic our French chef crew informed us there was a red liquid on his cabin sole and it tasted like wine. All was not lost, fortunately, as only a few cartons were crushed, but several were 'bruised' and obviously had to be drunk! Our house wine, popularly known as 'Chateau Cardboard' became 'Chateau Cardboard Pressé'!

REFRIGERATION

Engine-driven compressor units
with a holding plate are the
most popular refrigeration
systems with cruisers because
of their reliability, although
they are expensive. Since
the advent of solar panels
and good wind generators
12-volt compressor refrigeration is gaining in popularity. It is particularly convenient when plugged in at the dock or
when leaving the boat for a few days to
go travelling. The best arrangement is an engine-dri-
ven holding plate system with a 12-volt independent system in addition.
Both systems must be water cooled for the best efficiency. Coolers can
be divided, with the coldest area reserved for frozen foods and the rest
for refrigeration.

A holding plate acts like a storage container for 'coldness'. It is a sealed
tank containing a solution called eutectic fluid, usually a glycol/water
mix, which freezes at a temperature much lower than water. Running
the compressor freezes the fluid, then the compressor shuts down.
Thereafter, the fluid gradually thaws, absorbing heat from the cooler;
in a good system the compressor may not have to run for more than
an hour a day.

Systems without holding plates use evaporator plates like those
in your home 'fridge. As they are thermostatically controlled and run
intermittently, they require the battery charge to be monitored regularly.

The insulation of the cooler is paramount and production boats
are frequently deficient in this respect. Even if the capacity inside has
to be reduced make sure that you have at least 10 cm of insulation on
the sides and bottom and at least 8 cm on the top, including the lid.

Freon 12 used to be the common refrigerant used in marine units
but it has now been found to contribute to the depletion of the ozone

layer. It is still possible to get these units recharged, but as many western countries have strict laws banning the carriage of Freon in containers, it is becoming increasingly difficult to find. New units operate with more environmentally friendly gases, the most common in North America at present being HFC 134a. It would be prudent to carry recharge containers of this on long cruises, and to know how to use them.

Engine-driven compressors and some electric units use a sea water cupro-nickel heat-exchanger for cooling the compressed refrigerant. The heat exchanger may have a zinc sacrificial anode which needs regular replacement. The high power loads demand good quality. V-belts and spares should be carried. From time to time the filter/dryer cartridge will need to be replaced (an over-sized one is a good idea); a good marine system has valves either side of the filter so that this can be done with little loss of gas. Many cruisers include this job in their yearly routine maintenance.

For those who only have a refrigerator, vacuum packing is popular, prolonging the time you can keep meats. Dry ice can also help keep food cold for a long time; it is often available, even in third world cities. Frozen meats, etc. well wrapped in newspaper can be kept for many days in a solid state. As dry ice is frozen carbon dioxide, good ventilation is required. Although there is no odour and while carbon dioxide is not poisonous, it is heavier than air which it will displace in an enclosed space, reducing available oxygen. If all else fails, you can get regular ice everywhere but make sure it is frozen in the centre!

Lids on boat refrigerators have to be heavy because of the insulation necessary. Many manufacturers have a spring system to hold them up. These work well in calm waters but can collapse in a rough sea. Make sure a bolt or other securing system is fitted. Also, as boat fridges can be cavernous without a system of organisation it is easy to lose items. Plastic storage bins are used by several manufacturers to divide the fridge into sections and these work well.

As with your household freezer, clearly mark packages with the contents and the date. As the food in a boat freezer can be changing temperature by warming and then being cooled, a strict rotation of items should be observed.

ROUTE PLANNING and WEATHER

ROUTE PLANNING

The initial route you choose can contribute hugely to the success or failure of your trip. It is important to consider the experience and expectations of everyone concerned. Nothing turns people off boating more quickly than being cold and frightened, feeling totally inadequate and being yelled at by their easy-going partner who has suddenly become 'Captain Bligh'.

For a compatible life afloat it is preferable to ease into the cruising mode gradually, particularly for those who have less experience or who have young children on board. Stopping every night in a calm anchorage where goods and services are available and where there are interesting places to visit will greatly help in adjusting to life on board. Even after three years of cruising, having lived in one spot for a year leading regular lives, it took time to adjust again to life afloat as we headed up the Australian east coast from Sydney to Darwin. How much the children had grown was a particular shock and the corresponding reduction in space on the boat was remarkable!

Of the areas we have sailed, the Caribbean (including Central and South America) and the Mediterranean are ideal for cruising, as distances are short and navigation is generally not complicated. The Caribbean provides year-round tropical bliss, although one does have to be in certain areas or monitor the weather carefully during the hurricane season. The tragedies of the hurricanes in 1995 were a vivid reminder that you can never be complacent. The Mediterranean has a variety of seasons, and wonderful ancient cultures. Although very different, both provide many varied experiences and excellent cuisines.

Of course the route that is chosen is often dictated by the location of the boat. If the boat is in British Columbia, for example, complications set in right away. Whether you head down the coast to San Francisco or across to Hawaii this first passage route can be cold, rough, long, and by no means ideal for anyone who is uncertain about cruising in the first place. If your plan is to visit the South Pacific then an option for reticent crew member of flying to Tahiti should be considered. If you need replacement crew there never seems to be a shortage of people keen to have the experience of an offshore passage, as can be seen from the lists in the magazines of the offshore associations.

An alternative is to consider buying a boat in the area you wish to cruise. As our family was young, we decided to start our trip in Europe and spend a year mostly day sailing around the Mediterranean, so we sold our Beneteau in Vancouver and picked up a new boat from the factory in France. For Caribbean cruising there are often bargains to be had in Ft. Lauderdale, Florida, St. Martin and Antigua. Although the disadvantage is that you don't have time to work on your boat at home, many of these yachts have done previous long trips and are loaded with gear. The time you would have spent in transit from your home can be spent orienting yourself to the new boat on location and you have the added bonus of already being in the sun.

WEATHER

Weather is one of the biggest factors in a cruiser's life, whether regarding planning the long-term route or day-to-day sails.

Several people have commented that as we were out for six years we must have had no deadlines, and could stay as long as we wanted wherever we wanted. In fact, this is far from the reality. When cruising offshore one is constantly co-ordinating one's route with the world's seasonal weather patterns. Experienced sailors are cautious; they do not put themselves at risk by being in an area during the stormy season. They are familiar with meteorological terminology, weather symbols and charts, sources of forecasts and warnings and frequently listen to weather forecasts on the radio several times a day as this is fundamental to comfortable, crisis-free sailing.

In temperate and Arctic climes the four seasons are distinguished by large temperature variations and changes in frontal activity. In the tropics there are generally only two seasons: wet and dry.

In some areas the wet season is also the time for hurricanes, cyclones or typhoons, all names for the high winds which develop out of tropical storms. In the Indian Ocean and South East Asian waters there is also a seasonal reversal in wind direction, the monsoons.

Sailors in high latitudes are concerned with gales, blizzards, black ice, fogs and icebergs. In the tropics there are line squalls, lightning and tropical storms. Most cruising is done therefore in the dry or warm seasons. A typical South Pacific crossing, for example, is completed between April and November, when yachts either head down to Australia or New Zealand or go north of the equator, to avoid the cyclone season. Caribbean cruising is best from December to June with the north coast of South America being a nearby place to go for the rest of the year, as it is out of the hurricane belt.

Most circumnavigators are constantly on the move, with some flexibility for weather, travel and social events, then they 'winter' or 'summer' (depending on the hemisphere) through the cold season, such as in the Mediterranean, or outside the hurricane/cyclone season, often in one location. This is the time when boat repairs are completed, seasonal work is possibly obtained, or trips are made back home, and when cruising children may attend local schools.

(*See Navigation* regarding Routing and Pilot Charts, also Weather Forecasting.)

SAFETY

Although the cruising life is for the most part comfortable and enjoyable, inevitably there will be some excitement. Many of the worst situations can be avoided by preparing the vessel and crew; also by careful planning of routes and timetables. Hurricanes, cyclones and typhoons are for the most part seasonal as is much of the extreme weather, such as the fogs and gales of the higher latitudes.

As discussed in **Route Planning** we, like most cruisers, plan our route a year or more in advance to be in the right place at the right time, in the tropics moving north and south of the equator with the change in the hurricane seasons and in colder areas holing up for the winter. On passage the weatherfax is used to monitor developments around us and Ham nets, high seas broadcasts and ships provide additional information. On board, the barometer readings and wind strengths are logged hourly.

Nevertheless, unpleasant or extreme conditions will sometimes have to be endured. Lack of wind can cause delay, weather patterns can change quickly and forecasts can be wrong. We were lucky when crossing from Chagos to the Seychelles in the Indian Ocean that we were able to pick up weatherfax maps from distant French Reunion and Australia, as well as from the nearby US base in Diego Garcia. The first two showed an out-of-season tropical storm developing, which had become a full cyclone, 3 days before the latter recorded it. We were able to calculate that we would be safely in port well before we were threatened, but friends en-route to Madagascar would have been right in its path, had we not warned them in time to divert north.

PREPARATION

The purchase and outfitting of a yacht, ongoing maintenance, preparations for a cruise and one's daily routine at sea should all be influenced by the possibility of having to weather storms, survive a knockdown or deal with some major emergency. Everyone on board must be familiar with heavy weather gear, all safety equipment and with emergency strategies. They need to be able to cope even in the case where the skipper is incapacitated.

Before going offshore much can be done to minimize the devastation which may result from severe conditions. Hopefully you, like most cruisers, will never experience a knockdown or worse but it is prudent to think out the consequences and prepare for this and other emergencies.

ON DECK

Check the security of all gear. Will the anchors stay in place if you are rolled? What about the dinghy, liferaft and the outboard motor? Are all lockers secure and sealed; strongpoints and jacklines installed for life-harness attachment; companionway boards secured; bilge pumps adequate? Are sea anchor or drogue, warps, chafe gear, collision mat, heavy weather sails, bolt cutters ready for use?

THE LIFERAFT

Nearly all cruisers venturing offshore carry a liferaft. Buy a larger liferaft than the minimum for the crew on board. If there are only two, get a four man unit; if there may be four, then get the six man one. These rafts are sized assuming a very short time will be spent in them but this cannot be guaranteed. With four people in a four place raft there is no room to move, let alone to lie down.

Prepare for having to abandon ship, although this should never be done except when the vessel is actually sinking. There have been several cases where although the crew took to the liferaft and were subsequently lost the yacht was found later still afloat.

The liferaft requires regular servicing and restocking with flares, water, rations. We also include a knife, a waterproof flashlight, space blankets, a solar still and heliograph, an EPIRB, fishing gear and a medical kit with seasickness pills, vitamins, sunblock, antiseptic creams, aspirin and any current medications.

Jerry cans of water, a waterproof container with food packed in zip-lock bags such as dried fruit and nuts, condensed milk, energy bars and chocolate, also a mug and cutting board are ready to carry with us into the liferaft. We would also grab the hand-held VHF radio, the second EPIRB, passports and money.

THE RIG

Bagheera was new when we started our circumnavigation, but one of the changes we made was to go up one size on all the standing rigging and turnbuckles. Running backstays, which can be stowed by the mast when not needed, were added to take the strain of an inner forestay which is rigged so that it could be moved forward to a padeye and tensioned ready for a storm jib.

If preparing to cruise in an older boat, don't take chances with the rigging. Stainless steel wire loses strength without any obvious signs so replace it; go up in size if possible, also upgrade the chainplates, turnbuckles, toggles and tangs. Ensure that rig loads are properly transferred to the hull; some manufacturers still install inadequate chainplates with the load taken by the decks or by poorly secured bulkheads.

Before every passage, inspect the rig for wear *(see Chafe)*. This includes mast and boom fittings, standing and running rigging, blocks and furling gear, and look over the sails. Repairs are far easier at anchor than at sea and any failure will occur in the worst conditions.

Carry a supply of the correct sizes of Norseman or Sta-lok terminals and a length of rigging wire at least long enough to make a new cap shroud, and have the know-how and tools to do it. Heavy duty clamps enable two wires to be joined for temporary rigging repairs. It may be necessary to go up the mast in rough conditions carrying tools, so a good bosun's chair and crew training is needed.

BELOW DECKS

Severe damage and injury can result from heavy equipment being thrown about in a knockdown or in violent seas. Batteries have to be bolted down, not simply held in place by straps, and the stove prevented from jumping out from its gimbals. Five hundred litres of water, about 120 US gallons, weighs close to half a ton; check the installation of water, fuel and holding tanks. A holding tank bouncing around in the main cabin can sure spoil your day.

Add secure catches to all drawers; the kind which simply drop into a slot when closed will definitely fly open in the rough stuff. Spring and friction latches on lockers are rarely adequate and turnbuttons or barrel bolts may be needed. Floorboards can be screwed or latched in place, as can seat and berth locker lids.

When stowing provisions and equipment prior to a passage, make sure bottles, cans, tools and other heavy items are secure. Nothing should be allowed in the bilge which could affect the bilge pumps, such as labels which can wash off cans.

Alarm systems are frequently added to give warning of trouble. They are inexpensive and easy to install. Aboard *Bagheera* we have alarms for bilge water, explosive gasses, smoke, depth, low batteries, plus engine alarms for low oil pressure, no charging and overheating.

EQUIPMENT

Depending on the size of the yacht, the type of cruising planned and the budget a variety of safety and repair equipment should be carried *(also see Sails, Anchors, Chafe, Safety, Lightning, Electronics-EPIRBS, Steering systems).*

FIRES

A fire on board must be extinguished without delay and cruisers usually carry more fire fighting equipment than the basic Coast Guard requirements.

Extinguishers of the correct categories to fight fuel and engine fires, electrical fires, galley and any fire which might occur in bedding or lockers should be mounted where they can be reached quickly, and be inspected and recharged regularly. We strongly recommend a fibreglass fire blanket be stowed near the galley. This is the most effective way to extinguish a stove fire. Have a smoke alarm and an automatic or remotely operated extinguisher in the engine compartment with a fuel cut-off control operated from the cockpit that will isolate the fuel tank from the engine area in the event of a fire.

FLARES

Rocket parachute flares are the most favoured as they are the only ones which are likely to be seen at any distance, the hand-held ones are ineffective except at close quarters. Red smoke generators are good for daylight use, particularly with aircraft. A flare gun or Very's pistol is effective at medium ranges and is carried by some yachts as an emergency weapon.

LIGHTS

One's best insurance against being run down is to be seen in good time. Other vessels interpret what you are and which way you are going at night by your lights. High intensity navigation lights correctly installed to show the sectors precisely and where they are not obscured by sails or equipment are important upgrades for many production yachts. Aboard *Bagheera* a masthead trilight used offshore is visible at 8 miles and is less easily obscured at close range under the bows of a freighter, but for inshore work regular bow and stern (also when motoring mast-mounted steaming) lights are used as it is easier for small vessels to judge the distance between us.

An all-round white anchor light is necessary; automatic lighting units are available for use when the boat is not manned.

A searchlight is indispensible for flashing at ships and picking out channel markers or unlit vessels when entering a new anchorage.

PERSONAL EQUIPMENT

Each crew member needs a lifejacket which fits and is comfortable. See both the West Marine and BOAT/U.S. catalogues for excellent descriptions of the different types of personal flotation devices. The easiest to wear are the inflatable ones but they must be well maintained. Lifejackets should have a whistle and at night a light or personal strobe.

Lifeharnesses should also be adjusted to fit and need two clip-on lines. *They should have a strap which passes between the legs*, as people have been lost when hanging from a harness without this. Combination lifejackets with harnesses are available. Wet weather gear, survival suits etc. to suit the climate may also be needed.

JACKLINES

These are run from bow to stern along each side deck so that a life harness may be clipped on for deck work at sea, and are found on all cruising yachts that venture away from sheltered waters. Polyester webbing is popular for these because it lies flat on the deck, whereas wire can roll underfoot and can also be noisy when it moves on the deck as the boat heels. However, it must be remembered that polyester is subject to weakening due to ultraviolet rays and a season in the tropics may render it unsafe.

MAN OVERBOARD EQUIPMENT

Everything possible must be done to prevent a man overboard situation such as securing stanchions and lifelines with netting, having good handrails and non-skid deck surface, using harnesses and having crew discipline. Our rules are that no one may leave the cockpit to go on deck unless clipped on, with someone else there to watch. Anyone on a night or rough weather watch should be secured in the cockpit by a life harness; even in flat calm conditions rogue waves can roll the boat over unexpectedly. This happened to us in the Tuomotus. One of the most common overboard situations occurs because a man decides to pee over the side; even in good weather a bucket is safer!

A person overboard in the ocean is out of sight within seconds due to the ever-present swells; it is critical that the yacht's drill be based on bringing the vessel to a stop immediately. The commonly taught method of sailing on for a timed interval, then coming back on a reciprocal course doesn't work except in the classroom. Liferings, cockpit cushions and other floating objects thrown overboard immediately will help to mark the position and will give support to the person in the water. All life jackets should carry a light.

The recovery of someone who is exhausted or unconscious is difficult, particularly with high freeboard. A stern with a reverse transom and a ladder or boarding platform as is found on many modern designs is invaluable at this time. Otherwise a halyard taken to a winch, a block and tackle system from the boom or from a radar or wind generator mast needs to be rigged to get a person back on board. More cruisers are now carrying a Lifesling which greatly simplifies getting a person alongside and also acts as a lifting yoke. Practise the procedure.

When there are only two crew and one goes over the side a particularly difficult situation has developed and it is extremely important that the recovery drill should be discussed and practised.

COLLISION MAT

The oceans are unfortunately littered with debris, most of it man-made. Containers found floating are rare, but have been known to sink a ship. Oil drums, crates, logs and other large objects can cause enough damage to hole a small vessel.

A collision mat put in place over a breach in the hull will usually stem the flooding sufficiently for the pumps to cope until emergency repairs can be made. Make up in advance a square of canvas sized about twice the height of the freeboard, with nylon lines attached to strong grommets at the corners. A small sail can also be used effectively. Once over the hole, water pressure will hold the fabric against it and reduce the flow. With wood and fibreglass hulls a patch can then be put on the inside; use canvas smeared with underwater hardening epoxy paste backed by foam from cushions, wedged in with plywood and then screwed into place. When conditions permit an outside patch of plywood and epoxy should also be applied.

Metal hulls are more resistant to holing but it can happen. The metal plating is usually badly distorted and must be hammered flat before a patch can be wedged in place. As soon as possible secure an outside patch through the breach to the inner one.

A collision mat is very effective in that it enables temporary repairs to be made. It is not reliable if attempts are made to sail to shelter as it will almost certainly not remain in place, even if lines are lashed over it and around the hull. Heaving-to or lying to a sea anchor until the patches are in place is the best option.

STORM EQUIPMENT

A crew must be able to rig storm sails *(see Sails)* quickly, with halyard and sheeting arrangements known to all on board. Loads on the rig during a full gale are unbelievably heavy and all lines and fittings need to be sized accordingly.

Heaving-to, while useful for stopping in moderate conditions, has lost favour with some as a storm strategy as has lying a-hull. Modern designs should not lie beam-on to the seas but should present either the bow or stern *(see The Boat - effects of Displacement and Beam)*.

229

When conditions worsen, to the extent that sail can no longer be carried comfortably and there is sufficient sea room to leeward, consideration should be given to running before the wind under bare poles. If control becomes difficult or speed excessive then warps or a drogue towed behind will make steering easier and lessen the chance of broaching. A kedge anchor with chain and at least 200 feet of nylon makes an effective drogue; one can also be made up with tires and chain. There are several models of parachute drogues offered for sale which are excellent and stow easily.

Sea anchors have many detractors. I believe this is because the gear used was inadequate. To be effective a parachute sea anchor must be large, very strong and deployed from the bow with a substantial and long nylon rode. Air drop parachutes are too weak and many parachute sea anchors offered commercially are poorly designed. A sea anchor, therefore, must be custom-sized and chosen carefully. The size depends on the type of anchor chosen, the size of the boat and the length of rode needed for the wave height.

Multihulls in particular should consider carrying an adequate sea anchor because of their inability to recover from a capsize.

Whether towing warps, a drogue or lying to a sea anchor, protection against chafe is necessary for the lines *(see Chafe)*.

PUMPS

It is said that the most effective pump in a boat is a frightened man with a bucket!

Big is best where pumps are concerned. A high quality manual diaphragm pump which can remove at least 25 gallons a minute combined with a dose of adrenalin will move enormous quantities of water. This pump should be mounted in the cockpit near the helm so that one person can cope, and high enough so that a normal person can operate it for long periods without contortions.

Electric bilge pumps are fine for minor leaks but may not be reliable for sustained use in an emergency. Large capacity pumps driven by the engine through a clutch are excellent as long as they don't clog and the engine keeps running. A portable, usually gasoline driven fire pump is very effective *(see Bilges and Bilge Pumps)*.

SAILS FOR CRUISING

The average cruiser's sail inventory is surprisingly small, usually consisting of one mainsail, two or three headsails, a storm jib and sometimes a storm trysail for heavy going and a cruising spinnaker for the light stuff.

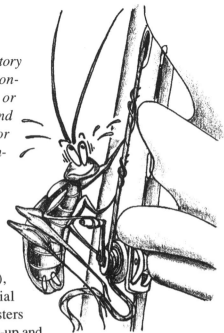

MATERIALS

Woven polyester, commonly known as Dacron (DuPont's trade name for this material), is still the most popular material with long-term cruisers. Polyesters themselves vary greatly in make-up and quality. For cruising sails, a cloth that has a tight weave, low resin content and is made by a reputable manufacturer will be a pleasure to handle and will last for many years.

The constant quest by racers for greater speed has led to the development of several new fabrics and films which, alone or laminated in combination, seek to minimise stretch and provide greater power for less weight aloft. Kevlar, Spectra, Mylar, carbon fibre are just some of these materials. These exotics should also offer benefits to cruisers, but the ability to retain their exact shape over a range of winds is of less importance to cruisers and many who have tried them offshore have reverted back to the proven, less expensive Dacron. New cruising laminates are appearing which are lighter in weight than polyester and which have excellent shape holding characteristics. They do, however, require more maintenance, are subject to mildew staining and are costly.

When ordering sails, remember that few sailmakers have extensive experience offshore and those that do have mainly been racing with a large crew and a determination to win. Their advice may be commercially motivated and not to your advantage. It is best to follow the experience of other cruisers and DuPont's own advertised information, where they advise the use of Kevlar for speed, but Dacron for the long haul.

Advantages of Dacron
1) Dacron is cheaper than even the most basic exotics and laminates.
2) It is more resistant to chafe and damage by flogging, shock loading, piercing and ultraviolet degradation.
3) It is comparatively soft and pliable and much easier to handle and fold for stowing than the shiny, slippery and stiff exotics.
4) Dacron can be repaired at sea by sewing, and patches are easy to apply.
5) Dacron has a very long working life, provided a good quality cruising cloth is used
Disadvantages are greater weight and gradual loss of shape with age.

HEADSAILS

Headsail furling gear is found on most cruising yachts, the problems associated with it in the '70s having long since been sorted out. Jamming is only likely if the sail is allowed to unfurl too quickly without the furling line being restrained, if the halyard does not lead to the top swivel correctly or if the gear itself is in bad condition. These problems are easily overcome by practice, preparation and maintenance.

Advantages of headsail furling gear
1) The sail is hoisted and ready for instant use; it rarely has to be dropped, folded and stowed below.
2) The sail may be used partially furled, and a smaller inventory of headsails is needed. This ability to easily reef a sail prolongs its life. Without furling gear, sail changes are often put off until long after they become necessary, particularly in tropical line squalls which are of short duration, when the temptation to allow some flogging is great.
3) Safety. The crew stay in the cockpit; the less it is necessary to go to the foredeck during a passage, especially in bad weather, the less the chance of an accident.
4) One person on watch can do everything, which is particularly important to the vast majority of cruising boats that just have a couple on board.

Because the sails are attached by a luff tape in a groove, the main **disadvantage of headsail furling gear** is that the sail is not restrained when lowered to the deck. This can be a problem if the sails are changed in a high wind.

Furling sails should be struck if storm force winds are forecast. If not possible use a spinnaker halyard to 'maypole' wrap the furled sail and lock the drum. All sails which are not full-hoist must have a strop between the head of the sail and the top swivel of the furling gear. This swivel should always be hoisted to full height to ensure the correct lead angle for the halyard. Failure to do this will inevitably cause the halyard to wrap and jam the gear.

Check that headsails, except storm jibs, have luff tapes that fit the foil. Many furling gears allow two sails to be hoisted together so that they can be winged out on each side. A foam insert at the luff is offered by many sailmakers and this helps the sail retain a reasonable shape when partially furled; sheet leads will move forward and car positions should be marked on deck.

In use, it is far better to change down to a smaller sail rather than partially furl, if it appears that the wind strength will remain high. This is not only because of increased efficiency, but also to prevent prolonged strain on the furling line. Before setting off, a method of locking the furling drum with a pin should be devised for those times when a sail change can't be made. Obviously, the furling line should be regularly checked as a failure could lead to a jammed system with too much sail unfurled for the wind strength.

All furling headsails should have their leeches protected from damage by the sun when the sail is furled. An acrylic sun strip will be long lasting but is thick and heavy and will distort the sail shape in light winds. Dacron covers which may need to be replaced about every two years are better for performance and appearance.

Storm jibs should not be used on the foil, but should have hanks to attach to an inner forestay which can be either removable or permanent.

Twin headstays are still popular; two hanked-on sails may be flown together downwind poled out on either side. One advantage of these hanked sails is that reef points can be sewn in to extend the wind range of the sail.

Yachts with a permanent inner forestay will find a self-tacking jib staysail useful to augment the headsail area in light winds and excellent when combined with a reefed mainsail in heavier weather.

Sailing wing-on-wing is stable and easy, and the common way to make fast passages in modern, moderately beamy and easily steered boats. Older, narrower designs tend to roll excessively and will be more comfortable, but slower, using twin headsails. A heavy-duty pole with one end permanently attached to a car on a mast track is used both for spinnakers and for sailing with the genoa poled out on the opposite side to the mainsail. The jaws at the outer boom end are clipped on to the windward sheet and the pole, which needs both topping lift and foreguy, is hoisted square to the apparent wind and levelled to the height of the headsail clew. With furling gear this can be done before unfurling.

It is particularly important that the sheeting arrangements and block positions be established when preparing for a cruise. The middle of the Atlantic with 50 knots over the deck is no place to be trying to work out how to lead your storm jib sheets.

MAINSAILS AND MIZZENS

In-mast and add-on furling gears are being increasingly used by cruising boats. The advantages of infinite reefing ability and the fact that everything can be done from the cockpit outweigh the loss of efficiency due to the lack of a battened roach and the potential for jamming. Hoisting, reefing and stowing a mainsail requires a lot of strength; this gear is a particular boon to the less physically able.

Boom furling systems offer the same reefing advantages as mast furling but allow for battens so retain an efficient sail shape. We now wouldn't be without our Profurl In-boom system.

Conventional mains should have luff slides locked into the mast groove, never a bolt rope, as these will restrain the sail when it is lowered. The headboard, batten pockets, reef points and cringles are all potential failure points if not made bullet-proof.

Full battens in mainsails reduce loss of efficiency with age, allow greater sail shape control with the ability to depower and eliminate flogging which helps extend sail life. With lazy jacks fully battened mainsails are easier to stow, but they are more expensive than regular mainsails, can be hard to raise and lower and have a chafe problem downwind. Wherever the battens rub against the shrouds there is enormous wear. Thick dacron webbing should be sewn on the wear points and replaced frequently, not only for the contact points for the whole sail but also at each point for every reef. The huge frictional forces and compression loads when hoisting or striking a fully battened sail can be overcome by using the Harken Battcars or equivalent at the luff. This additional expense is necessary for safety as without Battcars raising, lowering or reefing the mainsail in bad conditions can be difficult and many require more energy than an exhausted crew can produce.

A lazy jack system, essential with full batten mainsails, is also a great help with regular batten mains to help restrain them when being dropped and furled. Unfortunately there is a problem with chafe damage to the sail, particularly to seam stitching, from any contact between the cloth and the lines and blocks of the lazy jacks. Some cruisers have modified theirs so that the whole system is held forward of the sail until needed. At the very least, all blocks should be covered with soft padding.

When ordering a new sail be specific about the reefing dimensions. Virtually all stock sails have reef points that are only suitable for inshore cruising and racing; some even have a flattening reef which can result in a dangerously drooping boom end. For offshore sailing, the mainsail has to handle a vast range of winds and, when reefing, one wants to have a significant reduction in sail area. As with all other sails, seams should be triple stitched.

Aboard *Bagheera* our mainsail has the first reef at 20% of hoist, reducing the sail area to 64%. The second and third are at 40% and 50% respectively, giving areas of 36% and a pocket handkerchief 25% remaining after reefing. There are occasions when we have been thankful to have that third reef.

All crew members should be given practice in using the boat's reefing system so that anyone can do it in the darkest or windiest conditions.

When sailing downwind, a preventer system is needed both to hold the boom forward in the ocean swells and to prevent accidental gybes, should the self-steering gear be unable to stop the boat slewing in a particularly large wave. There is a danger of the boom dipping into the sea in a cross swell; several booms were broken when we did the Atlantic Rally for Cruisers. A preventer attached to the outboard end of the boom will prevent the spar bending or breaking if this happens. However, this makes gybing the sail in stronger winds more difficult as the line has to be detached and re-attached. A mid-boom attachment is more accessible but should have a 'weak link' which will break should excessive load be put on it, thus saving boom damage. On *Bagheera* we use a light shackle.

SPINNAKERS

Understandably most sailors prefer to make downwind passages and nearly all circumnavigations are in the tropics. Most sailing is done travelling east to west in the tradewinds which are usually less than 25 knots. Even if not circumnavigating, it is probable that a fair proportion of the cruise will be in light to moderate winds aft of the beam. Once boat speed drops significantly when sailing under twin headsails or wing on wing, a spinnaker comes into its own.

The symmetrical racing spinnaker is not really practical for cruising short handed, but we have to admit to a love affair with ours (which has *Bagheera's* big black panther head displayed) so it was used often when conditions were good. A spinnaker pole, double sheets and guys, foreguy and topping lift, together with multiple blocks, make hoisting, gybing and dropping this sail an interesting experience for only two people. We soon learned that however good the conditions, our 'chute' was best doused at dusk.

Far more practical for two to handle is the cruising spinnaker, which has a variety of names, such as Gennaker, Spanker and Flasher, depending on the sailmaker. These are asymmetrical sails which do not require a pole. Instead, they are tacked down at the bow with an adjustable guy led back to the cockpit. With two sheets led like jib sheets, they can be gybed without the need to go on the foredeck. For ease of hoisting and dropping, a sock or snuffer is a bonus as it restrains the sail. Some snuffers even allow for partial release, or spinnaker reefing. The clew can also be poled out for sailing downwind wing on wing.This gear is quite easy for two to handle and a large number of cruisers use a cruising spinnaker regularly.

A light-air genoa or drifter hanked on or flown free is also an option.

STORM SAILS

Every boat should have a strategy for dealing with heavy weather and a storm jib is an essential piece of gear - although, hopefully it will never leave its bag. Very heavy cloth and stitching, reinforced edges and corners, and secure hanks and cringles are needed to withstand the huge forces, from both the wind and also from breaking seas. The same applies to a storm trysail. Particular care must be taken to check that the sail track is secure if it has been riveted or screwed on to the mast.

A schedule should be established for ideal sail combinations in varying conditions.

SAIL CARE

Ultraviolet degradation and chafe are the two great enemies of sails. Chafe is preventable *(see Chafe)* but sun damage will be progressive, weakening the fabric to the point where it is no longer worth repairing. Luckily, modern woven polyesters will last many years provided their only exposure is when hoisted and that as soon as they are stowed they are covered. Remember to protect the dacron webbing at the corners from the sun with chafe tape or Sunbrella and to rinse salt and dirt out of sails regularly.

A comprehensive sail repair kit will include a sailmaker's palm and needles, threads of various sizes, twine, beeswax, dacron cloth in weights which match your sails, spare sail slides and hanks, dacron webbing, spare cringles, self-adhesive dacron chafe tape and nylon rip-stop tapes. Some even use contact cement to "stick it now - stitch it later". Also carry spare batten stock.

A course in sail maintenance and repair is strongly recommended. Small sailmakers' sewing machines are available and soon repay their cost, enabling one to repair or replace awnings, dodgers, sailcovers, etc. as well as maintain the sails.

SEASICKNESS

The ability to cope with potential seasickness can make or break any trip, whether coastal or offshore. Anyone can be seasick, although some are more prone than others, and it is important that there is understanding regarding the causes and effects. It is often hard for those who are not affected to fully realize how frustrating and debilitating mal de mer can be. As one who suffers, I say this with feeling!

Seasickness is primarily caused by a disruption to our balance system in the inner ear. Motion increases the activity of these cells in many people which leads to dizziness and nausea, and finally vomiting. Significant factors in its prevention are diet, alcohol abstinence and positioning on the vessel.

Most people adjust to the motion at sea in 48 to 72 hours, although this can change with differing conditions. One can have sea legs for a downwind motion but feel queasy again with the winds on the beam or ahead, as the boat moves in a very different manner. Once in calm water, recovery is generally rapid although I find it frustrating that once in harbour I lose my immunity very quickly. I might get away with one night but seldom two.

For short trips, seasick pills are commonly used; take them well in advance. As being alert on watch is paramount, it is important to find a brand that controls nausea but does not cause drowsiness. There are many types on the market and trying out different ones is really worthwhile. The most popular in Europe is Stugeron (Cinnarizine), which is available under different brand names in Australia and South Africa. Dramamine (Dimenhydrinate) and the similar Gravol, and Marzine (Cyclizine, by prescription) are brands commonly found in North America. When you find a type that works for you, buy plenty. You may not find them in the next country or even the next port. Once nausea has begun Phenergan suppositories can be taken.

For long trips the Scopolamine Transderm-V earpatch can be very successful in preventing seasickness and in reducing irritability produced by a constantly moving, hot, humid environment. The effect lasts for three days, with the option to use another patch if needed. The patch has to be stuck behind the ear several hours in advance; in fact I have to put it on twelve hours in advance, rather than the instructed five/six hours, for full effect. This can cause a problem if a decision is made to depart without enough advance warning. Taking a seasick pill to cover the interim period until the patch takes effect is not advised, as mixing drugs can cause a severe case of malaise. In many places patches are now only available under prescription for this reason. Although an ear patch can produce side effects, such as dryness in the mouth and temporary blurring of vision, they are popular when used correctly. Others prefer the 'Navy cocktail' of Phenergan (a depressant) an Ephedrine (a stimulant) which was developed by NASA for the astronaut programme.

Some people find the Dea pressure-point wrist bands, developed from Chinese acupuncture principles, very successful. Electronic bands are now on the market. I have also known people use pressure with their thumb for a few seconds with good results.

In addition to medicinal strategies at the time, preventative measures can be taken. Rich or spicy foods eaten the night before departure can affect reactions, as can alcohol. Coffee should not be taken by those who suffer, in fact if taken just before leaving will almost guarantee seasickness, and just the smell of bacon cooking is enough to send me off! Avoid these foods and drinks. Having warm, bland food in one's stomach, however, helps. Eating ginger, preferably raw but even ginger snaps, can work well, as can just eating! Bland foods such as crackers or bread nibbled slowly are best, with sips of carbonated drinks.

Staying in the fresh air, keeping busy, for example at the helm, and focussing on the horizon are all beneficial. Have a sweater at hand so as not to get chilled. Don't let yourself be talked into going below, particularly not to cook or to get something out of the back of a locker. It will be just when you are upside down that a big wave will hit, and that one lurch can ruin the rest of the day. If you have to go to the head, be quick. When below, open the hatches for ventilation, if possible, otherwise, lie down amidships where the motion is least. Frequent yawning is often a precursor to seasickness. In addition to the above take deep breaths of fresh air, but if all has failed don't fight it; once sick, one feels much better! Be sure to take fluids to prevent dehydration and nibble at something bland and starchy to settle the stomach.

This regime isn't as gruelling as it sounds. We seldom want much to eat when first at sea anyway, and prefer simple food that takes little preparation. Also, having stocked up the boat before leaving and enjoyed life to the full, one is generally tired on departure. I find my first two days at sea are a routine of taking my three-hour watch on deck and sleeping when off watch. It generally takes me two days to both catch up on sleep and to get my sea legs.

If you follow these practices I think you will be pleasantly surprised at the results. For example, one of our crew when crossing the Atlantic from the Canary Islands was a French girl who had been sorely afflicted while on a friend's boat. She was so ill on the trip to Madeira she lost her dentures overboard! (As an attractive girl in her thirties she was naturally terribly embarrassed but the local Madeira dentist immediately set her at her ease, assuring her she wasn't the first and certainly wouldn't be the last to suffer such a fate! Her new set of teeth were a much better fit than the old ones and at only $100 we urged her to get a spare set!)When I discussed the above precautions it turned out that she had failed on almost every account, in particular by having a rich spaghetti sauce on the eve of their departure. Not only was she not ill with us when crossing the Atlantic, but she was able to enjoy heartily the sumptuous meals prepared by our other crew member, a highly talented French chef.

STEERING GEAR

Mechanical wheel steering is the preferred system amongst cruisers. It is rare to find a long-distance cruiser without a self-steering system, either a windvane system or autopilot, or both.

Easy, powerful steering is a prerequisite for long term cruising. Avoid boats which are heavy to steer, have a mushy response or are directionally unstable. Many production yachts have steering systems that are inadequate for offshore work. The worse the conditions, the more you have to rely on them to get you safely to your destination.

The gear cannot be taken for granted and needs to be inspected before every passage.

MECHANICAL WHEEL STEERING

This popular system usually has a chain that runs over a sprocket on the wheel shaft which is attached at both ends to cables. These cables run over pulleys at the base of the pedestal and run aft to either side of a quadrant. Maintenance is straightforward involving regular inspection, lubrication and adjustment, if needed, of cable tension. Variations of this system include single or double 'push-pull' jacketed cables and rod systems. Some wheels are connected directly to the quadrant with a rack and pinion or even a worm gear system, the latter being preferred where rudder loads are too great to be comfortably held by hand.

HYDRAULIC WHEEL STEERING

When it is difficult to have an efficient cable run, such as in centre-cockpit designs, hydraulic wheel steering is favoured by builders. A hydraulic pump is operated as the wheel is turned which powers a jack attached to the quadrant through two thin hydraulic lines. This is a powerful system and works efficiently, but, except in the case of really good installations, there is no 'feel' at the wheel of rudder loads. In fact, some builders will use hydraulics to hide the fact that the steering loads are heavy.

Regular inspections for leaks are needed; one must know how to bleed air out of the system and replenish the fluid reservoir. Stock-up on the correct grade of hydraulic fluid as it may not be obtainable away from home, also have a spares kit with plenty of replacement seals. These should be checked carefully for size and quality before departure.

TILLER STEERING

Tillers are still found not only on older boats but also on smaller cruisers. They are simple to maintain and can be pushed up and away when not in use, a considerable advantage in a small cockpit. Inexpensive autopilots may be connected to the tiller and direct attachment can be made with lines for pendulum type-steering. Both self-steering systems require light, well-balanced rudders, however, and cannot operate on many of the older Colin Archer style designs which are heavy to steer.

EMERGENCY STEERING

Steering systems are subject to continuous loads under way and all systems can break down, even tillers. An emergency tiller, which attaches directly to the rudder post, is needed to control the boat until a safe landfall is made or repairs completed.

Damage to a rudder which renders it inoperable can result from collision with an object, or structural failure to the bearings or the rudder itself. One of the worst scenarios is a collision that results in the rudder being stuck to one side which makes the boat sail in circles. The only way out of this crisis is to force the rudder straight or get rid of it, both of which may be difficult. The latter solution favours spade rudders over skeg hung ones.

Getting home rudderless is possible in a well-balanced boat in good weather. If it is blowing hard there may be no option but to stream a drogue or sea anchor and wait it out. It might be possible to use wind vane steering gear if it operates independently of the vessel's steering system. The spinnaker pole lashed to the stern pulpit with a locker lid screwed in place as a blade, could also act as a rudder. If all else fails, attach a kedge anchor to a short length of chain and connect to the mid point of a 50- to 60-metre length of rope. Take the ends of the rope to either side of the transom and lead to the sheet winches. This will act as a crude steering device; winch in the port side to turn to port and vice-versa.

In heavy weather, when running before the wind with reduced or no canvas, accurate and powerful steering is needed to avoid the possibility of broaching. Towing warps or a drogue will help to keep the boat from slewing and will ease the loads on the steering gear.

SELF-STEERING AUTOPILOT, WINDVANE OR BOTH?

Cruising is particularly pleasant if your don't have to steer! Virtually all experienced cruisers have self-steering gear; it makes the trip much more relaxing and allows the person on watch to handle the sail trim and to navigate, so that the other crew member can have an undisturbed sleep. One of the most miserable passages you can make is when the self-steering system breaks down 1000 miles from your destination and two of you hand steer watch by watch until you get there red eyed and exhausted.

For this reason *Bagheera* has a powerful autopilot which works directly on the rudder quadrant, an Aries pendulum windvane mounted on the transom and a small tiller autopilot which works directly on the Aries in place of the vane or can be rigged to drive the wheel effectively.

AUTOPILOTS

Many cruising yachts carry an autopilot. The **advantage** of an autopilot is its reliability in steering a specified course regardless of the wind; this is particularly significant when sailing dead downwind or when extreme course accuracy is required. They can also be used while motoring. **Disadvantages** are power consumption and the possibility of failure - electronic, electric or mechanical.

An autopilot which is built-in, with the drive coupled directly to the steering quadrant and all the electronics other than the control secured below, is a worthwhile investment. Linear, rotary and hydraulic drives are available to suit virtually any steering system. They all steer to a compass heading as standard but most also offer a wind direction option.

A common mistake is buying a unit which is under powered. Manufacturers are competing for the enormous weekender market and recommend models which are simply unable to perform in serious weather, which is when you most need them. It is also important to buy a model from a manufacturer who has international representation; we chose Autohelm for this reason and are more than happy with their service.

The simplest units work directly on a tiller and are completely self contained except for the power source. They are inexpensive and can be adapted to operate directly in place of a vane on a wind self-steering gear for motoring or in lieu of an expensive built-in unit.

We found our Autohelm 800 worked surprisingly well with the Aries windvane, the only disadvantage over the Autohelm 6000 being our having to reef the sails sooner if the wind came up.

Bolt-on autopilots which operate directly on the wheel rely on very light steering loads for a reasonable life expectancy. They are really more suited to coastal cruising and if used offshore it would be prudent to carry a complete spare unit on board.

WINDVANES

Vanes vary in performance. Their **advantages** are that they do not rely on electrical power and that they are simpler units to maintain than autopilots. Their **disadvantages** are that they may wander, particularly in quartering seas, and when dead down wind a gybe is always a concern. Dodgers, biminis etc., that we now feel are necessities, can cause turbulence that further degrade their performance. However, many cruisers swear by their vanes and place complete reliance on them.

The three most common vane systems are:

1) **Servo-pendulum** which has a paddle suspended in the water that is turned in response to a change in wind direction. This makes the paddle swing to the side, which pulls a line that is attached to the tiller or wheel, thus altering the boat's course. Occasionally one sees the paddle operating directly via an arm which extends back from the rudder.

2) **Independent** where the vane operates its own rudder and the vessel's gear is not needed. This may not be as powerful as the pendulum but has the advantage of providing emergency steering, should the main gear fail. For centre-cockpit vessels this gear choice is obvious.

3) **Trim tab** where the vane operates a tab on the back of the rudder and moves it in response to wind direction. A simple system which works well provided the rudder loads are light.

For any sort of self steering, be it wind vane or autopilot, a balanced boat at all angles of heel and light rudder loads are requirements for accurate steering and reliability. If hard to steer by hand then the self-steering gear will not be reliable and this would not be a suitable craft for long-term cruising.

P.S. Partytime? Croquet using emergency tillers as mallets provides great entertainment for participants and spectators alike!

TRAVEL ASHORE

We are frequently asked "What was your favourite place during your circumnavigation?" In fact, we enjoyed every place we visited although would choose to go back to some sooner than others. Particular highlights include Turkey, Madeira, the San Blas islands (Panama), Galapagos, many remote South Pacific islands and everyone loved Australia. So much was exotic in Southeast Asia and the Indian Ocean; particular memories are Bali, in Indonesia, and Salomon, an uninhabited atoll in the Chagos group south of the Maldives. We were also fascinated by Africa and its amazing wildlife - and by so many other places en route.

Finding unique cultures, tasting their foods, and visiting wondrous sights is the adventure of cruising. It is constantly stimulating. There is always so much to plan, so much to see and so many new things to learn. Travelling by boat not only gives you the independence to go to out of the way places, it also provides flexibility as it is your transportation and accommodation. It is always exhilarating to arrive in a new place. Even the chores take on a different perspective as while exploring a town you come across the butcher, the baker and the market along the way. Because we weren't on the tourist route and for much of the time were going about our daily business like everyone else, we weren't really treated like tourists and having the flexibility of time we didn't feel pressured; if we didn't feel like sightseeing we could just stay at home.

ORGANIZATION

Enjoyment of a visit depends on many factors. If the officials are difficult, prices are high and the weather is bad it isn't a good start! These are variables you can't control but knowing some facts about a place, the sights to be seen and some aspects of the culture can greatly facilitate your enjoyment of time ashore. This is where travel books are indispensable. We find the backpackers' guides suit our kind of adventure travel the best; they are very informative regarding history, health, travel, culture, visas etc. as well as listing inexpensive accommodation when we go inland. There are several series; we favour the Lonely Planet Guides although also found the South Pacific Handbook by Moon Publications excellent. Buy these ahead of time as you probably won't find them at your arrival port. These guides also provide good reading while at sea. The boys were always involved in the research, which increased their interest and also added to their education. We have particularly fond memories of them joining us in our forward cabin to look at a wonderfully illustrated book on the Galapagos islands. As this trip turned out to be a slow one, it not only provided a diversion, we were also very knowledgeable about the wildlife on our arrival. Besides travel books reference books, on fish, coral, shells, birds, butterflies, animals etc. are in constant use aboard *Bagheera.*

Make sure you have the necessary visas in advance *(see Officialdom)*. Sometimes these are complicated to arrange as they are only issued in certain countries, and all have a time limit. This may affect your cruising plans, and may take you to a place that you had not originally planned to visit!

Language can sometimes be a problem although we are fortunate that the most common second language is English. A local phrase book is useful; it's surprising how far a few words, sign language and smiles can go. This interaction gives you a personal connection with the local people, and makes both parties feel more at ease, particularly when they come to visit you on the boat. We can get by in French and Spanish, and found both very useful but always made an effort to learn local greetings. It is not only fun to call out "Jambo" in Kenya, "Owya goin mate?" in Australia and "Bula" in Fiji, it is always much appreciated.

Also make sure you understand the local currency; you are particularly vulnerable when you first arrive. Those who have read *Just Cruising* may remember how instead of paying what we understood would be $15.00 for a bottle of champagne to celebrate Liza's 40th birthday it turned out to be $150.00! We're not sure who was shocked the most; ourselves for this outrageous charge or the waiter because if he didn't collect he had to foot the bill himself. In the end the bill was settled amicably and after dinner we were royally entertained on the house. Another instance was at the end of the Darwin/Ambon race, from Australia to Indonesia. A large group of yachties went out for dinner and agreed to split the bill. As so often happens with this kind of arrangement there were some resentments at the final division. In the end it was pointed out that although the figures were in thousands, in reality the amounts they were arguing over were cents!

Organising money is important for cruisers who do not want to wait around for bank transfers. (**See Budgeting** for mobilizing your funds.)

EXPLORING NEW COUNTRIES

Early on in our cruising we realised that where one can anchor safely is often not the best place for experiencing the culture, as it is either a commercial port or a tourist town. To really feel part of the country one needs to travel inland. Often a few miles will do it, in which case we catch local buses or even rent bicycles. Often we wouldn't have a specific destination in mind but it never mattered, we always had interesting experiences. Incidentally, if you take a bus away from the boat it is prudent to find out whether there is reliable return transportation that day!

At times there are specific sights that you would like to see. If these are well-known there are generally many methods of transportation. Taking a tourist bus is one choice; although these are often rushed there is usually an interesting commentary and you can decide whether any of the sights are worth a revisit. Renting a car is sometimes viable, particularly if you share the cost with another crew. Make sure your driving license is valid; although many countries used to require an international driving license this seems no longer necessary. Sightseeing is much more than going to the famous places, however. Some of our most memorable experiences were from 'just wandering around' or sitting in a taverna watching the world go by. In Turkey on one such evening, some people from Istanbul learnt it was Duncan's tenth birthday. Soon he was invited to dance with the rest of the men and the next day a birthday cake arrived at the boat accompanied by the local band. Although the evening before this band had only played wailing eastern music they were quite at home playing 'Happy birthday to you' on their exotic instruments.

LOCAL CUSTOMS

It is hard to emphasize too much the importance of dressing appropriately around the world and how much it means to people that you are paying them respect. Although we might prefer to wear shorts if it is hot, if a woman is wearing a skirt, or long pants, and the man long pants or conservative shorts, clearing-in with officials and doing daily business will probably go much more smoothly.

Many customs are quite different to ours and ignoring them can cause offence. Again, the travel books will inform you of local practice. In Tonga, for example, no work is supposed to be done on Sunday, so it is not a good day to check out the mast, particularly with a hammer! Many religions have rules about entering their holy places and it is important to set out that day in appropriate dress if you want to go inside. Sometimes you will be provided with attire. In Bali, for instance they gave Andy and Duncan sarongs to wear before entering the temple. Duncan made us promise not to take any photos of him! The more we travelled the more we realised the depths of some cultures compared to our own. Sadly however, particularly from the explosion in tourism, this is fast changing with everyone wanting to emulate western ways.

If you leave the boat for a period to travel inland you become a regular tourist. Check the food you are eating carefully, take precautions with the water and remember 'bugs' are far more prevalent ashore than they are on the boat. It's easy to forget you haven't the facilities at hand that you are used to on board. Particularly make sure you have had the necessary immunizations or have taken malaria prophylactics etc: Remember the laws of the land apply to you, these may be quite different to the one's you are used to. Always carry some form of identification. Be wise tourists, especially women; don't wear jewellery, have a safe place for your money and don't go to the disreputable parts of the city, especially at night.

Always ask permission before photographing local people, and never take photographs of military facilities, a harbour where there are naval vessels present or industrial installations such as oil refineries, or in security zones such as at border crossings. I made the mistake of taking a picture of Andy and the boys beside a man with a hat piled high with buns in the security area between Morocco and Ceuta. Instantly whistles blew and my camera was demanded. We had a battle on our hands to keep both the camera and film intact. If you do have any problems while travelling you can contact your country's consulates. Make sure you have a list of these because it is hard to find this kind of information when you can't speak the language. Canada for example has a booklet called Bon Voyage But... Tips for Canadians travelling Abroad which provides much useful information as well as all the addresses and phone numbers of the Canadian missions around the world. In addition there are information numbers to call in Canada to obtain the current conditions in a country.

LEAVING THE BOAT

Travelling inland requires leaving the boat unattended and this can be a problem. Ideally you leave the boat in a secure marina; with the increasing numbers cruising and the corresponding development of facilities, this is becoming more feasible in much of the world. If leaving at anchor you need to find not only a suitable anchorage but also need someone to mind the boat. Frequently cruisers do this for each other, then return the favour so the other crew can get away. Sometimes you can employ a local person. Those who have freezers which require the engine to be run need someone to do this on a daily basis wherever the boat is situated.

VISITORS' BOOK and BOAT CARDS

Something that you MUST purchase before you leave. Vivid memories will abound from your visitors' book; special times with people from different cultures, your fellow cruisers, visits from friends and unique events that are easily forgotten with the next new experience. Exchanging boat cards is also popular, providing a handy reference for names, addresses, boat names and email.

Some visitors will just sign their name and make a comment but a bound book with plain pages will encourage originality with drawings, photos, eloquent (or impudent!) lines, even poems. When fellow cruisers can take away the book for a few days, they come up with some veritable masterpieces and many a personal detail.

I quoted several of our visitors' book entries in Still Cruising. Here is another from Alison, my eldest stepdaughter, who came to stay with us in the Bahamas with her husband, Steve and sister, Vicky with boyfriend Rob. Cruising the islands lent itself to a very relaxing holiday, especially since we had been on the go most of the previous four months, sailing from South Africa. We particularly focussed on the beautiful turquoise waters, the essence of Bahamian cruising. Alison wrote:

To the Exumas we went
For a week full of sun,
On the fine yacht Bagheera
Always known for good fun.

Jamie dove deep
Finding shell after shell,
And each evening at dusk
Beat us all at 'Oh Hell'.

Then there was Colin
Always quick with suggestions,
On where to find lizards
And playing '20 questions'.

Duncan, fresh from school,
Caught fish and lobster tail.
His hair style is 'rad',
But he loves a good sail.

Vicky and Rob　　　　　　　*Andy of course*
Stargazed at night.　　　　*Thought all this a blast,*
They slept up on deck　　　*'Til he found it too noisy*
But got rained on at light.　*And retreated up the mast.*

Ali and Steve　　　　　　　　　　　*Then there was Liza,*
Dove for fish, shells and rocks.　　*Last, but certainly not least,*
Steve looked dressed for the office　*Who saw a good time was had*
In his long sleeves and socks.　　　*And prepared great big feasts.*

Thanks to all aboard Bagheera,
I hate to leave this bay.
(Do you think the office would notice
If I don't show up Tuesday?)

We celebrated our circumnavigation with two other families - Americans Tom, Jean, Dawn and Jennifer from *Jean Marie* and Canadians Peter, Tanis, Jennifer and Alex on *Wind Woman*. Tom's masterpiece says it all and definitely deserves a reprint.

SHIPMATES

Bagheera is a vessel with class we agree, equipped as a cruiser
　　sporting a racer's pedigree
Andy's her intrepid skipper - a mariner unmatched, his judgement
　　is sound though he's only partially thatched.
The Admiral's a redhead with freckles galore, Liza's never without
　　words. . . and she's never a bore.
Colin's a rockhound, he selects them by weight, the captain wants
　　to deballast, and let the boy pay the freight.
Jamie's a boat kid that much is quite clear, he's ready and able to
　　hand, reef or steer.
Duncan's 'Joe college' he matriculates ashore with studies and
　　rugby and coeds amour.
They're world class sailors, they've been all the way round with
　　friendship and strange sights their memories abound.
God Bless you each one, as you sail this grand sea, we'll think of you
　　often aboard the cutter Jean Marie.

You will also be asked to make entries in other cruisers' visitors' books so be sure to have some good photos and ideas at hand. A ships stamp is fun for visitors' books, and also useful for customs forms.

WATER

Water is the greatest necessity in life; being without it even for a day or two can be a major crisis. The advent of water-makers has potentially eased the situation for those who can afford one, although increasing, those that have them are still in the minority. A prudent skipper will want to be thoroughly familiar with his entire water system to be confident that there will be min-imal loss or waste on a pssage. A system that can be divided up into smaller units to avoid loss in the event of a leak is wise. Multiple tanks also help to isolate possible contamination if it should occur.

Before any ocean passage

1) Check and, if necessary, rein-force, the water tank attachment to the hull; water weighs one kilo per litre and a full tank is a huge strain on any inade-quate installation in the event of a knockdown.

2) Fit manual or foot-operated water pumps so that the pressure system can be bypassed.

3) Fit a manual salt water pump in the galley. An additional electric pump in line enables the sink to be filled with salt water effortlessly, thus encouraging the use of salt water over fresh.

On *Bagheera* we have 415-litre main tanks, 110 litres in aux-iliary tanks and on long passages carry 4 jerry cans of 23 litres each. How much water is needed depends on the temperature. In the high latitudes one can survive on less than one litre per day. In the tropics one needs double that as a minimum. Enough water should be carried in tanks and jerry cans to allow for three to four litres per person per day with at least a 50 percent reserve to allow for a slow passage. With proper conservation measures, it is unlikely that this amount will be used. However, arriving with tanks half-full is preferable to running out days before your landfall.

To have enough water for all the crew to shower before entering port adds to the pleasure of the landfall and will certainly make your welcome by the customs and immigration officials more friendly!

When not on a passage and with water supplies available, deck showers are popular. Some cruisers have an electric pump at the stern, particularly to hose down after swimming, while others confine themselves to 'sun showers', black plastic bags with a hose and shower head which can be purchased in most marine stores. When hung in the rigging in the tropical sun the water heats quickly. Other cruisers prefer a garden chemical sprayer, which is pressurized by pumping, as it gives a more powerful spray.

CONSERVATION

Unless the yacht carries more than the minimum water requirement, strict discipline must be followed to ensure that very little is used, other than for drinking and food preparation. A very small amount is needed for a wash with a cloth, for teeth and shaving.

By turning off the pressure water system at sea and using only the manual pumps a huge difference will be made in water consumption. This measure alone will go a long way in helping to achieve your consumption goals.

Washing-up can be done in salt water. Several dishwashing detergents, such as Joy or New Dawn, work well although the dishes won't sparkle quite as much and the dish towels will need to be rinsed out every time it rains. Wash vegetables and fish with sea water, and cook with a proportion of seawater rather than salting fresh water.

A salt water deck pump used for cleaning the anchor chain can also serve as a cockpit salt-water shower. Again, many shampoos work with sea water, such as Head and Shoulders, and those especially sold for the purpose. Only a little fresh water is needed for a careful rinse - depending on your hairstyle!

Needless to say, every warm rain squall is used for washing

bodies, towels and dishcloths, but don't get caught lathered-up when the rain suddenly stops!

WATERMAKERS

A watermaker increases comfort on board immediately when off shore cruising provided the output is large enough. A wide variety are now on the market, from tiny manual units for survival in a liferaft to huge commercial units which keep ships supplied. The basic components of these machines are a very high pressure sea water pump and a membrane filter which removes salt and any contaminants from sea water. The quality of the water is excellent.

The output is determined by the size of these components and is usually stated in the promotional literature as so many litres per day. These figures assume optimum conditions 24 hours a day, which in practice may never be achieved due to cold, saline or silty water, so always buy a size larger than you think you will need. Power can be provided by batteries, a generator or direct drive from the engine. Many DC units draw too much power to run without engine charging. We are very happy with our Spectra 12 unit that uses only 9 amps while producing 34 litres (9 US gallons).

Maintenance is quite straightforward but can be time consuming. It is important to ensure the watermaker is used only in pure seawater and not in contaminated harbours or silty river estuaries. Whenever the unit is shut down for a period the membrane must be flushed out and chemically inhibited. Failure to do this may result in having to replace the membrane which is expensive.

WATER COLLECTING

It cannot be assumed that piped water is available to fill your tanks even in quite large communities, so jerry cans must often be used. We carried four five-gallon ones for this purpose and on passages carried them filled and on deck ready to transfer to the liferaft. Quite often there are hefty charges for water, even in Europe and the Caribbean.

Aboard *Bagheera* we went for many months sailing off the beaten track in the Indian Ocean without access to water and had to resort to catching rain at every opportunity. To do this, we had arranged for our mainsail be cut so that the clew was several inches higher than the tack.

A sleeve fitted over the forward end of the boom to which a hose was attached which led into the water filler on the deck. During a rainstorm we would allow a few seconds for any salt to wash off the sail and then start to fill the tanks. The amount of rain that blew into the sail, found its way down to the groove in the boom and thence into the hose was amazing; a 20-minute tropical deluge would usually fill our tanks completely. Using the sail to catch rain was augmented by directing rain falling on our foredeck into the water filler by damming the flow with towels. Our large sun awning was also designed to catch rain when we were at anchor.

PURIFICATION

Sometimes water has to be obtained from questionable sources and purification is necessary. Excellent filters are available which are installed directly into the source for drinking water in the boat; these remove impurities and some will eliminate bacteria. If in doubt, add purification tablets, available in most countries. Or, if these cannot be found, then regular, (not scented) bleach may be used in the proportion of one teaspoon (4-6% bleach) to every 40 litres of clean water. (Bleach should not be used in aluminum tanks; here iodine may be considered.) There will be a faint chlorine taste at this dilution which can be eliminated by passing the water through a filter containing carbon. Our test is tea. If our early morning cup is palatable the filter has done a fine job!

FINALE

There you have it in a nutshell. As you can see the cruising life is not all 'gin and tonics' on the afterdeck but it is a huge amount of fun. It is one of the last great freedoms, where you are entirely in an adventure of your own making.

The message we have tried to convey throughout is to be prepared. You can't avoid all the problems but you can have the wherewithal to fix most of them.

Without doubt partners view the lifestyle in very different lights; be understanding and compassionate to each others needs. That some like certain aspects of cruising and not others in only natural; work around it so the life is enjoyable for all.

Make the most of the travel opportunities. Besides the well-known destinations there are so many places accessible to cruisers that the average tourist cannot reach. Get immersed in the cultures, taste their foods, dance to their music and appreciate the beauty of their lands.

Good luck with your plans, we hope *Cruising for Cowards* will help you, too, make your dreams come true. Be warned - once tasted, you will be hooked forever!

Appendix A
CONVERSION TABLES

WEIGHT: 1 kilogram (kg)   = 2.2 pounds (lbs)
              1 pound   = .455 kilograms
              10 pounds   = 4.545 kilograms
1 Imperial gallon of fresh water weighs 10 pounds, or 4.545 kilograms
1 U.S. gallon fresh water weights 8.333 pounds, or 3.787 kilograms
1 litre of fresh water weighs 2.2. pounds, or 1 kilogram
              1 Imperial gallon of gasoline weights 7.44 pounds, or 3.38 kilograms
              1 U.S. gallon of gasoline weighs 6.2 pounds, or 2.82 kilograms
              1 litre of gasoline weighs 1.64 pounds, or 0.744 kilograms
1 Imperial gallon of No. 2 diesel fuel weighs 8.04 pounds, or 3.66 kilograms
1 U.S. gallon of No. 2 diesel fuel weighs 6.7 pounds, or 3.05 kilograms
1 litre of No. 2 diesel fuel weighs 1.77 pounds, or 0.8 kilograms

DISTANCE: 1 metre   = 3.28 feet
              1 inch   = 25.4 millimetres
              1 foot   = .3048 metres
              1 yard   = .91 metres, or 915.5 millimetres.
              1 fathom   = 6 feet
              1 fathom   = 1.83 metres
              1 cable   = 120 fathoms
              1 nautical mile = 6076 feet; 8.5 cables; 1.852 kilometres
              1 statute mile   = 5280 feet; 7.4 cables; 1.609 kilometres
              1 nautical mile = 1.15 statute mile
              1 statute mile   = 0.868 nautical mile
              1 nautical mile = 1.85 kilometres

SPEED: Convert knots to miles per hour: Knots x 1.15
              Convert miles per hour to knots: MPH x .868
              Convert kilometres per hour to knots: Km x .54
              Convert knots to kilometres per hour: Knots x 1.85
              Convert metres/second to knots: M x 1.943
              Convert knots to metres/second: Knots x .514

TEMPERATURE:

Fahrenheit to Celsius
To convert temperature from Fahrenheit (F) to Celsius (C): ($°F$ - 32) x .555 = $°C$
Example: Convert 40°F to °C: (40-32) = 8; 8 x .555 = 4; thus 40° F = 4°C

Celsius to Fahrenheit
To convert temperature from Celsius (C) to Fahrenheit (F): ($°C$ x 1.8) + 32 = $°F$
Example: Convert 4°C to F: (4 x 1.8) = 7.992; 7.992 + 32 = 39.992; thus 4° C = 40° F

°C	°F		°C	°F		°C	°F		°C	°F
-20	-4		0	32		20	68		40	104
-10	14		10	50		30	86		100	212

THE BEAUFORT SCALE

#	KNOTS	DESCRIPTIVE TERMS	EFFECTS
0	under 1	Calm	Calm
1	1-3	Light air	Ripples
2	4-6	Light breeze	Small wavelets
3	7-10	Gentle breeze	Large wavelets; small crests
4	11-16	Moderate breeze	Small waves; some whitecaps
5	17-21	Fresh breeze	Moderate waves; some spray; many whitecaps
6	22-27	Strong breeze	Larger waves; whitecaps everywhere
7	28-33	Near gale	Sea heaps up white foam from breaking waves
8	34-40	Gale	Moderately high waves of greater length; foam blown in well-marked streaks
9	41-47	Strong gale	High waves; sea begins to roll; dense streaks of foam; spray reduces visibility
10	48-55	Storm	Very high waves with overhanging crests; sea takes a white appearance; rolling is heavy
11	56-63	Violent storm	Exceptionally high waves; sea covered with white foam patches; visibility still more reduced
12	64 & over	Hurricane	Air filled with foam; sea completely white with driving spray; visibility greatly reduced

VOLUME:

Imperial Gallons to Litres

> 1 Imperial gallon = 4.546 litres
> •To convert Imperial gallons to litres, multiply Imperial gallons by 4.546
> Example: 40 Imperial gallons x 4.546 = 182 litres
> •To convert litres to Imperial gallons, divide by 4.546
> Example: 182 litres / 4.546 = 40.035

U.S. Gallons to Litres:1 U.S. gallon = 3.7854 litres

•To convert U.S. gallons to litres, multiply U.S. gallons x 3.785
Example: 40 U.S. gallons x 3.785 = 151 litres
•To convert litres to U.S. gallons, divide by 3.785
Example: 151 litres / 3.785 = 39.89 U.S. gallons (round to 40)

U.S. Gallons to Imperial Gallons:1 U.S. gallon = .833 Imperial gallons

•To convert U.S. gallons to Imperial gallons, multiply U.S. gallons x .833
Example: 40 U.S. gallons x .833 = 33.32 Imperial gallons
•To convert Imperial gallons to U.S. gallons, multiply Imperial gallons x 1.20
Example: 33 Imperial gallons x 1.20 = 39.6 U.S. gallons

Litres to Imperial Quarts and Gallons

1 litre   = 0.88 quarts or 1.75 pints
1 quart = 1.14 litres
1 gallon = 4.54 litres

Litres to U.S. Quarts and Gallons

1 litre   = 1.0567 quarts, or 33.9 ounces
1 quart = 0.9467 litres, or 947 millimetres
1 gallon = 3.78 litres

COOKING
Convenient Cooking Measurements:

1 teaspoon	= 5 millilitres	l cup	= 16 tablespoons
1 tablespoon	= 15 millilitres	l cup	= 8.8 fluid ounces
1 cup	= 250 millilitres	l pint	= 20 fluid ounces

Liquid Measurements: (Imperial & Metric)

1 fluid ounce	= 28.41 millilitres	1 millilitre	= .04 fluid ounces
1 pint	= 568 millilitres	1 litre	= 1.75 pints
1 quart	= 1.14 litres	1 litre	= .88 quarts
1 gallon	= 4.54 litres	1 litre	= .22 gallons

Weight Measurements:

1 ounce	= 28.35 grams	1 gram	= .04 ounces
1 pound	= 0.45 kilograms	1 kilogram	= 2.21 pounds

Temperature Equivalents:
32° Fahrenheit (F) = 0° Celsius (C)

212° F = 100° C	375° F = 190° C
300° F = 150° C	400° F = 200° C
325° F = 160° C	425° F = 220° C
350° F = 180° C	450° F = 230° C

INTERNATIONAL MORSE CODE & PHONETIC ALPHABET

A	ALPHA• —	N	NOVEMBER— •
B	BRAVO— •••	O	OSCAR— — —
C	CHARLIE— • — •	P	PAPA• — — •
D	DELTA— ••	Q	QUEBEC— — • —
E	ECHO•	R	ROMEO• — •
F	FOXTROT•• — •	S	SIERRA•••
G	GOLF— — •	T	TANGO—
H	HOTEL••••	U	UNIFORM•• —
I	INDIA••	V	VICTOR••• —
J	JULIET•— — —	W	WHISKEY• — —
K	KILO— • —	X	X-RAY— •• —
L	LIMA•— ••	Y	YANKEE— • — —
M	MIKE— —	Z	ZULU— — ••

DISTRESS - SOS ••• — — — •••

USEFUL EMERGENCY RADIO FREQUENCIES AND RESOURCES
VHF Channel 16 - calling and distress, reliable range 20-30 miles
SSB 2182 KHz - worldwide distress frequency, reliable range about 300 miles
HAM Maritime Mobile Nets are active almost worldwide 24 hrs a day between 14300 - 14320 MHz (Anyone can use a Ham frequency in an emergency.) There are generally Ham, SSB and often VHF nets in most popular cruising areas. When using Ham/SSB the greater the distance, also the higher the sun, the higher the frequency generally needed. Propagation can vary hugely depending on atmospheric conditions.
REED'S Nautical Almanacs (Email jdk@ReedsAlmanac.com) are invaluable for Pilot information, Tides, Currents, and includes an Ephemeris for Celestial Navigation, as well as data regarding Communications, Weather, Electronic Navigation, Notices to Mariners and Cruising Guides. They are updated annually.
WEATHER for those in the Atlantic and Caribbean Herb Hilgenbert (Southbound two, VAX-498) broadcasts daily on 12359 MHz at 2000 UTC. Local cruisers' nets also often give weather. WeatherFax software is popular among ocean cruisers.

Appendix B - USEFUL ADDRESSES

CRUISING ASSOCIATIONS

CANADA
Bluewater Cruising Association
8886 Hudson St.
Vancouver, BC V6P 4N2
Tel. (604) 266-3361 message
Email bluewater@geocities.com

World Cruising Club
C/o Jim Winslow,
338 Howland Ave.
Toronto, Ont M5R 3B9 Tel. (416) 978-2680 (work) (416) 535-3319 (home)
Email winslow@spine.med.utoronto.ca

UK
The Cruising Association
C.A. House
1, Northey St.
Limehouse Basin
London, E14 8BT
Tel. 0171 537 2828
Fax 0171 537 2266
Email ca@cruising.org.uk

Ocean Cruising Club
Anthea Cornell, Club Secretary
28 Molyneux Street,
London, W1H 5HW
Tel./Fax 0171 262 1579
Email antheajc@compuserve.com

UNITED STATES
Seven Seas Cruising Association
1525, S. Andrews Avenue, Ste 217
Fort Lauderdale, Florida, 33316
Tel. (954) 463-2431
Fax. (954) 463-7183
Email office@ssca.org

Little Ship Club
Bell Wharf Lane
Upper Thames St.
London EC4R3TB
Tel. 0207 236 7729
Email cluboffice@little-ship-club.co.uk

Royal Yachting Association
Romsey Road
Eastleight, Hants SO5O 9YA
Tel. 023 8062 7400
Fax. 023 8062 9924
Email admin@rya.org.uk

EDUCATION

Worldwide Education Service
Unit 2, Telford Road, Bicester,
Oxfordshire OX26 4LD UK
Tel. +44 (0) 1869-248682
Tel. +44 (0) 1869-248064
Email office@weshome.demon.co.uk

Calvert School
10713 Gilroy Road, Suite B,
Hunt Valley, MD 21031
Toll Free. (888) 487-4652
Tel. (410) 785-4300
Fax. (410) 785-3418
Email inquiry@calvertservices.org

MARINE INSURANCE (who insure for couples)

Blue Water Insurance
1016 Clemons St. Suite 200
Jupiter, FL 33477 USA
Tel. (800) 866-8906, (561) 743-3442
Fax. (561) 743-8751
Email bluewater@blueh2oins.com

Pantaenius
Marine Building, Victoria Wharf
Plymouth, Devon P14 ORF
Tel. 01752 223656
Fax. 01752 223637
Email info@pantaenius.co.uk

MEDICAL RESOURCES

International Association for Medical Assistance to Travelers (IAMAT)
40, Regal Road, Guelph
On., N1K 1B5 Canada
Tel. (519) 836-0102

736 Center Street
Lewiston NY 14092 USA
Tel. (716) 754-4883
Also contact your local Health Department's Travel Clinic

Hospital for Tropical Diseases
4, St. Pancras Way
London, NW1 OPE, UK

Centers for Disease Control (CDC)
1600 Cliften Rd NE
Atlanta, Georgia 30333 USA
Tel. (404) 639-3311

MEDICAL INSURANCE

PPP International
Phillips House, Crescent Road, Tunbridge Wells
Kent, TN1 2PL, UK
Tel. 0198 277 2002 (Outside U.K.)
Tel. 0 800 33 5555 (U.K. Only)

Healthcare Global
Wallace & Co.
P.O. Box 480 Middleburg
VA 22117 USA
Tel. (800) 237-6615, (540) 687-3166
Also check with your Automobile Association for extended health plans for travellers

Blue Water Insurance
1016 Clemons St., Suite 200
Jupiter, FL 33477 USA
Tel. (800) 866-8906, (561) 743-3442
Fax. (561) 743-8751

TRAVEL

Many coutnries now have services that give pertinent information for travellers such as dangerous situations, health hazards etc.
Canadians should call Canada (800) 267-6788, US Citizen Services (800) 529-4410.
Also obtain a list of your country's consulates around the world.

BOAT CHARTER COMPANIES

Look in the yachting magazines for information on charter companies.
Examples are:

The Moorings	USA (800) 535-7289	UK 01227776677
Sunsail	USA (800) 327-2276	UK 01705222222
Sun Yacht Charters	BVI (800) 772-3502	
Caribbean Yacht Charters	USA (800) 225-2520, (727) 559-7142	

Examples of crewed charter companies where crews have considerable offshore experience:

Ann-Wallis White
Charter Yacht Brokers
Box 4100 Annapolis, MD 21403
Tel. (410) 263-6366
Fax. (410) 263-0399

Nicholson Yacht Charters Inc.
432 Columbia St.
Cambridge MA 02141-1043
Tel. (800) 662-6066, (617) 661-0555
Fax. (617) 661-0554

Appendix C – READING SUGGESTIONS

Anchoring
Complete Book of Anchoring and Mooring, 2nd Ed.
Earl Hinz - 1993

The Boat
SAIL'S Things that Work
SAIL Magazine - 1993
Complete Guide to Choosing A Cruising Sailboat
Roger Marshall - 1999
Understanding Rigs and Rigging
Richard Henderson - 1990

Boating Experience
Essential Seamanship
Richard Henderson - 1994
Handbook of Sailing
Bob Bond - 1992

Budgeting
Ocean Cruising on a Budget
Anne Hammick - 1990
Voyaging on a Small Income
Annie Hill - 1993

Electricity
Managing 12 Volts
Harold Barre - 1996
The 12-volt Doctor's Practical Handbook
Edgar J. Beyn - 1983

Electronics
GPS User's Guide
Ken Englert - 1995
Small Boat Guide to Radar
Tim Bartlett - 1991

Engines
Marine Diesel Engines
Nigel Calder - 1991

Knots
Knots/Chapman's Nautical Guides
Brion Toss - 1990

The Ashley Book of Knots
Clifford W. Ashley - 1944
Splicing Handbook
Barbara Merry - 1987

Life on Board
Self-Sufficient Sailor 2nd Ed.
Lin & Larry Pardey - 1997
Cruising Rules
Roland Sawyer Barth - 1998

Maintenance
Complete Guide to Boat Maintenance and Repair
David G. Brown
Boatowner's Mechanical and Electrical Manual, 2nd Ed.
Nigel Calder - 1995
Canvas Work and Sail Repair
Don Casey - 1996
Sailboat Refinishing
Don Casey - 1995

Medical
AMA Handbook of First Aid and Emergency Care - 1990
Travellers Health: How to Stay Healthy Abroad
Dr. R. Dawood - 1992
Advanced First-Aid Afloat, 4th Ed.
Peter F. Eastman, MD - 1995
Dangerous Marine Animals
Bruce W. Halstead, MD - 1995

Navigation
Chapman's Piloting, 61st Ed.
Elbert S. Maloney - 1993
One Day Celestial Navigation
Otis Brown - 1993
Practical Celestial Navigation
Susan P. Howell - 1987
Navigation Rules: rules of the Road
Edited by David Burch - 1992

Small Craft Piloting and Coastal Navigation
Al Saunders - 1988
> *Walker Commonsense Log Book*
> Milo and Terry Walker - 1990

Officialdom, Visas and Paperwork
World Cruising Handbook, 2nd Ed.
Jimmy Cornell - 1996

Provisioning
Boat Cuisine
June Raper - 1994
> *Galley K.I.S.S and Cruising K.I.S.S Cookbooks*
> Corinne Kanter - 1987 and 1996

Cruising Cuisine
Kay Pastorius - 1997
> *Great Cruising Cookbook*
> John Payne - 1996

The Joy of Cooking
Irma Rombault - 1985
(Excellent general purpose)
> *Keeping Food Fresh: How to Choose and Store Everything you Eat*
> Janet Baily - 1993

Sail Away! A Guide to Outfitting and Provisioning Your Boat for Cruising, 2nd Ed.
Paul and Sheryl Shard - 1998

Safety
Heavy Weather Sailing, 5th Ed.
K. Adlard Coles - 1999
(Updated by Peter Bruce)
> *The Sea Anchor and Drogue Handbook 1995*
> Daniel Shewmon

Storm Tactics Handbook
Lin and Larry Pardey - 1997

Route Planning
World Cruising Routes, 4th Ed.
Jimmy Cornell - 1998

Travel
Yachtsman's Ten Language Dictionary
Barbara Webb, revised by Mishael Manton - 1995
> *Travel with Children*
> Maureen Wheeler - 1990

Handbook for Woman Travellers
Maggie and Gemma Moss - 1991
> *Lonely Planet Travel Guides*

Weather
Sailor's Weather Guide
Jeff Markell - 1995
> *The Weather Handbook*
> Alan Watts - 1995

Understanding Weather Fax
Mike Harris - 1997

Also read the yarns of earlier cruisers - the Guzzwells, Joshua Slocum, Susan and Eric Hiscock, Hal Roth, Tristan Jones, Beryl and Miles Smeeton and Clare Francis, to name a few - but remember cruising is far more comfortable these days! A popular children's series about boating adventures is by Arthur Ransome - Swallows and Amazons, We didn't Mean To Go To Sea etc.

Thanks go to Robert Hale and Co., Nautical Book Distributors and The Nautical Mind Marine Booksellers and Chart Agents (800) 463-9951 or (416) 203-1163 for their suggestions in compiling this list.

APPENDIX D

GLOSSARY OF TERMS
(Definitions specific to *Cruising for Cowards*)

ABEAM Off one side of the boat

ABOUT To change direction in sailing, when the wind fills the sails from the other side. To come about; change course

ADRIFT Drifting, or broken loose from a mooring. Dragging anchor

AFT At the back of the boat; behind

ALOFT Up above; as up in the rigging or up the mast

ANEMOMETER An instrument for measuring the velocity of the wind

ANTIFOULING Bottom paint, to deter growth of weed, barnacles etc.

ASTERN To go backwards; behind the boat

AUTOPILOT Electro/mechanical steering device for automatic course keeping

BACKS, BACKING When the wind changes in an anti-clockwise direction

BACKSTAY Wire supporting the mast which attaches to back of boat

BAGGYWRINKLE Material on the shrouds, to stop chafe damage to sails, traditionally made out of old rope

BAROMETER An instrument for registering the atmospheric pressure

BATTENS Stiffening pieces usually of fibreglass or plastic traditionally wood. Used to support the roach of a sail.

BEAM REACH Sailing at about 90° to the wind direction

BEAM Width of a boat at its widest point; 'On the beam'at right angles to the direction of the boat

BEAR AWAY To alter course away from the wind

BEARING The angle between and object and north

BEATING To sail into wind by zig-zagging (tacking) towards it

BEAUFORT SCALE International scale of wind strength, Forces 0-12

BELOW Inside the boat

BERTH A bed; To berth, to come into the dock; A berth, the space in which a boat lies at the dock

BILGE Space under the floor boards

BINNACLE A stand in the cockpit on which the compass in supported

BITTER END The extreme end of a line

BLOCK A pulley

BOAT HOOK A device for catching hold of a ring bolt or grab line in coming alongside a pier or picking up a mooring

BOOM Horizontal spar supporting the bottom of the mainsail

BOOM VANG Tackle from the boom to the deck to keep the boom from lifting (also called a kicking strap)

BOSUN'S CHAIR A chair for going up the mast generally made from wood and canvas and hoisted by a halyard

BOW The front of the boat

BROACH Heading up into wind uncontrollably

BULKHEAD A structural 'wall' which divides the yacht into compartments

BUOY Floating device anchored to the sea's bottom. Used as markers for navigation, automatic weather reporting, enables vessels to tie up, as fishing net markers etc.

BURGEE A triangular flag used to identify a yacht club

CAPSTAN A winchlike drum on a windlass used for hauling in rope

CAST OFF Undo a mooring or towing line

CATAMARAN Boat with two hulls

CHAFE Damage due to abrasion

CHAIN PLATES Hull attachments for standing rigging

CHART Nautical map showing navigational aids, depths, hazards and land forms

CHRONOMETER A highly accurate clock used by navigators

CLEAT Fitting on which to secure a line

'CHUTE Spinnaker

CLEW Aft bottom corner of a sail

CLINKER Lapstrake planked (hull), planks overlapping like clapboards

CLOSE-HAULED Sailing as close to the wind as possible

CLOSE-WINDED A craft capable of sailing very close to the wind

COAMING The raised protection around a cockpit

COCKPIT A recessed part of the deck in which to sit and steer

COMPANIONWAY Entry and stairway to get below

COMPASS An instrument using a pointer which indicates magnetic north

CRADLE A frame used to hold a boat when she is hauled out of the water

CRUISER Any boat having arrangements for living aboard

CUTTER A single masted sailboat in which the mast is set amidships and having split headsail rig. (See SLOOP)

DEAD RECKONING (DR) Estimate of the boat's position based on course & speed

DEATH ROLL Side-to-side uncontrollable motion when going downwind

DECKHEAD Underside of the deck (ceiling in a house)

DEPTH SOUNDER An electronic instrument that measures the depth of the water

DEVIATION Angular difference between compass bearing and magnetic bearing caused by the effect of iron aboard ship. Effect varies for each point of the compass

DINGHY A small boat or tender

DRAFT Depth of the boat below the waterline

DRAGGING When an anchor slips along the bottom

DROGUE A device trailed behind a boat to create drag

EBB The outgoing tide

ENSIGN A national flag flown on a boat

EPIRB Emergency Position Indicating Radio Beacon

FAIRLEAD A fitting which changes the direction of a sheet or halyard led through it

FATHOM A measurement of depth (1 fathom =6 feet)

FEND OFF To push the boat away from an object so no damage occurs

FENDERS (bumpers)Inflated cylinders used to protect the sides of boat when berthed

FIDDLES Strips of metal or wood to stop objects from sliding e.g. on the stove or table

FLOOD TIDE A rising tide

FLOTSAM Floating debris

FOOT Bottom edge of a sail

FOREDECK Deck at the front of a boat

FOREGUY (downhaul) Line to pull down the spinnaker pole

FORESTAY Wire supporting the mast which is attached to the front of the boat

FORWARD Towards the front or bow

FREEBOARD The height of the hull between the water and the deck

FRONT Leading edge of a moving mass of cold or warm air. Cold fronts are usually associated with rain, lightning and squalls. Warm fronts are associated with heavy clouds and rain

FURL Mainsail: To drop and lash to the boom. Genoa: To roll round a vertical aluminum extrusion which rotates around the forestay

FURLING GEAR Equipment used to enable furling of the genoa

GALLEY Boat kitchen

GANGPLANK A moveable bridge used to get from the dock or pier to a boat or vice versa

GENOA Large foresail (overlaps the mainsail)

GIMBALS A device to enable an object, such as a compass or galley stove, to remain horizontal regardless of the boat's motion

GO ABOUT (to tack) To turn the bow through the wind when sailing

GOOSENECK Hinged fitting which attaches the boom to the mast

GPS (GLOBAL POSITIONING SYSTEM) Position indicating electronic navigational aid

GROUND TACKLE Anchor, cable, etc., used to secure a vessel to the bottom

GUST Sudden increase in wind

GUY Windward spinnaker sheet that attaches to pole

GYBE (jibe) To change course downwind so that the sails change sides (can be dangerous when unplanned)

GYPSY (wildcat) A revolving sprocket on a windlass which has pockets to engage the links of chain

HALYARD Line for hoisting sails

HANKS Clips for attaching foresail to the forestay

HARD OVER Placement of the wheel, or tiller, when it is put over as far as possible to one side or the other

HATCH An opening through the deck

HAUL To draw a boat or net out of the water

HEAD OF SAIL Top corner of the sail

HEAD UP To luff or turn towards the wind

HEAD(S) Boat toilet

HEAD-TO-WIND When the front of the boat, or bow, points into wind

HEADSAILS Sails that attach forward of the mast

HEADSTAY (forestay) Rigging wire from the bow or foredeck supporting the mast

HEAVING-TO A method of stopping the vessel and allowing it to maintain a comfortable attitude, usually with a reefed mainsail, backed jib and lashed helm

HEEL When boat leans over at an angle (most severe when beating in a strong wind)

HELM To steer; steering device

HOIST Pull up

HULL Main body of the boat

JIB foresail (in front of the mast)

KEDGE A small anchor

KEDGING To move a boat by hauling on a kedge anchor

KEEL Appendage under the hull running fore and aft, needed for vertical stability and to prevent leeway

KETCH A two-masted sailing vessel with smaller aftermast stepped forward of the stern post

L.O.A. Means length over all and refers to the longest measurement of the boat as compared to the length at the waterline

LANYARD A line fastened to an article, such as a pail, whistle, knife, or other small tool, for purpose of securing it

LATITUDE Distance in degrees north or south of the equator

LAZARETTE Storage lockers on deck aft of the steering wheel

LEE CLOTH Length of Canvas secured at the side of a berth to keep occupant in when boat heels or rolls

LEE SHORE Coast onto which the wind is blowing

LEE SIDE, (LEEWARD) Side of the boat away from the direction of the wind

LEECH The trailing edge of a sail (back edge)

LEEWAY Sideways drift

LIFELINE Lines around the boat to stop people falling overboard

LIFERAFT Specially designed inflatable raft with food, water and an EPIRB for use when the yacht has to be abandoned

LIFERING Floating ring to throw to a person who has fallen overboard

LIMBER HOLES Holes bored horizontally on the frames of the boat near the bottom to allow water in the bilge to drain to the lowest point where it can be pumped out

LINE A term for any rope used aboard a boat

LOCKER A storage compartment on a boat. A chain locker is a compartment where anchor chain is kept. A hanging locker is a closet sufficiently large for hanging of clothing

LOG Measures speed and distance through the water

LOGBOOK, OR THE LOG Regular record of boat's progress with position, speed, weather etc.

LONGITUDE A measurement of distance expressed to degrees East and West of the meridian of Greenwich, England

LUFF Front edge of a sail

LYING A HULL A technique useful in heavy weather, with bare poles and helm lashed such that the vessel lies beam on to the seas

MAINSAIL Large sail attached to aft side of main mast

MAKE FAST To belay or tie a line securely

MARLINSPIKE A pointed wooden or steel instrument used to open up the strands of rope and wire

MAST Vertical spar which supports the sails

MASTHEAD Top of the mast

MILE At sea the nautical mile is one minute of latitude at the equator, or 6,080 feet; used as a measure of distance

MINUTE One 60th of a degree of latitude or longitude; also, one 60th of an hour

MIZZEN The shorter mast aft on a yawl or ketch.Same as mizzenmast

MOOR To secure a boat between two posts, to a dock, or to a buoy

MOTORSAILER A vessel combining the features of both a sailboat and a motorboat

NAVIGABLE Water that is deep enough to permit passage of boats

NAVIGATION LIGHTS Lights used at night. Red faces port (left side) and green faces starboard (right), white faces aft

NEAP TIDES Smaller changes in the height of the tide, occur twice monthly at the half moon (alternate with spring tides)

OARLOCK, OR ROWLOCK Fitting which acts as a pivot point for an oar

OFF THE WIND Sailing on a reach or run

OFFSHORE WIND The wind when it is blowing from or off the shore

ON THE WIND See close-hauled

ONE-DESIGN CLASS A number of sailboats that are built and equipped exactly alike

OUTBOARD Outside the perimeter of the deck; portable engine for a dinghy

OVER STAND To sail beyond an object, such as a buoy

OVER ALL The boat's extreme length. Abbreviated LOA

OVERHAUL To overtake or gain on another vessel at sea. Also to do a complete repair to an engine or boat

PADEYE A fitting on deck used for attaching lines or blocks

PAINTER Bow line by which a small boat is towed or made fast to a mooring

PARALLEL RULES A pair of straight-edges fastened together so that the distance between them may be changed while their edges remain parallel. Used for transferring lines from one part of a chart to another

PAY OUT To let out a line

PILING Vertical timbers or logs driven into the water's bottom to form a support for a dock or to act as a breakwater

PILOT A man qualified and licensed to direct ships in and out of a harbour

PILOTING Coastal navigation

PITCH The up and down motion of a boat about a central axis. Also, the angle of the propeller blades

PLANING When a boat rides on top of the water

PORT CAPTAIN The official at a port who is in charge of all harbor activities

PORT SIDE Left side of the boat when looking forward

PORT TACK When the wind comes on the port side,(sails will be to starboard)

PRAM A small dinghy, usually bluff bowed

PREVENTER Line leading forward which holds the boom at right angles to the boat when going downwind, to prevent a gybe

PULPIT The railings at the bow of a yacht

QUARTER Between astern and abeam (back and middle) of the boat

RACE A very strong tidal current

RADAR Electronic instrument for detecting other vessels, land and storms

RAFT UP Tie alongside another vessel

REACH Sailing with the wind on the beam, the sail in approximate half way out. Can be a close reach, beam reach, orbroad reach

REEF A ridge of rocks which is at or near the surface; a portion of sail furled and tied down to reduce the area exposed to the wind

RHUMB LINE A course that crosses all meridians at the same angle

RIG To prepare a boat for sailing; the mast and its supports

RIGGING The gear which supports and controls the spars and the sails such as sheets, shrouds, stays and halyards

RULES OF THE ROAD The international regulations for preventing collisions at sea

RUNNING BACKSTAYS Adjustable lines supporting the back of the mast

RUNNING LIGHTS Lights used at night by vessels to identify type and indicate direction when under way

RUNNING To sail with the wind behind the boat

SAIL TIES Webbing strips used to tie the sails when furled

SAILS Shaped dacron, or other strong material, used to catch the wind and propel the boat through the water

SATELLITE NAVIGATION, OR SAT NAV Electronic device that aids navigation

SCHOONER A sailboat with two or more masts, the aftermost one being of equal or greater height than those ahead

SCOPE The length of mooring or anchor line in use

SEA ANCHOR A drag device, usually canvas, steamed from the bow and used to keep a boat headed into the wind during very heavy weather

SEA COCK A valve attached to a through-hull fitting

SECURE To make fast

SET Trimming a sail for the wind direction; course error due to current; the shape of the sail

SEXTANT An instrument used to aid navigation by measuring altitudes of celestial bodies and hence determining position of the boat

SHACKLE A U-shaped piece of metal with a pin which secures the open end

SHEET A line used to trim a sail

SHIPSHAPE Well-kept, orderly, clean

SHROUDS Wire supports on either side of the mast

SKEG A fixed fin near the stern, often supporting the rudder

SLACK To ease off a line

SLACK WATER The short period of time when the ebb (low) and flood (high) remain stationary

SLOOP A single masted sailboat in which the mast is set forward of amidships and usually using a single overlapping headsail

SNUB To check or stop a line

SOLE Floor of the interior of the boat

SPAR Term for masts, booms, spinnaker poles, etc.

SPINNAKER Lightweight, parachute-like sail (usually colourful) used when the wind is aft of the beam

SPINNAKER POLE A boom attached to the mast at one end and the spinnaker at the other, used to support and control the spinnaker

SPLICE To join rope or wire by tucking the strands together, such as short, long, eye and back splice, etc.

SPREADERS Short struts between mast and shrouds to add support to the rig

SPRING LINES Docking lines used to prevent a boat from moving fore and aft

SPRING TIDES Greatest change in the height of the tide, occurs twice monthly at the new and full moons (alternates with neap tides)

STANCHIONS Vertical supports for lifelines

STAND BY An order employed to alert crewmen, or on radio to ask receiver to wait

STANDING RIGGING The shrouds and stays which support the rig

STARBOARD Right side of the vessel when looking forward

STARBOARD TACK Sailing with wind on the starboard (right) side of the boat, (sails will be to port)

STAY Wire supporting the mast fore and aft

STEERAGE WAY Sufficient forward speed to allow rudder control

STERN The back of the boat

STOWING Securing or putting away

STRIKE To lower a sail or flag.

STUFFING BOX A device around a propeller shaft that permits it to revolve freely without letting water into the hull

SWELL Nonbreaking, long, easy waves. The expansion of wood when wet

TACHOMETER An instrument used to record the r.p.m. of an engine

TACK Act of passing the bow through the wind when sailing; the front lower corner of the sail

TACKLE A system of blocks and line to give mechanical advantage

TELL-TALE A short piece of ribbon or wool tied to a shroud or attached to a sail to indicate the flow or direction of the wind

TENDER A small boat employed to go back and forth to the shore from a larger boat

TIDE The rise and fall of the sea level due to gravitational pull of the moon and sun

TOPPING LIFT (uphaul) Lines supporting main boom and spinnaker pole

TOPSIDES That portion of the hull above the water line

TRANSOM Flat part across the back of boat

TRILIGHT A navigation light carried at the masthead combining port, starboard and stern lights.

TRIM Fine tune a sail

TRIMARAN Boat with three hulls

TRISAIL A storm sail used in place of a mainsail.

TROUGH The valley between two waves

TRUE COURSE The actual course relative to true north, or compass course when corrected for deviation and variation

VARIATION The difference in degrees between true and magnetic north

VEER When the wind changes in a clockwise direction

WAKE The eddies and swirls left astern of a boat in motion

WASH The waves made by a boat moving through the water

WATCH A period of duty on board a vessel

WATERLINE Demarkation between portion of hull above water and below

WAY Movement through the water of the boat

WEATHER FAX Instrument for receiving graphic weather charts

WEBBING Woven tape or strapping

WEIGH To raise the anchor

WINCH Round metal drum with detachable handle for winding in lines

WIND GENERATOR Wind driven electricity-producing device

WIND INSTRUMENTS Devices that measure wind speed and determine its direction

WIND VELOCITY Rate of motion of the wind

WINDLASS Mechanical or electrical device to lift anchor and chain

WINDSHIFT Change in wind direction

WINDVANE A device which automatically steers a boat at a pre-set angle to the wind

WINDWARD Direction from which the wind is blowing

WING ON WING Sailing downwind with the genoa and mainsail on opposite sides

YAWL A sailboat similar to a ketch but with smaller aftermast stepped abaft the stern post

SEND A COPY TO A FRIEND!

If not available at your local bookstore, please order through

Romany Publishing,
3943 West Broadway, Vancouver, B.C. V6R 2C2
Tel: (604) 228-8712 / Fax: (604) 228-8779
email: Romany@telus.net
website: www.aboutcruising.com

Please send:

☐ *JUST CRUISING* - Europe to Australia ($18.95)

☐ *STILL CRUISING* - Australia to Asia, Africa and America ($18.95)

☐ *CRUISING FOR COWARDS* - Strategies, Boats and Equipment Preferred by Experienced Cruisers ($24.95)

☐ *COMFORTABLE CRUISING* - Around North and Central America. ($19.95)

☐ *VIDEO - JUST CRUISING* Based on 'On Board 5 for six', a finalist in the CANPRO TV Documentary Awards, this video shows the lure of life afloat around the world, besides giving much practical boating and travel information. 55min. ($24.95)

(PLUS $5.00 SHIPPING AND HANDLING)

To:
Name: _____

Address: _____

City: _____ Prov/State: _____

Postal Code: _____ Country: _____

☐ Payment enclosed (Sorry, no CODs)
☐ By cheque (made payable to Romany Publishing)
☐ Or credit card by tel/fax